NUMBER TEN
Texas A&M University Economics Series

Also by David Reisman

ADAM SMITH'S SOCIOLOGICAL ECONOMICS
RICHARD TITMUSS: Welfare and Society
GALBRAITH AND MARKET CAPITALISM
STATE AND WELFARE: Tawney, Galbraith and Adam Smith
THE ECONOMICS OF ALFRED MARSHALL
ALFRED MARSHALL: Progress and Politics

The Political Economy of James Buchanan

David Reisman

Texas A&M University Press

COLLEGE STATION

Published in Great Britain by THE MACMILLAN PRESS LTD. 1990

LIBRARY OF CONGRESS CATALOGING-IN-PUBLICATION DATA

Reisman, David A.
    The political economy of James Buchanan / David Reisman.
      p.   cm. — (Texas A & M University economics series ; 10)
    Bibliography: p.
    Includes index.
    ISBN 0-89096-430-0
    1. Buchanan, James M. 2. Economics—United States—History.
I. Title. II. Series. III. Series: Texas A & M University
economics series ; no. 10.
HB119.B67R45 1990
330.1—dc20   89-4435
                                               CIP

Contents

Acknowledgements

The author and the publishers wish to thank Professor James M. Buchanan and the following who have kindly given permission to reproduce copyright material:

Academic Press for quotes from *Democracy in Deficit* by J.M. Buchanan and R. Wagner; The University of Chicago Press for extracts from *Limits of Liberty* by J.M. Buchanan; The University of Michigan Press for quotations from *Calculus of Consent* by J.M. Buchanan and G. Tullock; Texas A & M Press for permission to quote from *Freedom in Constitutional Contact* by J.M. Buchanan; Liberty Fund, Inc., for the use of quotes from *What Should Economists Do?* by J.M. Buchanan; Cambridge University Press for material from *Reason of Rules* by H.G. Brennan and J.M. Buchanan; and Professor J.M. Buchanan for permission to quote from *Liberty, Market and State* published by Wheatsheaf.

1 Introduction

James Buchanan, reflecting on the state of economic science as it was at the time when he was awarded the Nobel Prize in that subject, was capable of branding much of the work of his colleagues and contemporaries as little more than a waste of resources:

> As it is practiced in the 1980s, economics is a 'science' without ultimate purpose or meaning. It has allowed itself to become captive of the technical tools that it employs without keeping track of just what it is that the tools are to be used for. In a very real sense, the economists of the 1980s are illiterate in basic principles of their own discipline . . . Their motivation is not normative; they seem to be ideological eunuchs. Their interest lies in the purely intellectual properties of the models with which they work, and they seem to get their kicks from the discovery of proofs of propositions relevant only for their own fantasy lands . . . I do deplore the waste that such investment of human capital reflects.[1]

Economists should be teaching and studying the mutually-supportive relationships between market exchanges and other free institutions, between the decentralisation of decision-making processes and the primacy of the individual, between democratic structures and an atmosphere of perceived consent. Instead, economists retreat into mathematical demonstrations of allocative efficiency in static conditions of scarce endowments which shed all too little light on the central economic and social issues of modern times:

> Our graduate schools are producing highly trained, highly intelligent technicians who are blissfully ignorant of the whole purpose of their alleged discipline. They feel no moral obligation to convey and to transmit to their students any understanding of the social process through which a society of free persons can be organized without overt conflict while at the same time using resources with tolerable efficiency.[2]

This development Buchanan deeply regrets – so deeply, indeed, that the whole body of his work is characterised by nothing so much as the missionary's zeal to bend the bent rod in order to make it straight again.

In bending the bent rod, Buchanan has placed particular stress on the

invisible hand of self-interested searching ('perhaps the major intellectual discovery in the whole history of economics'[3]) and on order via
spontaneous coordination ('perhaps the only real "principle" in economic theory as such'[4]), and thus on the ideas and insights of the classical
liberals and classical political economists, however unfashionable and
even radical they might appear today: 'We find ourselves in the bizarre
position where those of us who seek to define our central research
programme as it was defined for the first century and one-half of our
discipline's history are now the methodological revolutionaries.'[5]
Among those classical liberals and classical political economists,
moreover, it is for the ideas and insights of Adam Smith that Buchanan
clearly has the greatest respect. It was Smith, after all, who, at a time of
considerable other-directedness, undertook that crucial task 'which is,
at base, the discipline's primary reason for claiming public support': he
explicated, lucidly and eloquently, 'the simple principle of laissez-faire,
the principle that results which emerge from the interactions of persons
left alone may be, and often are, superior to those results that emerge
from overt political interference. There has been a loss of wisdom in this
respect, a loss from eighteenth century levels, and the message of Adam
Smith requires reiteration with each generation.'[6] It was Smith, further-
more, who, in sharp contrast to the approach adopted by the well-
meaning pragmatists of his time and ours, eschewed case-by-case,
policy-by-policy analysis in favour of across-the-board rules and
unambiguous constitutional regulations:

> Adam Smith sought to free the economy from the fetters of
> mercantilist controls; he did not propose that the specific goals of
> policy be laid down in advance. He did not attack the failures of
> governmental instruments in piecemeal, pragmatic fashion; he
> attacked in a far more comprehensive and constitutional sense. He
> tried to demonstrate that, by removing effective governmental
> restrictions on trade, results would emerge that would be judged
> better by all concerned.[7]

Smith, in short, made himself the champion both of mutual advantage
through free market exchange and of '*ordered* anarchy' (in the sense of 'a
regime described by well-defined individual rights and by freedom of
and enforcement of voluntary contracts'[8]); and Buchanan in both
respects very much shares his vision and his perspective. As did, of
course, Buchanan's mentors in the Chicago School of Frank Knight,

Henry Simons, Lloyd Mints and Aaron Director – libertarians as well as investigators, and scholars who impressed upon their young student that 'the basics of economics were those of *price theory*, not formal mathematics, and *price theory applied to real world issues*'.[9] Except for an early flirtation with central planning, *dirigisme* and socialism such as was not uncommon among intellectuals with a strong sense of moral obligation when confronted with the human and economic tragedy of the Great Depression, Buchanan has never deviated from the pro-individualist, pro-capitalist stance of Smith and of Chicago – from a deeply-felt conviction, in other words, that the 'solid arguments of economic theory' cannot but demonstrate to any believer in human dignity 'that the choices in the market are not arbitrary, that there are narrow limits on the potential for exploitation of man by man, that markets tend to maximize freedom of persons from political control, that liberty, which has always been his basic value, is best preserved in a regime that allows markets a major role.'[10]

Buchanan is pro-individualist and pro-capitalist but he also believes that there must be limits to liberty lest conflict-resolution in the sense of Smith (i.e. the reaping of reciprocal gains from trade) degenerate into 'warre' in the sense of Hobbes (i.e. the state of nature in which life for the individual is 'solitary, poor, nasty, brutish, and short'[11]). There must, in other words, be, at the very minimum, a 'protective State', a 'legal-governmental system that enforces property-rights and contracts'[12] and without which the separate actions of individuals through interrelated markets would produce a network of coordinated agreements worth not much more than the paper on which they were written. For there to be what Buchanan calls maximal liberty, there must clearly also be what Nozick calls the minimal State.[13] Buchanan would have no cause to disagree with Milton Friedman's dictum that 'the consistent liberal is not an anarchist'.[14] Like Friedman, however, he would say that the consistent liberal is afraid of Leviathan as well as of anarchy, and wishes therefore to see State as well as citizen constrained by rules. The consistent liberal is not an anarchist. The consistent liberal *is* a constitutionalist: 'I remain, in basic values, an individualist, a constitutionalist, a contractarian, a democrat – terms that mean essentially the same thing to me.'[15]

It is in the circumstances eminently suitable that Buchanan and his colleagues should (in 1957) have founded their Thomas Jefferson Center for Studies in Political Economy at the University of Virginia; and that its successor, the Center for Study of Public Choice, should have remained rooted – located as it was first at the Virginia Polytechnic Institute in Blacksburg (1969–82) and then at George Mason University in Fairfax – in that one of the United States which has such uniquely close historical ties with the Founding Fathers of the American Constitution. The Founding Fathers saw the need to impose from the start limits on the freedom of the State to infringe the freedom of the individual; and the arguments of *The Federalist Papers* and other writings were at an early stage translated into a written Constitution with a Bill of Rights and what appeared to them to be adequate protection for the principle of 'no taxation without representation'. The Founding Fathers could not have foreseen the subsequent growth in government and still less that its Leviathan-like tendencies would threaten personal liberties (such as the right to live without inflation) at least as much as their better-known counterparts in the area of civil rights (such as the rights of assembly and of speech) – with the obvious result: 'The American constitutional structure is in disarray.'[16] Even so, however, 'the United States citizenry has surely come closer to an embodiment of a set of constitutional attitudes than any other people in the history of the world';[17] and Buchanan is confident that his fellow-countrymen, given their particular openness to the constitutional mentality alongside that well-known individualism which has so powerfully drawn them to free enterprise, will grasp the constitutional nettle and proceed to a '*consensual redefinition* of individual rights and claims',[18] revising and extending but not rejecting or scrapping the exemplary contribution to social order that was made by the Founding Fathers.

The teachings of Jefferson, Hamilton, Madison, Jay – and of George Mason himself – had a considerable influence on the development of Buchanan's constitutional political economy. So did the arguments contained in less than a hundred pages of a then-completely-untranslated book published in 1896. The book bears the not instantaneously arresting title of *Finanztheoretische Untersuchungen*. Of its author Buchanan has written: 'Wicksell is the primary precursor of modern public choice theory.'[19] Knut Wicksell, after all, 'was the first scholar to recognize that a rule of unanimity for reaching collective decisions provides the institutional analogue to two-person trade in strictly private or partitionable goods';[20] and there can be few topics that are more fundamental to Buchanan's perspectives than are the gains from trade. No person who reads Wicksell having read Buchanan can fail to be impressed by the similarities between the two authors. Consider Wicksell on the conscious search for social consensus:

There are hundreds of ways of distributing the costs of a proposed state expenditure among the separate classes of the people . . . Provided the expenditure in question holds out any prospect at all of creating utility exceeding costs, it will always be theoretically possible, and approximately so in practice, to find a distribution of costs such that all parties regard the expenditure as beneficial and may therefore approve it unanimously.[21]

Or Wicksell on that civic pride (as opposed to alienation and malintegration) that is so significantly fostered by the system of 'approximate unanimity in tax approval': 'Each member of society would be happy in the knowledge that the goods which taxation withdraws from his private use are destined solely for purposes which he recognises to be useful and in which he has a genuine interest, be it for purely selfish or for altruistic motives. Surely this would do more than anything else to awaken and maintain the spirit of good citizenship.'[22] Or Wicksell on the complementarity of interests beneath the constitutional umbrella: 'It is not the business of the science of public finance and of tax legislation to do away with the egotism of the social classes, but to assign it its proper place as a safeguard of legitimate particular interests. This force, to which so much ill will has been imputed, may then yet produce some good'.[23] Or Wicksell on subjectivity ('When it comes to benefits which are so hard to express numerically, each person can ultimately speak only for himself'[24]) and thence on the impotence of even the most benevolent of despots meaningfully to compare extra benefits with extra costs: 'If the individual is unable to form an even approximately definite judgement on this point, it is *a fortiori* impossible for anyone, even if he be a statesman of genius, to weigh the whole community's utility and sacrifice against each other.'[25] Impossible means impossible, to Buchanan as to Wicksell; and there must accordingly be a strong inference that that which is impossible ought not to be attempted lest we end up in the Machiavellian, non-democratic, oligarchy-ridden world of De Viti De Marco, Puviani, Pantaleoni, Barone, Einaudi, the older Pareto, and the other Italian fiscal theorists of the period roughly from 1880 to 1940 with whose work Buchanan came into contact when Fulbright Research Scholar in Italy in 1955–6. Buchanan was familiar with the pluralist-democratic theory of the State and was committed to voluntary consent. The Italians' emphasis on coercion (as opposed to consultation and participation) clearly made him think carefully about his own assumptions, and the origins of his analysis of manifestations of dissensus such as the taxpayers' revolt[26] may perhaps be found in his exposure to the Italian literature – as where, reflecting on the idea that a small ruling elite should impose its will (if need be, by force) on the total citizenry, he says: 'It would be unreasonable to expect that individuals who do not participate in the choice process should voluntarily accept and comply with such decisions as may be made.'[27] Such dissensus does not arise in the world of Adam Smith – where the butcher has power over the baker with respect to meat and the baker over the butcher with respect to bread. Nor does it arise in the world of Knut Wicksell or of the Founding Fathers – where a constitutional order reflecting unanimity and consensus strictly limits the powers of the vassals to play at being the Lord.

Nor does such dissensus arise in the constitutional political economy of James Buchanan and his colleagues with which we shall be concerned in this book.[28] Our discussion will proceed by way of The Constitution and Operational Rules through Institutional Failure to A Charter for Democrats, and thence to the Democratic State, The Moral Dimension and, finally, Economics and Beyond. Our overall conclusion will be that the economics of political and social order is a somewhat more unusual field of study than is, let us say, the economics of money and banking or the economics of industry and trade; and that Buchanan's attempt to bend the bent rod cannot but be taken very seriously indeed.

2 The Constitution

Buchanan is an economist who believes that economics is not about maximisation in conditions of static scarcity so much as about what Hayek and other Austrians call 'catallaxy',[1] i.e. the processes of voluntarily exchanging and agreeing as between autonomous individuals. These processes are to be observed in far more areas of social life than merely the trading of apples for oranges, and one of those areas must inevitably be the polity: 'By a more or less natural extension of the catallactic approach, economists can look on politics and on political processes in terms of the exchange paradigm.'[2] It is thus in terms of the exchange paradigm that the constitution must be conceptualised: 'As an economist, I am a specialist in contract,'[3] Buchanan states, and the contract in question, he might well have added, can just as easily involve all citizens in a society as both trading-partners in a green-grocer's shop.

Buchanan's analysis of constitutions proceeds in three stages – the first relating to the individual, the second to the agreement, and the third to the notion of justice.

2.1 THE INDIVIDUAL

Some theorists have conceived of politics as a positive science devoted to uncovering and revealing essential and absolute truths concerning the 'public interest' and the 'good society'. The more elitist of these theorists have sometimes called for a philosopher-ruler in touch with authentic national objectives (perhaps because these represent the divine will of the Gods as revealed in Scriptures, perhaps because these are consonant with natural laws such as that of gravity) to ignore the false perceptions of his unenlightened fellow-countrymen in order to home in on the lasting and the general. The more democratic of these theorists have frequently spoken of a social welfare function which allows all possible positions of allocative equilibrium to be ranked and a unique welfare optimum to be selected on behalf of the community by a specialist policy-maker – always assuming, needless to say, that he himself may be taken as being, essentially and absolutely, omniscient, beneficient and personally disinterested. Neither the more elitist nor the more democratic of these theorists would have much in common with James

Buchanan, who categorically denies the very existence of 'some higher form of truth, revealed only to those who hold the sacred keys and hence undiscoverable and unchallengeable, even to those who might qualify as scientists'.[4] Instead of starting with the macrocosm and working their way down to the individual, Buchanan argues, theorists should begin with the individual and work their way upwards to the whole: 'The critical normative presupposition on which the whole contractarian construction stands or falls is the location of value exclusively in the individual human being. The individual is the unique unit of consciousness from which all evaluation begins.'[5] Logically so – for only the individual can experience utility and disutility, rank alternative states of welfare, formulate beliefs concerning *ought-to-bes*, make his way through the thicket of risk and uncertainty in the direction of an expected objective the nature of which it may be impossible for him fully to articulate to others. That which is sought for, both in politics and economics, cannot in the circumstances be anything that exists independently of the attitudes and interests, preferences and purposes of the discrete individuals who make up the society: 'The first and most critical presupposition that provides a foundation for any genuine democratic theory is that which locates sources of value exclusively in individuals.'[6] *Virtuosi* and moral absolutists will no doubt be shocked by the radical ethical relativism to which this points: 'Values are widely acknowledged to be derived from individuals, and there are not absolutes. God has been dead for a century, and attempts to revive him are likely to founder.'[7] God is dead, Henry Dubb remains, and Buchanan's advice to would-be Stalins and Ayatollahs is therefore unambiguous: values have no external existence or objective content independent of each individual's choice calculus.

The rejection of the organicist model (in which the social whole is seen as being other than simply the sum of its parts), the departure from idealist systems of philosophy (in which the ultimate aims of the rational individual are identified much in the same way as a detective identifies a criminal), thus points directly to methodological individualism (that, in other words, 'all theorizing, all analysis, is resolved finally into considerations faced by the individual person as decision-maker'[8]) and to revealed preference (since there is no alternative mode of assessing another person's choice problems) – and to *homo economicus*: '*Homo economicus* offers a better basic model for explaining human behavior than any comparable alternative.'[9]

Homo economicus is a methodological construct which has long been employed in economic theory and which offers a model of economic man as a rational, purposive actor who maximises (subject to constraints ranging from resource endowments to other people) that which he conceives to be in his own self-interest to maximise – *whatever* it might be. Of course *homo economicus* can (and frequently does) involve the single-minded pursuit of the market participant's net wealth. Central to the correct employment of the construct is, however, the perception that any other goal would fit just as well into the schema, provided only that economic man himself – and not an authoritarian Other – defines the objective to be pursued. *Homo economicus* does not, therefore, in any way exclude the possibility that Robinson Crusoe's utility function might incorporate Friday's happiness as an argument; or that Crusoe might allocate time and other resources to hunting meat for Friday when his maximand could just as easily have been catching fish for himself. Self-interest in no way excludes altruistic and benevolent conduct of this kind. Simply, the *homo economicus* construct stipulates that, if the model is indeed to yield good predictions, it must be the case that Crusoe himself expects to derive pleasure from what he anticipates will be the pleasure of Friday in eating the meat. Crusoe might be disappointed *ex post* with respect to his own pleasure (as where he finds, in the event, that he feels surprisingly indifferent as Friday eats and eats) or – still more likely – with respect to the anticipated subjective sensations which he imputes to Friday (who might turn out to be a vegetarian). Such disappointment is regrettable (although, of course, endemic to all future-oriented action where uncertainty is present) but it does not weaken the force of the contention being defended – that the *homo economicus* construct is compatible with a wide range of micro-motives indeed.

Human nature being human nature, Buchanan argues, the self-seeking orientation of *homo economicus* is likely to be found in a wider range of areas than simply the making of specifically economic exchanges; and one of the areas into which he feels the contractarian paradigm might usefully be extended is political science. At one level this means that the motivation of voters, politicians and bureaucrats ought to be reassessed in terms of the rational maximisation of individual utility (Anthony Downs, visibly influenced by *Capitalism, Socialism and Democracy*, had pioneered this analytical approach in 1957[10]); while at another level this means that non-market actors who speak of the 'public interest' ought to make clear that they are only expressing their own personal assessments and judgements as to the welfare of the whole. The institutional setting of politics is different from that of the economic market. Human nature, however, is standard, uniform and the same.

Not, however, always very beautiful; for, while the self-interest axiom can undeniably account for real-world observations that give little comfort to the cynic or the pessimist, it is also the case that conflict is ubiquitous and the Hobbesian 'warre' an ever-present possibility. A model predicated on individuality and contract cannot but conclude that, 'ceteris paribus, the liberty inherent in anarchistic order without law is the most desirable state of affairs',[11] that 'the ideal society is anarchy, in which no one man or group of men coerces another'[12] – but, sadly, *ceteris* is not *paribus* and human nature seems not to be the friend of amicable cooperation and State-less interdependence. The problem is not scarcity alone: 'Even if all 'goods' that might be 'economic' should be available in superbundance, conflict among persons might still arise. Social strife might arise in paradise.'[13] The problem is dominance: 'In a strictly personalized sense, any person's ideal situation is one that allows him full freedom of action and inhibits the behavior of others so as to force adherence to his own desires. That is to say, each person seeks mastery over a world of slaves.'[14] If God had not been dead for a century he might legitimately be had up for faulty workmanship and asked to improve on that which he made only with coarse clay. That option not being on offer, the imperfect individual has no alternative but to turn to the second-best solution of the constitution.

2.2 THE AGREEMENT

In economic or market exchange, the motive for the agreement is mutual advantage and the gains from trade that are reaped from participation: both parties to the contract gain and neither loses – or else each would not voluntarily have given his assent. Where Crusoe and Friday exchange fish for coconuts (dividing their labour according to differential endowments and comparative advantage) or collaborate in order to build a fort (combining their labour in collective action because neither unaided is up to the task both regard as desirable), there conflicting interests are reconciled through unanimous agreement between the two individuals and perceived welfare is heightened as a result.

Political exchange is no different, as Buchanan, together with Gordon Tullock, spelled out in their important book of 1962 on *The Calculus of Consent*: constructive social cooperation yields benefits to all parties (whereas force and fraud generate advantages only for the winners in what then becomes a zero-sum game) and, precisely because social order is a good thing, 'it is rational to *have a constitution*'.[15] Early theorists such as Hobbes were therefore right, as Buchanan, together with Geoffrey Brennan, pointed out more than two decades after *The Calculus of Consent* in *The Reason of Rules*, to speak in terms of a 'social contract': 'At the most fundamental level, rules find their reason in the never ending desire of people to live together in peace and harmony, without the continuing Hobbesian war of each against all'.[16] Thus the *raison d'être* of the 'protective State', as Buchanan, writing on his own, explained in *Liberty, Market and State*:

> The fundamental role for politics, inclusively defined, is that of providing the legal framework within which individuals can go about their ordinary business of seeking to further the values they choose to seek, without overt conflict. The enforcement of rights and contracts is a necessary task for government in any liberal regime. The argument extends quite normally to the guarantee of internal and external order.[17]

Buchanan states that 'anarchy is ideal for ideal men' but that 'passionate men must be reasonable';[18] but he also concedes that there can exist a regulatory rule even in the anarchic state of nature. There are, specifically, three instances in his work of cases where a regulatory rule obtained or could have obtained even in the absence of judges and constables, night-watchmen and referees.

The first such instance is that of *self*-government, which in Buchanan's view both precedes the institution of formal government and paves the way for it by demonstrating the utility of rules. Thus it is that even in a state of anarchy isolated man anxious to plan and predict sets his alarm clock and in that way 'makes contracts with himself': 'The alarm clock becomes, for Crusoe, the enforcing agent, the 'governor' whose sole task is that of insuring that the contracts once made are honored. For effective enforcement, the 'governor' must be external to the person who recognizes his own weaknesses.'[19] Man is evidently by nature a purposive, gratification-deferring, future-facing being; and thus by nature a being enthusiastic to accept the orderly behaviour-patterns that are associated with rules – even where those rules are entirely *self*-imposed.

The second such instance involves normative constraint and ethical standards such as antedate the embodiment of your beliefs and mine in laws and statutes. Thus 'there may be near-universal agreement on many elements in a structure of legal rights. Laws against murder, rape, assault, and theft may command almost unanimous consent. Such laws represent the translation into politics of widely held and commonly shared moral values'.[20] You and I may have had an intrinsic revulsion to such violations of the individual's autonomy even before our unanimously-agreed rules were formalised and codified; and to that extent the state of nature was not a state of *anomie*.

The third such instance concerns non-conflictual conventions such as rules of the road:

> Rules of the road serve the function of allowing persons to pursue their separate and independent courses, which may conflict in the absence of such rules . . . Road rules have a social function, which is to facilitate the achievement of the purposes of all persons who use the facility, regardless of what these purposes might be. And the rules are adjudged in accordance with their ability to satisfy this criterion.[21]

Robin Hood and Little John, meeting on a narrow bridge in the anarchic state of nature, are on course for a reciprocally destructive collision or, at best, for the winner-take-all situation where the one pushes the other into the river. Robin Hood and Little John could, however, hypothetically, have laid down criteria in advance such as govern primacy of access; and it is hard to see why they would delay instituting such a rule merely because there was no government to promulgate it. Buchanan accepts that the rules of grammar can perform yeoman service even in the state of nature – since even there it is in everyone's interest to convey his meaning and make himself understood. This result may usefully and logically be extended to the case of all non-conflictual conventions. Even in the anarchic state of nature, after all, it is difficult to believe that some rational men would persistently drive on the right-hand side of the road, others on the left: masterless men who invent governments in a bid to save their lives are hardly likely to indulge in suicidal conduct of this kind if a spontaneous agreement, even in the anarchic state of nature, can possibly be negotiated.

There are, in Buchanan's work, three instances of cases where a regulatory rule obtained or could have obtained even in the anarchic state of nature – those, respectively, of *self*-government, normative standards and non-conflictual conventions. In none of these three cases is political intervention indispensable and inevitable if harmonious social interaction is peacefully to continue. Sadly, however, and precisely because men are made of coarse clay, these three cases do not tell the whole story. The reference to non-conflictual conventions makes no allowance for the zero-sum antagonisms that arise when I covet your property: 'We require rules for living together for the simple reason that without them we would surely fight.'[22] The reference to normative standards makes no allowance for 'the explicit flaunting of traditional codes of conduct, the direct and open disregard for what had previously been considered to be acceptable standards for elementary "good manners" '[23] that arise when I ride roughshod over what the community takes to be right: 'To the extent that more and more human interactions exhibit conflicts at the boundaries, institutional means for resolving these will emerge, and the set of formalized rules will expand. If men abide by rules implicitly, formalization is not required. If they do not do so, formalization, implementation and enforcement become necessary.'[24] And thus is the State born, *as if* guided by a conscious desire to purchase protection against violation of person and property in a world where established conventions and economic exchanges are seen to be unable to produce adequate mutual tolerance for a viable social order.

The decision to hire a governor is a conscious and rational one: 'Just as our Crusoe may choose to govern himself by the alarm clock, two or more persons may rationally choose to be governed by prior selection and implementation of enforcement institutions.'[25] It is also cost-effective, where each of the parties in consequence of the enforcement contract can than disarm and disinvest in defence and predation: the mutual consent here serving as the 'genuine basis for the emergence of property rights', both parties 'agree to and accept the assignment, which carries with it the complementary agreement that they will not behave so as to violate the terms. Both parties can, therefore, reduce their private investment in attack and defense.'[26] It is also, like all exchange relationships freely entered into, positive-sum and welfare-enhancing – by definition, in fact: 'The essence of any contractual agreement is *voluntary* participation, and no rational being will voluntarily agree to something which yields him, in net terms, expected damage or harm.'[27] It is also firmly rooted in unanimous consent; for every rational person who joins a club or enters into a game will only do so, being rational, if he feels that he will be better in than out. We are in because we want to be in, every participant believes he derives benefit from participation, and this result holds true even if we happen to be a chess-club where my win is your check-mate and vice versa:

> The zero-sum characteristic applies to the 'solution' of the game; it does not apply to the 'contract' through which all participants agree on the rules. At this second level there must be mutual gains, and the rule of unanimity must apply. At this level there is no way in which a zero sum

solution could apply; the game simply would not be played unless all participants expected some individual benefit at the time of entry.[28]

Even where I lose I win because I play within the rules laid down by that fundamental political contact called a constitution.

Because the constitution is a contract and because a contract will not voluntarily be signed unless all the signatories believe they stand to gain from it, the constitution clearly cannot contain clauses that discriminate as between social groups and interests: 'The requirement that, at the ultimate constitutional stage, general agreement among all individuals must be attained precludes the adoption of special constitutional provisions or rules designed to benefit identifiable individuals or small groups as these rules operate over a time sequence of collective decisions.'[29] Fortunately, of course, the very fact that constitution-making is by definition antecedent to decision-making within the framework of the constitutional rules is a force militating in favour of full consensus at the earlier stage – since, quite simply, the *future* interests of even the most rational of utility-maximisers cannot realistically be assumed to be known to him *now*: 'Essential to the analysis is the presumption that the individual is *uncertain* as to what his own precise role will be in any one of the whole chain of inter-collective choices that will actually have to be made. For this reason he is considered not to have a particular and distinguishable interest separate and apart from his fellows.'[30] If only the individual knew in advance what his future sectional, class, group or even individual interests would be, he would no doubt press – rationally so – for partisan rules that favoured those particular interests. As he *cannot* predict 'with any degree of certainty' the future roles and coalitions in which he will be involved, he has no choice but to assume that 'occasionally he will be in one group and occasionally in the other. His own self-interest will lead him to choose rules that will maximise the utility of an individual in a series of collective decisions with his own preferences on the separate issues being more or less randomly distributed.'[31] An omniscient individual would demand a constitution that satisfied his own identifiable objectives and – if his fellow citizens were also omniscient – general agreement would be difficult if not impossible to obtain. The very fact that we have a constitution at all may therefore be taken as tangible proof that people are not omniscient and that no one, however wise, can predict the course and outcome of a future chain of occurrences: 'The uncertainty that is required in order for the individual to be led by his own interest to support constitutional provisions that are generally advantageous to all individuals and to all groups seems likely to be present at any constitutional stage of discussion.'[32] Randomness and unknowledge may thus become, at the stage of constitution-making if nowhere else, the guarantors of the public interest: because of them, after all, the rational individual 'may tend to act, from self-interest, *as if* he were choosing the bet set of rules for the social group. Here the purely selfish individual and the purely altruistic individual may be indistinguishable in their behavior.'[33]

Time is evidently central to Buchanan's understanding of the veil of uncertainty as it relates to the business of constitution-making, the comparison being to a proposed game (of chance or skill) where the players first iron out conflicts of opinion and agree upon appropriate rules and only then begin to play: no player can know in advance what rule will most benefit him at what stage of what future match, and the best that any participant can do is to join with his fellows in attempting 'to devise a set of rules that will constitute the most interesting game for the average or representative player'.[34] Given the veil of uncertainty and taking the long-run perspective, it is thus in the self-interest even of a potential law-breaker to ensure that the constitution contains clauses that yield him personally the benefits of law and order:

> Conceptually, men can reach agreement on rules, even when each party recognizes in advance that he will be 'coerced' by the operation of agreed-on rules in certain circumstances. A potential thief, recognizing the need for protecting his own person and property, will support laws against theft, even though he will anticipate the probability that he will himself be subjected to punishment under these laws.[35]

Given man's radical unknowledge of future plays of the game and recognising that history-to-come is a very extended sequence indeed, it is even in the self-interest of a person who today thinks of himself as rich not to oppose inter-group transfers:

> Under our assumptions, the individual, at the time of constitutional choice, is uncertain as to his own role on particular issues in the future. If the inference suggested here is correct, the individual, because of this uncertainty, *will not expect positive external costs to be imposed on him by purely redistributive transfers of real income.* The reason is evident: he will see that the external benefits which he may secure through imposing external costs on others on certain occasions will tend to equal the external costs which others will impose on him on different occasions.[36]

Things would, of course, be very different if the gamester, the criminal and the plutocrat could see into the future; for then the gamester would, at the constitutional stage, demand rules friendly to the four aces which he knows he will always hold (and discriminating against the king of spades which will never be his trump), the criminal would call for lenient punishments in view of his certain knowledge that he will steal your diamonds whereas a counterpart villain will only make off with his cat-food, and the plutocrat would resist all downward transfers of property and privilege because of the fact that he will himself never occupy a lower position on the social scale. Yet none of these persons can in reality see into the future; and each must, like the rest of us, make his decisions in time present without any significant knowledge of what time-to-come will bring. Thence their concord – on the grounds that a social contract is undeniably preferable to the anarchic state of nature. Thence their agreement – on general rules decided upon by full consensus. Thence the constitution.

2.3 THE NOTION OF JUSTICE

There can be few constitutionalists who do not want their rules to be fair. There cannot be many contractarians who think that order is a social necessity but justice merely a classroom luxury. The notion of justice is in fact absolutely central to the whole constitutionalist-contractarian approach as formulated by Buchanan and his associates, and the reason for this is intrinsic to the whole conception of the calculus of consent: 'A "fair rule" is one that is agreed to by the players in advance of play itself, before the particularized positions of the players come to be identified. Note carefully what this definition says: a rule is fair if players agree to it. It does not say that players agree because a rule is fair.'[37] No rule is fair without reference to the consensus that performs the 'basic normative function':[38] 'Justice takes its meaning from the rules of the social order within which norms of justice are to be applied. To appeal to considerations of justice is to appeal to relevant rules. Talk of justice without reference to these rules is meaningless.'[39] Any rule is fair if it is the product of genuine agreement among freely-contracting social actors: 'A rule is legitimate, and violations of it constitute unjust behavior, when the rule is the object of voluntary consent among participants in the rule-governed order. Why is this so? Because the provision of consent on a voluntary basis amounts to offering a *promise* to abide by the rules. Just conduct is conduct in accord with promises given.'[40] God has been dead for a century, natural laws and natural rights have no foundation in fact, Platonic ideals and essences have all the characteristics of wishful thinking – but you and I exist, and that means that, however contingent, history-dependent, non-teleological and 'relativistic',[41] so too does justice exist: 'What justice requires depends on what particular rules individuals happen to have agreed to',[42] and for that reason it is entirely endogenous (not external) to our own particular community.

Just conduct is conduct in accordance with prevailing rules to which prior consent has been given, rules which have emerged in the course of a decision-making process on which you and I unanimously confer the accolade of legitimacy: 'To discuss policy alternatives or options independently of processes in which policy choices take place almost necessarily involves reversion to or maintenance of the notion that non-individualistic sources of value and valuation exist, whether these be expressed as the efficiency criteria of the economists or as the common-good vector of the philosophers.'[43] Such non-individualistic standards simply do not exist, and the implication is clear: 'Evaluative criteria must be applied to rules or processes rather than to end states or results . . . There is no external standard or scale through which end states can be "valued". End states must be evaluated only through the processes that generate them. What emerges from a process is what emerges and nothing more.'[44] Just processes produce just rules, just conduct is conduct in accordance with those rules, 'injustice springs from a violation of . . . rules that are legitimately expected to be applied by participants or affected parties',[45] but more than that the democratic relativist simply cannot say on the precise nature of the just outcome for which the community opts: 'Any outcome may be acceptable, provided the rules are fair and are adhered to.'[46]

Justice is rooted in consent, but the consent must be voluntary and freely given. In the case of duress it clearly is not; and no one would criticise the victim of a blackmailer or a mugger offering a bargain of the 'your money or your life' type for subsequently failing to live up to his promise to honour his contract. Buchanan and Brennan even extend this result from extreme duress to extreme adversity, as where they observe that 'a starving man who agrees to run inordinate risks for a crust of bread cannot necessarily be held to be bound to the agreement.'[47] Interestingly, they do not apply their concept of coerced or involuntary contract to the more general case where the relative bargaining strength of the parties is dramatically unequal – partly, one suspects, because they believe that consensus does in fact regard such bargains as morally binding, partly because of the painful but inescapable truth that 'we live in a society of *individuals*, not a society of *equals*'.[48] There are many things we can do to assist the less privileged, and there is every chance that our community will wish (especially when situated behind the veil of uncertainty) to undertake some or all of those things. What we cannot do is to encourage the less privileged to default on their agreements simply because they are weak and their trading partner is strong. Justice is rooted in consent. They gave their consent, and a promise is a promise. Besides which, unequal contracts are as old as the very process of contracting itself: 'In Hobbes's model, there are, by inference, considerable differences among separate persons in a precontract setting. To the extent that such differences exist, postcontract inequality in property and in human rights must be predicted. For my purposes, there is no need to discuss in detail the degree of possible inequality among separate persons in the conceptual state of nature.'[49] If, in the circumstances, we wish to argue that unequal endowments or unequal power are justifiable grounds for defaulting on contract in the here-and-now, there will hardly be a large number of contracts that can reasonably be regarded as inviolable.

Justice is rooted in consent, but the fact is that few of us have actually been shown the original contract, let alone been asked to sign it. Buchanan is not a strict constructionist with respect to the original contract and recognises that there is no empirical evidence that supports its putative existence: 'Historically, an explicit stage of constitutional contracting may never have existed; the structure of rights may have emerged in an evolutionary process characterized by an absence of conscious agreement.'[50] An evolutionary process starting from a dismal base, moreover, should it prove true (as is perfectly logical and fully in keeping with the spirit of Hobbes) that the state of nature was transcended not by the state of consensual compacting but by the state of force and dominance, the state in which order is established by means of the strong enslaving the weak: 'Under such conditions societies will tend to be controlled by some groups which will tyrannize over other groups.'[51] The construct of the original contract is clearly not intended to be descriptive. It is an *as if*, but a valuable *as if* to any social theorist or concerned citizen who values order above chaos and believes that the ideal agreement is one based upon unanimous consent. That being, in Buchanan's view of the human condition, all or most of us, the precise whereabouts today of the original contract is evidently of little importance, while the objection that few of us have been asked to sign it would appear to be rooted in a misapprehension: we may not have signed the *original* contract, but our continuing participation in the social game testifies to our having given tacit consent to the social rules currently in force. Our consent is not coerced in view of the fact that we do have a genuine option not to participate – as witness the alternatives represented by suicide, emigration and revolution, to name but three (not one of them as attractive, it must be recorded, as, let us say, a month's holiday in Tahiti): Our consent not being coerced, it must be voluntary; and there will be few of us indeed who will maintain that a man who plays a game is exempted from arousing in others the normal expectation that he will abide by the rules merely because he did not have a hand in their being drafted. Most of us will rather argue that 'voluntary participation amounts to agreement to the rules. It constitutes a tacit promise to abide by prevailing rules, and the breaking of such a promise is equivalent to unjust conduct because it involves treating others in ways in which they do not deserve to be treated.'[52] Justice is rooted in consent. Striving through legitimate democratic channels to change the rules is therefore just. Unilateral action is, however, unjust. You did not design the rules of the game but you began to play according to the rules of the game inherited from the past. You now say that you want to play the game of chess according to the rules of whist. We will listen to your proposals with interest; but, when all is said and done, you are not the only player.

Justice is rooted in consent, but the consent in question ceases to be social currency the moment that it has been spent on the purchase of the constitutional order. Every child knows what, apparently, some economists do not, that you can't have your cake and eat it too:

> In some economists' discussions of the law, one obtains the impression that choosing whether to abide by the rules is like selecting a drink at a soft-drink machine; that is, one either abides by the rules and pays no penalty or fails to abide by the rules and simply pays the price of so doing, as reflected in the rules. But the legislated punishment is not to be construed simply as the 'price' of an alternative course of action; it also symbolizes the fact that a 'wrong' has been committed. Making a choice among alternative drinks is a morally neutral act; choosing between legitimate and illegitimate modes of behavior is not morally neutral (or at least not if the legitimacy springs from the prior consent of the chooser).[53]

Gary Becker would appear to be the target in this connection, and most of all where he treats fines and imprisonment (suitably weighted by the likelihood of apprehension and the probability of conviction) as the going market price for an economic good or service where illegally obtained: 'A fine can be considered the price of an offense, but so too can any other form of punishment; for example, the "price" of stealing a car might be six months in jail. The only difference is in the units of measurement: fines are prices measured in monetary units, imprisonments are prices measured in time units, etc.'[54] Becker's position is that of the positive economist seeking to account for real world occurrences and he has no *a priori* objection to the hypothesis (holding constant other variables such as biological traits and family upbringing, and setting aside irrational impulses such as those associated with crimes of passion) that the same calculus may reasonably obtain with respect to the theft of a loaf of bread as in the case of its legitimate purchase: 'The approach taken here follows the economists' usual analysis of choice and assumes that a person commits an offense if the expected utility to him exceeds the utility he could get by using his time and other resources at other activities. Some persons become "criminals", therefore, not because their basic motivation differs from that of other persons, but because their benefits and costs differ.'[55] Buchanan's position (while unambiguously sharing Becker's assumptions and predilections in areas such as those involving rationality of choice, empirical evidence and the application of economic theory to non-market situations) is somewhat different. Buchanan does not deny that *homo economicus* (if on, say, £5000, or perhaps unemployed) might rationally choose to spend one year of his time on a prison-sentence in exchange for the £25 000 which he steals from a bank. What Buchanan does say is that *homo economicus* has no moral right to exchange punishment for profit in this way for the simple reason that he, *homo economicus*, has already spent his consent on social order and therefore no longer possesses the option of spending his non-consent as well: 'Consent is to the *rules*, and the moral force of promise keeping is such that one is obligated to other players to play by those rules.'[56] Buchanan would, one suspects, have far more sympathy (despite the profound difference of approach to social reform which inevitably separates the democrat from the revolutionary) with the attitude of a criminal who states that he never freely gave his tacit consent to rules and games which he always found repugnant than he would with the free rider who seizes short-term personal advantage while hoping that others will continue to act in such a way as to ensure the survival of the stable institutional order to which all voluntarily gave their consent. Justice is rooted in consent, and no one but a scoundrel,

Buchanan clearly believes, would publicly give that consent only then privately to withdraw it again. While the scoundrel is bound to reflect that it is the successful free rider who today enjoys the picnic, the suckered good citizen who tomorrow (in the form of the radical decay of social order) has to pay the bill, neither the free rider nor the good citizen, one feels sure, could fail to note the high moral tone which characterises the notion of justice as it appears in the work of James Buchanan.

Nor could either, always provided that he is a serious student both of Buchanan's writings and of *A Theory of Justice*, fail to note the close and important parallels which can be drawn between Buchanan and another influential contractarian thinker, John Rawls. Four in particular would seem to be of particular interest.

First, Rawls, like Buchanan, denies that justice is 'maximizing the good' (in the sense of outcomes or final positions linked in some way to fixed exogenous absolutes or to known endogenous endowments). Justice, to Rawls as to Buchanan, is not a matter of end states and results. Justice refers instead to a process governed by rules:

> In justice as fairness one does not take men's propensities and inclinations as given, whatever they are, and then seek the best way to fulfill them. Rather, their desires and aspirations are restricted from the outset by the principles of justice which specify the boundaries that men's systems of ends must respect. We can express this by saying that in justice as fairness the concept of right is prior to that of the good. A just social system defines the scope within which individuals must develop their aims, and it provides a framework of rights and opportunities within and by the use of which these ends may be equitably pursued.[57]

Second, Rawls, like Buchanan, makes use of a construct which Rawls states is 'purely hypothetical'[58] and which allows both authors to tease out consensual propositions by means of assuming the total suppression of all relevant knowledge of a personal nature such as might bias choices in the direction of specific rather than of general interest. This construct in the work of Rawls is known as that 'original position' which exists when all parties to a shared decision are situated behind a 'veil of ignorance' so thick that none can see how the various alternatives will affect him in his own unique and individual capacity. Behind that veil, in other words, the truth of the matter is that the parties have no basis for bargaining in the usual sense. No one knows his position in society nor his natural assets, and therefore no one is in a position to tailor principles to his advantage. We might imagine that one of the contractees threatens to hold out unless the others agree to principles favorable to him. But how does he know which principles are especially in his interests?[59]

He does not, and from such ignorance is justice born.

Third, Rawls, like Buchanan, has a strong belief in the value of individual liberty – so strong, in fact, that he is able confidently to predict that rational individuals situated in the 'original position' will deliberately assign priority to that first principle which states that 'each person is to have an equal right to the most extensive total system of equal basic liberties compatible with a similar system of liberty for all'.[60] As this 'first principle' is nothing other than an alternative formulation of that fundamental condition which stipulates unanimity of consensus at the stage of constitutional contracting, Buchanan clearly shares Rawls' confidence that free citizens, like moral philosophers, may be relied upon to opt for individuality and autonomy in preference to paternalism and direction by others.

Fourth, Rawls, like Buchanan, sees the representative individual as in essence a risk-averter rather than a risk-preferrer. The asymmetry of orientation which this produces is well-illustrated by the example of a rational decision-maker wondering whether or not to make an occupational move that might carry a higher stipend and then deciding that he derives more satisfaction from cutting his potential losses than he would do from increasing his potential gains: 'It is not worthwhile for him to take a chance for the sake of a further advantage, especially when it may turn out that he loses much that is important to him.'[61] Risk-aversion in Rawls' work is closely associated both with the first principle of equal liberty (given that no one in the 'original position' can know *ex ante* if he is down to play the victor or the victim) and with the second principle of levelling redistribution (given that any rational person behind the 'veil of ignorance' will expect to suffer more if he turns out to be poor than he will gain in happiness if he is revealed, once the veil is drawn, to be rich); while risk-aversion in Buchanan's system is at the very root of constitutional contracting (to end the state of nature at the cost of some personal liberty), voting rules and compensation tests (to ensure that the rights of minorities on particular issues are properly respected), and constitutional reform (to protect the vast bulk of the citizenry from the violence and depredation of politicians and bureaucrats). In the theories of both authors, clearly, the concept of the vulnerable striving to insure is the basis of predictions that the mercenary soldier or even the natural entrepreneur might find difficult to comprehend.

Four parallels between Buchanan's writings and *A Theory of Justice*. Now, however, two differences, referring, respectively, to those two central principles of social justice that Rawls anticipates will emerge, as if guided by an invisible hand, from the intellectual darkness of the original position.

(a) The first principle

With respect to the first principle, Rawl draws the conclusion that it is 'irrational' for an affluent society to rank 'further economic and social advantages' over 'the interests of liberty':

> Beyond some point it becomes and then remains irrational from the standpoint of the original position to acknowledge a lesser liberty for the sake of greater material means and amenities of life. Let us note why this should be so. First of all, as the general level of well-being rises (as indicated by the index of primary goods the less favored can expect) only the less urgent wants remain to be satisfied by further advances, at least insofar as men's wants not largely created by institutions and social forms. At the same time the obstacles to the exercise of the equal liberties decline and a growing insistence upon the right to pursue our spiritual and cultural interests asserts itself.[62]

Buchanan would be far less confident, far more tentative, in predicting other men's future revealed preferences; in asserting that some wants are 'less urgent' than others; in postulating (even in the context of a thought-experiment) a trade-off between freedom and prosperity when the two are perhaps better seen as complements than as substitutes; or in describing as 'irrational' that which many (participants and philosophers alike) would merely describe as 'undesirable'. Buchanan, because his principal focus is on the democratic calculus of consent, is able to show what the Rawlsian 'original position' cannot, namely in what manner rational individuals articulate and coordinate discrete non-market choices. As a believer in individual autonomy at the initial stage of constitutional rule-making, it is at the very least to be inferred that Buchanan hopes his fellow citizens will not then sell (or lend) their birthright for a mess of pottage. That they retain an absolute right to do so, however, is not, in Buchanan's view, in question.

An agnosticism with respect to the income-elasticity of liberty which, to be frank, one would have expected to find in the work of Rawls as well. Rawls' celebrated 'Archimedean point for assessing the social system without invoking a priori considerations'[63] is, after all, the state of ignorance in which the rational individual is in a state of radical unknowledge even insofar as his own value-system is concerned: 'Nor, again, does anyone know his conception of the good.'[64] Faced with such unknowledge, it does appear inconsistent and over-confident to assert that the maximal system of equal basic liberties will hold out such exceptional attraction to the representative individual trapped in the original position. Even if material wants in his society do remain 'compelling', he might say, still it is his opinion that it can never be 'rational for the persons in the original position to agree to satisfy them by accepting a less than equal freedom':[65] even ten thousand naked savages, he might suggest, will find it rational to assign priority to liberty over wealth where the perceived price of planned progress is the Gulag, the killing fields and the crocodiles. Meanwhile, and crossing the cut-off point beyond which only the 'less urgent [material] wants remain',[66] even there, the representative individual might insist, nonetheless it continues to appear rational to him to put economic gains above political liberties: even if the sacrifice is as great as that of political democracy for rapid growth (and particularly if it is as small as mid-day prayers on Tuesdays in exchange for a new car every week), it is a burden, he might maintain, which he elects to bear. Little can be said, in other words, about the probable attitude of the representative individual to a putative trade-off as perceived from a hypothetical position of unknowledge. Nor about the conceptual validity of the trade-off itself: 'The parties in the original position are assumed to know the general facts about human society',[67] Rawls observes reassuringly, but the sad truth is that the rest of us do not share their grasp of the relationship between market and plan, direction and affluence. Nor can much be said about the precise position of the trigger threshold (the conspicuously uncertain 'certain level of wealth')[68] below which it can be rational to trade rights for well-being and above which it is not. Nor about the political problems that would arise if some citizens believed the key level was so high that it had never yet been reached by any known civilisation while other citizens insisted that it was so low as to have been reached long ago by all societies economically more developed than is Samoa. Nor about the important difficulty that rational choice with respect to the trade-off presupposes accurate information about the stage of economic development of one's own society – and this information the assumption of the veil of ignorance itself is intended to render inaccessible. Little can be said, it must be concluded, about quite a wide range of issues that are thrown up by Rawls' first principle, that of the primacy of liberty.

The penumbra of confusion surrounding the Rawlsian prediction does harm by detracting attention from the Rawlsian procedure. The core message in Rawls' theory is a simple one: 'Pure procedural justice obtains when there is no independent criterion for the right result: instead there is a correct or fair procedure such that the outcome is likewise correct or fair, whatever it is, provided that the procedure has been properly followed.'[69] Such a core message expressly rules out of court all talk of content, consequences, outcomes and end states: 'The idea of the original position is to set up a fair procedure so that *any principles agreed to* will be just.'[70] *Any principles agreed to* – a lesson which every student of economic systems (whether personally a libertarian or a *dirigiste* by inclination) must take to heart, assuming only that he retains a belief in the meta-principle of justice as fairness such as binds Rawls to Buchanan: 'Throughout the choice between a private-property economy and socialism is left open; from the standpoint of the theory of justice alone, various basic structures would appear to satisfy its principles.'[71] Buchanan shares Rawls' commitment to justness of decision-making procedures. He also shares Rawls' commitment to individual liberty. More cautious than his fellow contractarian, however, he is unprepared to share as well Rawls' confident prediction that good processes will in the event produce liberated institutions. A market-minded economist with a belief in consumer sovereignty, the most Buchanan is prepared to do is to wait and see.

(b) The second principle

With respect to the second principle, Rawls, adopting as is his perhaps unwarranted custom the posture of the impartial logician ('Principles of justice may be conceived as principles that would be chosen by rational persons'),[72] anticipates the social choice of a levelling strategy according to which inequalities in access to those primary goods 'that every rational man is presumed to want'[72] will only be permitted by the community to the extent that they command popular support: 'All social values – liberty and opportunity, income and wealth, and the bases of self-respect – are to be distributed equally unless an unequal distribution of any, or all, of these values is to everyone's advantage.'[74] He also anticipates that that which is 'to everyone's advantage' will generally be taken to mean that which is to the advantage of the worse-off and the less-privileged – and the cause, therefore, of a ground-swell of opinion in favour of the maxim that 'social and economic inequalities are to be arranged so that they are . . . to the greatest benefit of the least advantaged'.[75] The primary logic that powers this preference could well be intuitive altruism and sympathetic fellow-feeling, an emotive commitment to a common culture and a form of 'social union'[76] in which human beings regard one another as 'partners', have 'shared final ends', 'value their common institutions and activities as good in themselves';[77] in which individuals transcend self-interest by acknowledging 'the duty of help[ing] another when he is in need or jeopardy, provided that one can do so without excessive risk or loss to oneself';[78] in which a citizen who 'would never act as justice requires except as self-interest and expediency prompt' is not only 'without ties of friendship, affection, and mutual trust', but, far worse, is also popularly taken to be deficient in 'certain natural attitudes and moral feelings of a particularly elementary kind' such as are normally 'included under the notion of humanity'.[79] Such a wretch none of us would want to be; and that is why references in Rawls to the non-rational, non-calculative side of human nature will please more advocates of right relationships than just Tawney (who believed that, when it came to one of God's creatures, 'one can't look a gift cherub in the mouth'[80]) and Titmuss (who, convinced as he was that man has 'a social and a biological need to help',[81] was pleased to be able to show that 'voluntary blood donor systems', in the case of Britain, 'represent one practical and concrete demonstration of fellowship relationships'[82]).

References to background values and generally-accepted opinions abound in Rawls – to such an extent, indeed, that Hare, commenting on the repeated use of phrases such as 'commonly shared presumptions', is able to state, with some surprise, that 'from page 18, line 9 to page 20, line 9, I have counted in two pages thirty expressions implying a reliance on intuitions'.[83] His surprise is simply explained; for the fact is that it is not intended to be the moral sense which supplies the primary logic, in *A Theory of Justice*, that powers the levelling preference of Rawls' second principle, but rather the calculative rationality of the nervous risk-averter when he awakes one morning to find himself behind a thick veil of ignorance in none other than the original position. Such a representative individual may be assumed to have 'a conception of the good such that he cares very little, if anything, for what he might gain above the minimum stipend that he can, in fact, be sure of by following the maximin rule'[84] (although the conflicting assumption that actors in the original position 'do not know their conception of the good'[85] undeniably renders his ultimate choice a singularly difficult one); and he may further be assumed to be drawn by his anxieties to 'rank alternatives by their worst possible outcomes'[86] (although the 'principle of insufficient reason' which dwells in the darkness of a position that admits no probability calculus will have no choice but to cry out to him that this effort cannot succeed, 'objective probabilities'[87] being by definition unknown and unknowable). As with the maximin of the representative individual, so with the maximin of the society of which he is a part; and it is in this way that Rawls arrives at his result that self-interest and calculative rationality will lead a collectivity, consciously maximising the minimum pay-off, to make the lot of the least favoured as advantageous as possible. A chain of reasoning which, as it happens, can hardly be expected to satisfy either the economic psychologist (who will point out that so cautious an approach to the incentive of gain as compared with the risk of loss augurs poorly for the alleviation of scarcity) or the rigorous reasoner (who will remind the reader that maximax is just as likely as maximin precisely because, as *A Theory of Justice* clearly explains, the actors in the original position cannot be informed as to their own attitudes to risk-taking: 'The veil of ignorance also rules out the knowledge of these inclinations: the parties do not know whether they have a characteristic aversion to taking chances.')[88] Nor will the Rawlsian chain of reasoning, relying so heavily as it does on the language of that which is 'lexicographically prior'[89] (the second principle of justice *after* the first) and on the methodology of ordinal ranking (the welfare of the rich *after* that of the poor), entirely satisfy the residual cardinalist obsessed with the *by how much* – a reservation about his analytical schema which Rawls himself captures in his reflection that it 'seems extraordinary that the justice of increasing the expectations of the better placed by a billion dollars, say, should turn on whether the prospects of the least favored increase or decrease by a penny'.[90] Nor, finally, does the Rawlsian second principle extend any particular attraction to James Buchanan; and this despite the strong similarities in approach that link the two distinguished contractarians.

At the applied level, Buchanan says, it is difficult to have any great confidence in the Rawlsian prediction for the simple reason that it so transparently refers to a world which is not our own. The Rawlsian second principle relates to choices made *as if* behind a thick veil of ignorance. The real world provides little scope, however, for the making of such choices: the veil having already been drawn aside, it is now too late, removed as we are from Paradise to the east of Eden, to make the requisite decisions *as if* still unaware of social attributes and external characteristics. The veil having been drawn aside, social actors have access to the knowledge that was expressly denied them in the original position (knowledge, for example, about 'place in society', 'class position', 'natural assets and abilities', 'the particular circumstances of their own society'[91]) and are in consequence of that knowledge rendered incapable of showing the impartiality that is the precondition for justice. Real world actors, in short, *know* who they are – and that they are not all equal (or even equally ignorant): 'A nation of small freeholders, perhaps roughly similar to the United States of 1787, would fit the model well',[92] Buchanan and Tullock observe, but they also say that equal endowments are not to be expected in the real world of today. Nor is equal unknowledge an everyday occurrence. A model which relies so heavily on something which does not exist is, Buchanan concludes 'narrow and distracting'.[93] It is hardly the sort of model which is likely to be of much assistance at the applied level to citizens and policy-makers wishing to be fair.

Meanwhile, at the theoretical level, Buchanan notes, Rawlsian ignorance is static (the blank photograph of a unique moment in historical time) whereas reality is dynamic (the moving picture rather than the singleton snap) – and once the subject is changed from that of ignorance about today to that of uncertainty concerning tomorrow, so too does the focus shift from the nervous sharing-out of the difference principle to the enthusiastic gambling of the rules-governed fair game. Yet it is in truth one thing to assert that the fortunate and the well-endowed, if temporarily posted to the veil of ignorance, will there promise to share their advantages with the worse-off, and quite another indeed to predict that a colony of poker-players, gathering voluntarily in the veil of uncertainty in the expectation of a satisfying game, will agree in advance that everyone must win and everyone have prizes. That they *might* so agree is not, of course, in question; and an important cause of that agreement (so consonant with the spirit of maximin) might, Rawls-like, be the self-interested sympathy with self which every individual experiences when imagining the dreadful shipwrecks that might befall him in the course of life's uncharted journey. Such sympathy with self (and not, let us say, the exploitative bashing of the successful few by the jealous many) could, to take one example, lie at the root of the rational individual's support for the multiperiod institution of progressive income taxation:

> Under this institution, he knows that he will be subjected to heavy taxes only if he is fortunate enough to receive large incomes; if he is

unlucky in the economic game and secures only small incomes, he is assured that his taxes will be more than proportionately reduced. On the basis of this sort of calculus, and quite apart from any feelings for his fellow man, feelings which can be partially translated into demands for explicit redistribution as a 'public good', a certain logic of progressive taxation can be developed.[94]

The fact that the players *might* agree to share the prizes is, however, a million miles from the prediction that they *will* so agree. Perhaps they will, Rawls-like, so agree – or perhaps they will, Nozick-like, insist that the essence of justice lies not in the outcomes at all but rather in the rules within the firm framework of which the patterns emerged. As Nozick explains it, writing in support of good procedures such as the unfettered competition of the free market:

> The entitlement theory of justice in distribution is *historical*; whether a distribution is just depends upon how it came about . . . Almost every suggested principle of distributive justice is patterned: to each according to his moral merit, or needs, or marginal product, or how hard he tries, or the weighted sum of the foregoing, and so on. The principle of entitlement we have sketched is *not* patterned . . . The system of entitlements is defensible when constituted by the individual aims of individual transactions. No overarching aim is needed, no distributional pattern is required.[95]

Buchanan the economist would be quick to agree with Nozick that the economic market involves good procedures not least because it is indifferent as between end states: 'My natural proclivity as an economist is to place ultimate value on process or procedure, and by implication to define as "good" that which emerges from agreement among free men, independently of intrinsic evaluation of the outcome itself.'[96] Buchanan the *political* economist would immediately add, however, that not just the economic market but the political too can be defended by strict reference to the standard of process: 'Political actors operate under a set of more or less clearly defined rules, and they make choices among the options available to them so as to maximize their returns (which may, here as in other settings, involve ethical as well as economic objectives)'.[97] One of the policy options which those political actors might democratically select, moreover, is, inevitably, none other than distributive justice in the sense of Rawls. They might buy the bundle – or they might leave it on the shelf. The question of their choice is an empirical one. *Ex post* all will be revealed. *Ex ante* even the moral philosopher is compelled to dwell in darkness with respect to those end states which sovereign citizens will choose to regard as just.

3 Operational Rules

Democracy, Buchanan believes, better reflects individuals' preferences than does any of the well-known alternatives such as the military junta, the single party dictatorship, the elitist ruling committee, or the benevolent depot with a propensity to play at being God. Politics being a process of discovery aimed at identifying the 'public good', the advantage of the democratic mode of search-activity is that it seeks to consult the maximum feasible constituency and to reconcile the separate interests of the largest possible number of social actors. The task is not an easy one given the quintessential individuality of the participants in the drama of collective action and Buchanan's repeated assertion that the 'public interest' is nothing other than 'what the individual says it is. Moreover, each individual will have a meaningful conception of what he conceives to be the public interest; there will be as many social-welfare functions as there are individuals in the group.'[1]

The task is not an easy one but it is as important as the Hobbesian *bellum* is undesirable; and in this chapter, following on from our previous discussion of constitutional contracting, we shall examine Buchanan's views on the nature of the operational rules that might usefully be introduced, once the firm foundation of the constitutional compact is in place, in an attempt to maximise potential gains from the institution of the democratic order. The first topic to be considered is decision-making on the basis of consent that is less than unanimous; the second topic the redefinition of Pareto optimality such as to refer to rule-governed processes and not to positions of equilibrium or to end states; and the final topic the morally-sensitive but economically-sensible expedients of vote-selling and vote-trading. None of these topics would be worth considering – and nor would the constitutional compact itself – if man were by nature a recluse and a hermit, a creature in whose essence it were to prefer individualistic solitude to membership and attachment. Yet the fact is that most individuals are not natural refugees from society but rather natural participants in it: 'The preferred direction for institutional reform will require the difficult balancing of the values of independence, self-reliance, and liberty on the one hand, against those of community, fraternity, and dependence on the other. Individuals simultaneously want to be free *and* to belong to a community.'[2] It is this duality of desire which makes the study of the whole democratic enterprise worth undertaking and which lends legitimacy to the examination of the three topics to be considered in this chapter.

3.1   THE DECISION-MAKING RULE

At the constitutional stage, when the fundamental rules of the game are being forged, there is only one decision-making rule and it is 'unanimity of consensus':[3] so central are the ground-rules that are then being hammered out to the way we live, work and play, that there cannot conceivably be any rational maximiser of expected utility who would wish to absent himself from participation in the process of discussion, bargaining and compromise that culminates in contract – nor any group of self-defined democrats that would seek to exclude even one sane adult from the formulation of 'a set of rules that is agreed upon in advance and within which subsequent action will be conducted'.[4] At the constitutional stage, clearly, public choice most nearly resembles market exchange since then, in the one case as in the other, unanimity of agreement based on subjective assessment of mutuality and reciprocity in reward is and must be the sole test of that which is right and proper to do.

Unanimity is good but, as is so often the case with good things, it is also expensive: the larger the number of persons whose assent must be won for a single alternative prior to collective action being undertaken, the greater the investment of time and effort in higgling and bargaining that must be made for a joint decision to emerge, the higher, in other words, the 'decision-making costs' incurred in securing consensus. These costs can be very high indeed, and not least because of the curious fact that, each voter having an absolute monopoly with respect to his own vote, each voter has, where the decision-making rule becomes more inclusive, more personal power rationally to exploit an essential scarce resource for his own private advantage: 'If we include (as we should) the opportunity costs of bargains that are never made, it seems likely that the bargaining costs might approach infinity in groups of substantial size . . . Near unanimity, investments in strategic bargaining are apt to be great, and the expected costs very high.'[5]

Unanimity is good but it is also expensive, and the most obvious way of cutting corners is by cutting percentages – by introducing, that is to say, a decision-making rule which specifies not 100 per cent consent but something less than 100 per cent. Such a rule does lead to a saving on 'decision-making costs'. Sadly, however, it at the same time generates new costs of its own, namely the 'external costs' imposed on the minority which voted *against* by the majority which voted *for*. Where there is a rule of unanimity, no citizen must live with an outcome to which he has not personally consented. Where there is a rule of less than unanimity,

there is a genuine possibility that an individual might find himself
obliged to put down his dog (because the majority are cat-lovers), put up
with an inadequate bus-service (because the majority have cars) or pay
taxes to support the construction of a road which he will never use on the
basis of a decision which he vociferously opposed: 'The private
operation of the neighborhood plant with the smoking chimney may
impose external costs on the individual by soiling his laundry, but this
cost is no more external to the individual's own private calculus than the
tax cost imposed on him unwillingly in order to finance the provision of
public services to his fellow citizen in another area.'[6] Clearly, 'the
necessary condition for the presence of external costs, as we have used
this term, is some difference in the distribution of the benefits and costs
of collective action among members of the community'[7] (as where you
experience subjective gain and I suffer subjective loss from a collective
decision to prohibit the consumption of alcohol on commemorative
holidays). These costs can be very high indeed, and not least because of
the very conception of unbridled individuality in which Buchanan's
system is rooted: no one likes to pay 'external costs' by being compelled
to live in a way other than that in which he would himself have chosen to
live.

Hence the problem: as unanimity is approached 'decision-making
costs' rise but 'external costs' fall while the roles are reversed where
collective decision-making moves in the direction of one-man rule.
Aggregating the two types of cost (Buchanan and Tullock term the
resultant composite 'interdependence costs') what emerges is the
familiar U-shaped curve, with number of individuals required to take
effective action on the horizontal axis and (the present value of) expected
costs on the vertical – and thence the required decision-making criterion:
'For a given activity the fully rational individual, at the time of
constitutional choice, will try to choose that decision-making rule which
will *minimize* the present value of the expected costs that he must suffer.'[8]
Once, in other words, the all-inclusive rule of unanimity (with zero
external and maximal decision-making costs) is rejected, for an unambiguously-specified proposal in the field of collective action, on the
grounds that it is too expensive, 'there seems to be nothing to distinguish
sharply any one rule from any other. The rational choice will depend, in
every case, on the individual's own assessment of the expected costs'.[9]
There is, needless to say, no more reason *a priori* to expect that
individual always to opt for a simple majority than there would be to
expect a rational diner always to opt for a *truite au bleu*: 'The $(N/2 + 1)$
point seems, a priori, to represent nothing more than one among the

many possible rules, and it would seem very improbable that this rule should be "ideally" chosen for more than a very limited set of collective activities. On balance, 51 per cent of the voting population would not seem to be much preferable to 49 per cent.'[10] It is in the circumstances much to be regretted that so many people treat 51 per cent as if it were 100 per cent and thereby elevate simple majority to the status of the unanimity rule. Democratic decision-making on the operational, day-to-day, post-constitutional level presupposes participation and coordination. It does not presuppose 51 per cent – one proportion among many and in no sense the essence of the democratic system.

The adoption of the less-than-unanimity rule increases the probability that a majority will impose its will (in the sense of felt external costs) on a minority. It is important, however, to appreciate that 'a' minority is not necessarily coterminous with 'the' minority and that the opportunity to form new coalitions sharply reduces the profitability of investment by individuals in strategic bargaining. Under a rule of 100 per cent, each and every voter has the power alone to cause a given project to be abandoned and, knowing that, the incentive to conceal his true preferences (the opposite of revealed preference in non-strategic situations) in order to sell his tolerance of the external cost for the maximum possible *quid pro quo*. Under a rule of less than 100 per cent, the social waste that is represented by the allocation of time and effort to such non-productive transferring is also less: if the 51/100th individual threatens to drop out of the game unless he is given only slightly less than the whole of the mutual gains from trade, his bluff can quickly be called and one of the 49/100 watching idly from the sidelines rapidly summoned to take his place. The new coalition is still a majority government able to impose external costs on a minority, but there is nonetheless a significant difference: the identity of the 51 and the 49 has been altered, 'a' majority still decides for the whole but it is not 'the' majority that ruled before the realignment, and the specific external costs in question — while only likely to fall to zero in the genuinely exceptional case where the 49 think precisely as the 51 do but pretend to think otherwise as a strategic ploy – are such as now to menace cats whereas previously the threat was to dogs. Unless, of course, and even under a rule of less than 100 per cent, the membership of the coalition were to be stable and not shifting – as would be the case if either of two not-unrealistic conditions were to hold. The *first* condition is captured by the idea that it is better to be in the influential majority than in the passive minority: the bargaining range as between the members of a governing group is significantly reduced by the spectacle of a reserve army of alternative participants eager to join the incumbents should an existing governor have to be excluded because of his greed, but this diminution in the power of the avaricious to hold their brothers for ransom is, frankly, less than likely to cause them to drop out of the coalition altogether. Some power, they are bound to conclude, is better than no power at all; and they will therefore, if rational, moderate their personal demands to the extent required in order to remain in the team. The *second* condition is associated with permanent social division (caused, say, by the institutionalised inequality of opportunity represented by racial discrimination): 'So long as some mobility among groups is guaranteed, coalitions will tend to be impermanent',[11] Buchanan and Tullock state, but they also see that impeded mobility can be the cause of long-lasting alliances. At the stage of constitution-making, of course, the veil of uncertainty conceals all permanent characteristics and ensures that there is no predictable basis for future coalitions. The post-constitutional position is somewhat different, exposed then as we are to the terror of the truth that you and I are doomed for the foreseeable future to be not 'a' majority but 'the' majority precisely because the only possible interloper is unacceptable to either of us.

The choice of the decision-making rule is to be determined *ceteris paribus* by the criterion of cost-minimisation, in the model of the calculus of consent that is developed by Buchanan and Tullock. What is important to remember is that the cost-curve in question has a height as well as a shape, an intercept as well as a slope; and that it is not insensitive to displacement such as would and does occur when causal variables other than number of individuals required to take effective action are in operation. Causal variables such as the size of the decision-making group and the degree of cultural homogeneity by which it is characterised.

With respect to the size of the decision-making group, the point is an obvious one, that, even if the rule adopted were to be the same (simple majority, let us say) in both cases, yet less time and effort will need to be invested (other things being equal) to win the consent of 51 voters out of 100 than would be required were the task to involve 501 out of 1000: 'The expected costs of organizing decisions, *under any given rule*, will be less in the smaller unit than in the larger, assuming that the populations of each are roughly comparable.'[12] Faced with the responsibility of a particular activity or choice, therefore, and keen to keep decision-making costs to the minimum, a rational collectivity is likely soon to hit upon the idea of devolution, decentralisation and local government: 'One means of reducing these costs is to organize collective activity in the smallest units consistent with the extent of the externality that the collectivization is designed to eliminate.'[13] Externalities, of course, are notoriously careless when it comes to schemata such as these; and even if our village should go teetotal, it might still be possible for you to impose the tax of your drunkenness on us as a result of your activities in the decision-making unit just down the road. Were our two villages to opt to act as one, needless to say, investment in decision-making costs would rise as each tried to persuade the other to standardise along its own particular lines. Depending upon how much the wet village enjoys its wetness relative to how much the dry village enjoys its dryness, those costs could be very considerable indeed, and not least when compared with the perceived discommodity of the externality in question. The optimal size of the decision-making unit should in the circumstances be established with one eye on each of the two types of cost and thus in accordance with the following rule: 'The group should be extended so long as the expected costs of the spillover effects from excluded jurisdictions exceed the expected incremental costs of decision-making resulting from adding the excluded jurisdictions.'[14] The outcome cannot be predicted in advance, save to say that some collective decisions are likely to be made by the family (the smallest supra-individual political unit) while others will be settled at the level of the nation or the league of nations. Such diversity, such differentiation, such competition even, can hardly be unattractive to any believer in individual autonomy and freedom of choice. In this case, however, they result from nothing more philosophical than a straightforward comparison of relative costs.

With respect to the degree of cultural homogeneity by which the decision-making group is characterised, the point is, once again, a not-abnormally implausible one, that the higher our initial level of consensus, the smaller the investment of time and effort that will be required in order to secure adequate agreement: 'The over-all costs of decision-making will be lower, given any collective-choice rule, in communities characterized by a reasonably homogeneous population than in those characterized by a heterogeneous population.'[15] A culturally-homogeneous community could clearly afford the luxury of a highly-inclusive decision-making rule, so low are the costs of winning consent with respect to the representative proposal advanced. Alternatively, such a community might opt for the lowest-possible rather than the highest possible decision-making proportion, reasoning to itself that consultation is costly and the probability of genuine externalities modest: it is just such a community, for instance, that is most likely to delegate all decision-making powers to a single ruler or a single assembly and then (subject to the fail-safe device of elections held at regular intervals) give the leadership a free hand to act on what it perceives to be the sense of the national meeting. A culturally-heterogeneous community is, however, an altogether different sort of beast: 'By contrast, the community that includes sharp differences among individual citizens and groups cannot afford the decision-making costs involved in near-unanimity rules for collective choice, but the very fears of destruction of life and property from collective action remain very high in such communities.'[16] One implication of this result is that the range of activities undertaken by governments in communities that lack basic consensus on fundamental values (some of the multi-tribal societies of the Third World, for example) might have to be severely restricted precisely because of the high economic costs of political democracy: 'The implication of this is the obvious conclusion that the range of collective activity should be more sharply curtailed in such communities, assuming, of course, that the individualistic postulates are accepted. Many activities that may be quite rationally collectivized in Sweden, a country with a relatively homogeneous population, should be privately organized in India, Switzerland, or the United States.'[17] A second implication of this result is that a culturally-heterogeneous community, if experiencing a breakdown of law and order in the society, many nonetheless be reluctant to opt for a restoration of law and order at the level of the polity. A loose way of formulating this point would be to say that much of life simply cannot be made subject to formal governance by codes and statutes:

> Many aspects of social intercourse are organized anarchistically, which means that the observed orderly behavior depends critically on mutual acceptance of certain informal precepts by all parties. Life in society, as we know it, would probably be intolerable if formal rules should be required for each and every area where interpersonal conflict might arise. An indirect test of the cohesiveness of a society may be offered in the range of activities that are left open to informal rather than formal control.[18]

A stricter and harsher way of making the same point would be to say that if you are anti-drink and anti-dog while I am anti-abstinence and anti-cat, neither of us will agree on the precise specification of the laws and the orders which both of us would *ceteris paribus* like to see the judges and the constables enforce. Our culturally-heterogeneous community is desperately in need of law and order precisely because we are culturally heterogeneous – and yet, for the very reason that we are culturally heterogeneous, the interdependence costs involved in democratic intervention may be so high as to render a political solution too expensive to contemplate. The *complete* breakdown of law and order presents no problem since we then return to the stage of constitution-making and do so in peril of our lives. It is in the circumstances not total but rather partial chaos which would seem to generate the greater challenge for the decision-making rule at the operational or post-constitutional stage in a modern political democracy.

3.2   PARETO OPTIMALITY

The concept of Pareto optimality refers to the case where no one economic actor can be made better off without another economic actor being made worse off. Imbued with individualistic ethics and the conviction that the acting individual alone is in a position to judge of his own best interests, economists who make use of the concept state clearly that no external observer is capable of comparing the subjective perceptions of discrete persons. Such welfare economists accordingly rely exclusively on revealed preferences (deducing, for example, that if an individual moves from A to B he does so because his expected utility is higher at B than it was at A) and take care not to rank the infinity of points of Pareto optimality one against another (lest they be accused of making inter-personal comparisons of utility such as suggest that our country would contain within it more felt happiness if only some of Peter's income could be redistributed in favour of Paul). All of which is well and good – no one can seriously object to the taking-in of slack through greater efficiency in the use of a fixed endowment, or to measures which increase the perceived welfare of at least one member of the group without any other having to make a perceived sacrifice – save for one thing: the concept refers explicitly to end states and positions of equilibrium and yet some economists are likely to point out that inertia and *statis* are constructs singularly out of keeping with the human condition. All is flux, these economists will insist, the future outcome of a current process is by definition uncertain, and too great an emphasis on equilibrium states is bound therefore to shunt the car of economic science on to a wrong line. Among these economists ('The relationship to the Austrian and near-Austrian perspective on economics should be evident'[19]) is James Buchanan, who with Geoffrey Brennan, has written as follows of the complex, the continuous and the unknowable: 'We can act only now: we cannot act in the past. But neither can we act in the future. We confront choice options now, not later, and although the action that we take now may influence the choice of options available to us later, along with our possible orderings of these options, the fact remains that we cannot, in the present, make choices in future time.'[20] We will make those choices, but cannot do so now; those choices will lead to still other choices; and in the circumstances the quietude and the peace of equilibrium states seems singularly out of keeping with the true nature of our economic activities.

Which is not to say that Buchanan rejects the legitimacy of the search for opportunities to make one economic actor better off without simultaneously making another worse off. On the contrary, and such a search is an important part of his own work. What he does argue, however, is that the search should be directed not to results and to outcomes but rather to the institutional-legal structure within which voluntary exchanges are situated: 'In the subjectivist-contractarian perspective, "efficiency" cannot be said to exist except as determined by the process through which results are generated, and criteria for evaluating patterns of results must be applied only to processes.'[21] Here as usual, in other words, it is the rules which constitute the centerpiece of the argument: 'If the rules are nonoptimal, there must be reforms that will benefit everyone.'[22] Here as usual, moreover, it is 'the Wicksellian test of conceptual unanimity' which 'offers the only defensible normative criterion for evaluating reform proposals': 'If an existing institutional structure is genuinely inefficient, there must exist some means of changing or reforming elements of this structure so as to benefit *all* persons and groups in society.'[23]

The focus is not, as it would be in traditional welfare economics, upon allocative efficiency. Rather, in Buchanan's rethinking of welfare economics, it is on the rules that provide the normative framework within which the spontaneous interaction of social processes then proceeds. Thus it is that the introduction of a wealth tax by itself could never be Pareto optimal: 'In this case, persons who have accumulated wealth have made prior choices under other rules. A change in fiscal rules of this sort violates all criteria of "fairness" and could never lay claim to Pareto superiority.'[24] The introduction of such a tax could, however, be made Pareto optimal by compensating the taxed accumulators (i.e. inducing them voluntarily to exchange one right for another): this would leave them feeling no worse off while the rest of us (as is proven by our initial support for the tax) now feel better off. The compensation in this case could not take the form of a direct cash payment as that would by definition only restore the *status quo ante* with respect to stocks of wealth and thus defeat the object of the exercise. There is no reason, however, why it should not take the form of changes in still other rules – an expedient which might appeal, let us say, to a dairy farmer who is enriched by governmental price-fixing in the case of milk but impoverished by such practices in fields such as transport and veterinary services: 'He might strongly oppose a specific reduction in milk price supports, since such action will almost surely reduce his net wealth. At the same time, however, he might support a generalized rule that would eliminate political interference with any and all prices for services or goods.'[25] Agreement, clearly, is all, but with one reminder – of 'the prospective nature of any change in rules that qualifies as Pareto superior'.[26] The dairy farmer makes a guess *ex ante* as to the future utility-function which he expects to experience *ex post*. He might, of course, live to regret the agreement into which he entered in the light of that expectation. But business is business and agreement is all.

Inter-personal comparisons of utility cannot be made, and for that reason total social welfare can never be said to rise unless each and every member of the community has given his prior consent to the change in the rules: 'All less-than-unanimity decision-making rules can be expected to lead to nonoptimal decisions by the Pareto criterion.'[27] Unless we all happen to think alike, in other words, anything less than all-inclusive involvement can be expected to generate external costs by any criterion at all: 'To be able to go beyond the Pareto rule and to judge a change "desirable" when all parties do not agree, the economist would find it necessary to compare the utility of one individual with that of another, a comparison which must by nature introduce prospects of disagreement among separate persons.'[28] Such disagreements, such external costs, can be eliminated by the adoption of a rule of unanimity such as is always employed in the assessment of 'betterness' at the constitutional stage: 'Only if a specific constitutional change can be shown to be in the interest of all parties shall we judge such a change to be an "improvement".'[29] The elimination of external costs in this manner is, however, not a free good, and thus it happens that a rational individual will frequently seek to economise on decision-making costs at the operational level by accepting a rule of less-than-unanimity such as he would find totally inadequate were more important issues to be settled: 'This suggests that even the most rationally constructed constitution will allow some decisions to be made that are "nonoptimal" in the Pareto sense. This inference is correct if attention is centred on the level of specific collective decisions.'[30] *Specific* collective decisions — since even if one decision is sub-optimal (as measured by unanimity of consensus) the constitution itself might be optimal (as measured by the same standard) and there might in addition be general support for the practice of minimising interdependence costs through the adoption of the second-best decision-making criterion of majority rule. All of this would seem to suggest that decisions which are demonstrably 'nonoptimal' when looked at in isolation can nonetheless be regarded as slightly more attractive when seen in the constitutional context which alone legitimated the departure from unanimity: 'The selection of a decision-making rule is itself a group choice.'[31] Indeed it is, and revealed preference, here as elsewhere in the discussion of Pareto optimality, has *prima facie* a strong claim to our respect.

The fact that individuals are continuously being asked to reveal their preferences, the repeated reference to non-comparability of utility-fields, the reiterated emphasis on unanimity of consensus, the strongly-held belief above all that not one should lose out as the price of others' gain – Buchanan's world is obviously a world of noble ideals. The opposite side of the coin is that it is also a world in which change of any kind is exceptionally cumbersome and expensive to bring about. Elementary microeconomic theory teaches that inconvenience and cost *ceteris paribus* are a deterrent to consumption. The fear must inevitably be that the consumption of change will prove prohibitive given the conditions that must be satisfied; and that the community will remain in consequence frozen into a *status quo* which is sub-optimal. Of course some rights are well-specified (the registered title, say, to a plot of land) and by nature non-controversial (the case with the voluntary exchange of a share-certificate for an agreed purchase-price). Other rights, however, are more nebulous (the issue, say, of whether A's reasonable expectation of normal capital appreciation for his home imposes a duty to pay compensation upon B, a new black neighbour, or C, an adventure-playground sited next door). Yet other rights are as free from ambiguity as they are a cause for resentment on the part of those trapped in their seamless web: a worker who accepts that he has signed a contract of employment will, if also an avid reader of the famous economist, Karl Marx, maintain that he only consented under duress to alienate his labour-power in favour of an idle coupon-clipper dwelling in Monte Carlo – the duress in question being merely another name for the celebrated freedom of choice between low pay and no pay which, the avid reader of the famous economist will say, must be transcended by the revolutionary abrogation of the labour contract and not, by definition, by tinkering amelioration. Buchanan's view of rights is that they are normally well-specified and non-controversial. Even in such circumstances the burden of renegotiation and transfer is a considerable one. Where rights are more nebulous and/or a cause for resentment, that burden increases; and therewith the danger that the consumption of change will prove prohibitive. Pareto optimality in such a case may well prove as much a distant mirage as a noble ideal.

Where the State is itself player as well as referee, the problem of change becomes more complicated still. For one thing, there are the difficulties involved in winning consent – a major constraint on legislated reforms: 'Since persons disagree on so much, these schemes may be a very limited set, and this may suggest . . . that few changes are possible. Hence, the status quo defended indirectly.'[32] Such an implication of political *stasis* is perhaps an odd bed-fellow for the economist's more usual expectation of entrepreneurship (including the taking of initiatives with respect to the exchange of rights) and growth (which is fostered *inter alia* by an improved allocation of scarce resources). It is an implication, however, which follows inevitably from Buchanan's acknowledgement of social division with respect to the proper course of social change – as it does from his conviction that compensation must be paid as the moral counterweight to a liability being imposed. The need to part with effective demand is a great disincentive to collective action, as it is to private. What this means in simple terms is that even if current consensus demands intervention, still a cautious leadership will keep that involvement to the minimum: once it regulates industry (air-fares are a case in point), once it provides services (a free-on-demand National Health Service being one), it thereby makes the State the hostage to future swings in public opinion. Expectations once formed are difficult to cancel and a *quid pro quo* is indispensable if a subsequent change is genuinely to meet the test of Pareto optimality. Buying out the contractual rights of the civil servant who was promised lifetime tenure may be just but it is also costly. One option is for the State to leave those rights where they lie (even if that then means that resources desperately required elsewhere prove impossible to shift). A second option is for the State not to promise such privileges at all (even if the painful consequence is serious under-recruitment of key professionals with scarce skills). Both options involve inaction. Both options point to the *status quo*.

The honest man's insistence on paying for all transfers of title will provoke raucous laughter in the slave-quarters in the event of liberation: those in servitude having no relevant rights, it is the logic of Buchanan's position that compensation from the limited national budget should go to the slave-owners and not to the slaves. This too is a dimension of the *status quo*, for Buchanan makes absolutely clear that his posture is not that of the avenging angel anxious to rectify past injustices nor even that of the impartial historian curious to learn how existing assignments of property-rights (whether by labour and exchange or force and fraud) actually came into existence, but rather that of the moral-minded economic philosopher who is concerned to ensure that good practices are observed in the future while simultaneously prepared, letting by-gones be forever by-gone, to forget the past:

> I do not especially like the status quo defense that my methodology forces me into, but where can I go? . . . In my vision, the status quo does have a unique place, for the simple reason that it exists, and hence offers the starting point for any peaceful (contractual) change . . . My defense of the status quo stems from my unwillingness, indeed inability, to discuss changes other than those that are contractual in nature . . . The status quo has no propriety at all save for its existence, and it is all that exists. The point I always emphasize is that we start from here and not from somewhere else.[33]

Of course we start from here; but to make as much of the fact as Buchanan does has the unintended outcome of building a deceptive asymmetry into his intellectual system. Looking backward, we are asked to ignore the acknowledged immoralities of conquest and trickery and to invoke instead the trusty *as if* of unanimity or quasi-unanimity – *as if* we had some good reason apart from the convenience of tidyness for so doing: 'Again it is necessary to repeat the obvious. The status quo defines that which exists. Hence, regardless of its history, it must be evaluated as if it were legitimate contractually.'[34] Looking forward, meanwhile, we are asked to regard the hypothetical *must* and the equally-musty *as if* with the same respect that we would accord to an explicit deed of covenant signed and sealed in the presence of two solicitors of unquestionable integrity. So asymmetrical an approach to rights is profoundly unconvincing – and not least because Buchanan himself, in the occasional unguarded moment, does seem to confess that the power to create rights is even today not spread evenly throughout the community. Thus, talking of freedom and unanimity, the individual and the State, Buchanan adds a tantalising rider which the reader hardly expects to encounter: 'This is not, of course, to suggest that imperfec-tions in democratic process are absent or that all persons possess equal power of influencing governmental policy in the modern world, and in America in particular.'[35] Buchanan, regrettably, never spells out the precise nature of the power-imbalance which he has in mind. A public choice economist who has read his Downs and knows his Niskanen, however, he does make observations in certain places which suggest that he sees it principally as a public sector problem – the following, for instance: 'As students of political economy have long recognized, producer interests tend to dominate consumer interests, and the producer interests of government employees are no different from those of any other group in society.'[36] Such an admission is in itself sufficient to sow the seeds of doubt as to whether it is genuinely realistic and acceptable that the *status quo* be 'evaluated as if it were legitimate contractually'. Once the principle has been established that privileged access might produce legislated conventions that deviate from ideal standards, moreover, then it is difficult not to speculate as to whether the deviance in question might not originate in *loci* of concentrated power in the *private* sector such as figure hardly at all in Buchanan's world-view. Campaign contributions, bribes, promises of future employment, bureaucratic symbiosis, old-boy networks, interlocking élites, the exchange of favours and the common interest – these and other characteristics of the modern economic and social system are frequently cited by those who are strongly opposed to the 'here' from which 'we start' in support of the contention that even today the power to create rights is not spread evenly throughout the community. Nor should one forget that the courts alongside the parliaments, in Buchanan's words, 'do legislate and always have'[37] – and that both the inordinate financial burden of legal representation and the unrepresentative cultural background of unelected arbitrators may well tend to build a certain bias even into judge-made law. That 'the rich' might as a group have significantly greater influence on the 'here' from which 'we start' than do 'the poor' as a group is not, however, a possibility that looms large in the political economy of James Buchanan. A populist through and through, his methodology compels him to speak of discrete individuals where the Galbraithian would talk of corporate groups and the Marxian of social classes. A committed contractarian first and foremost, Buchanan fully supports the honest man's insistence on paying for all transfers of title – however the title was established. His theory of Pareto optimality will provoke raucous laughter in the slave-quarters. Raucous laughter is, however, infinitely preferable to tears – tears such as the tears of frustration which are bound to come to the eyes of even the most sympathetic conservative when he encounters a defence of the *status quo* along the lines of the typically tolerant reply Buchanan made to the criticisms of a not-unfriendly social democrat: 'You say that my position "places too much power in the hands of the already privileged". I accept this, and agree with it, as a value judgement. But who are you and I to impose our private values as criteria for social change. Each man's values are to count as any other's, at least in my conception.'[38] It is by no means easy to have a bar-room brawl with a man like that.

3.3   THE MICROECONOMICS OF CONSENT

No concept figures so prominently in economic theory as does that of voluntary exchange – logically so, since so much of economic theory tends to focus on the maximisation of subjective satisfaction and so much of that maximisation, given well-specified individual property-rights in clearly-differentiated goods and services, presupposes the opportunity to swap the lesser-valued for the higher-valued utility with another economic actor whose preferences are equal but opposite. Each trading-partner must expect to benefit from the transaction as otherwise he would not freely have concluded the contract that he did. Each, it is to be inferred, would rank market renegotiation of property-rights above the non-exchange alternative which leaves the one stuffed with corn but thirsty for wine, the other drowning in wine but starved of corn, and neither with the opportunity to attain that maximum of happiness which would have been his if only the *quid* had been allowed to come to the *quo*. Yet both, it is fair to conclude, would view with surprise and even distaste the proposition that that which is appropriate for corn and wine, for deer and beaver, is also appropriate for votes. Buchanan and Tullock question the logic of that reaction. Markets are markets, they argue, people are people, and it is in the circumstances desirable at least to reflect upon two distinct cases in the microeconomics of consent.

(a)   Vote-selling

A vote is a scarce commodity. A scarce commodity has a tendency to acquire a price. The bribe paid by a lobby to a politician in exchange for his vote on a bill is an illustration of that price. Such self-seeking behaviour is unethical. It is also fully rational. Both parties gain. Neither party loses. The only threat is from the principals who employ the agents. The shareholders in a corporation react negatively to the news that the executives whom they employ to maximise profits are in receipt of second salaries from competitors, suppliers or retailers whose interests are such as to cause profits to drop. The voters in a constituency

are no more pleased with the news that the representative whom they
elected because of his declared commitment to peace has in the event
voted for war in exchange for a generous endowment of corn, wine, deer,
beaver, and, last but not least, cash. Both the shareholders and the voters
will describe the conduct of their agents as corrupt and immoral. No
doubt the profferers of the bribe would say more or less the same (albeit
more privately) should the executives or the representatives re-rat and
refault. The language is that of moral standards but the real problem,
arguably, is straightforward conflict of interest. The executives and the
representatives, it would appear, simply made the mistake of making
more contracts than they could reasonably honour. Whether the
shareholders and the voters would have spoken of immorality and
corruption had the self-seeking behaviour led, respectively, to higher
profits rather than lower, peace rather than war, must remain at the very
least an open question. It is one that is unlikely to be answered in view of
the obvious fact that no rational bribist bribes a man to do something he
would have done in any case. Be that as it may, the authority vested in a
politician is clearly fiduciary rather than absolute, and the presumption
against his selling of his vote on a bill must derive from one of the most
fundamental principles of the capitalist market economy – that no man
has a right to alienate a property not his own.

Where the property is his own, then, of course, the situation is
different. The rule of one adult/one vote is frequently cited as being
essential to political democracy, and for the reason that all adults are
essentially equal in citizenship-rights. If, however, rational adults
possess rights which are absolute rather than fiduciary, then, Buchanan
and Tullock insist, it is important to justify (or, by implication,
reconsider) our present-day prohibition on the selling of votes for
money. If, for example, the citizen should (subjectively speaking) feel
that his vote is next-to-worthless to him in a particular election or
referendum, he would have the opportunity, were there to exist an open
market in votes, to exchange his vote for money and subsequently
to exchange the money for a good or a service which yields greater utility
to himself personally than does national policy on the issue or issues in
question. Votes, he will reason, are, like blood, self-renewing, and the
decision to sell his option on one occasion is therefore not a permanent
loss: he expects, after all, to be given a new vote in the next election, to
cast, to sell, or to waste as he pleases. Meanwhile, clearly, there is a
presumption that the citizen who buys the vote is less indifferent on the
given issue or issues at staked than is the one who sells; and thus a
suggestion that gains from trade are being reaped that would never have

come into existence had vote-selling been (like the sale of alcohol in the United States of the 1920s) prohibited on paternalistic or ethical grounds. Which is not to say that the citizen will be compelled to indulge in such trading if he finds it not to his taste – only that he be given the choice to do so should he wish to reveal his preference in this way. *De gustibus non est disputandum*, and a vote *is* an economic commodity.

Vote-selling raises the welfare of both parties where A sells to B, but C may feel threatened, despite the fact that in the open market he too had the chance to buy A's vote. Not that the problem of minorities is unique to vote-selling; and Buchanan and Tullock draw particular attention to the plight in the present system of a Downsian 'passionate minority' of 49 per cent in the case where the members of the simple majority are only slightly more than totally apathetic on the issue in question. But C's fears are nonetheless fully comprehensible with respect to the external costs which he, C, anticipates, once B has two votes, C has one vote, and A has cash but no vote at all.

Buchanan and Tullock do not, to be fair, entirely allay those fears. They accept that if B is rich while C is poor, A's decision to put his vote on the market will lead to a situation in which the distribution of political power is skewed in favour of those (individual or classes) who also hold economic power.[39] What they do add, however, is that the inequalities of economic power as between A, B, and C are less important than is commonly thought. At the stage of constitutional choice, this is because A, B and C cannot know *ex ante* which of them will be rich and which poor at some later stage: differences in future economic position, as seen from the veil of uncertainty, are unknown and unknowable. At the stage of operational choice, the reason is that bundles of votes (unlike mergers in industry) are by definition short-lived in view of the fact that the next election is always in the offing. Admittedly interest-groups and analogous coalitions might last longer than a single parliament – but in that case, Buchanan and Tullock say, A might choose to sell to B precisely because of his knowledge from experience that B will cast A's vote in the very manner that A himself would have done. Here B transfers money to A (who is evidently the better bargainer in redistributional matters such as these) but no *de facto* change in voting-patterns then occurs as a consequence of the *de jure* shift in rights of proprietorship.

To all of which C will reply, one suspects, that his fears with respect to the external costs he anticipates as a result of A's selling to B are not entirely allayed by Buchanan and Tullock's reassurances. At the objective level, C will say, Buchanan and Tullock do not show that a rich man (or perhaps a consortium of such rich men) *cannot* buy up the votes of enough poor men to be able to run the nation in such a way as to benefit the rich – only that alternative scenarios can be envisaged, principally connected with changes in circumstances over time. At the subjective level, C will point out, the very fact that a vote on a particular issue can have a high subjective value to B as compared to A (and this irrespective of their relative wealth) means that he, C, can be put at risk by a lunatic or a fanatic who gets *immense* satisfaction or pleasure – the reason why he is willing to pay such a high price for A's vote – from butchering C's dog and razing C's pub. In such an account B corresponds to nothing other than one of those terrifying 'utility monsters' who are described as follows by Nozick: 'Utilitarian theory is embarrassed by the possibility of utility monsters who get enormously greater gains in utility from any sacrifice of others than these others lose. For, unacceptably, the theory seems to require that we all be sacrificed in the monster's maw, in order to increase total utility . . . Utilitarianism is notoriously inept with decisions where the *number* of persons is at issue.'[40] Vote-selling in such a case has the implication that average happiness in our nation would rise if the interests of C (who likes his dog and his drink but does not love them) were to be sacrificed to the interests of B-cum-A (who is observed to froth at the mouth at the sight of a hound or a pint). This implication is unlikely to have any greater appeal to the minority represented by C than is Nozick's subsequent reflection that the same line of argumentation could be used to defend minority-rule as well provided only that the minority in question is sufficiently passionate: 'Maximizing the average utility allows a person to kill everyone else if that would make him ecstatic, and so happier than average.'[41] Slaughtering the majority of the people in a nation is a major decision and one which, in the sense of Buchanan and Tullock, would have to be labelled as constitutional and settled by the rule of unanimity. Killing C's dog or closing C's pub, being a smaller issue, is the greater problem. Under the numerical system of one adult/one non-transferable vote the suppression of minorities by majorities is apparent even to the naked eye. Under the utilitarian system of one adult/one marketable vote the tyranny of the majority is perpetuated, with the single difference that the numbers constituting the majority are smaller than in the previous instance precisely because the A's of this world have agreed to exchange their voting-rights for compensation which they say is adequate.

If A is to be compensated, perhaps C should be compensated as well –

perhaps, in other words, each and every actor should be offered a bribe such as just induces him voluntarily to sell his consent. The outcome of such a network of exchanges would be *as if* collective action involving operational choices were to be governed by the constitution-making norm of total consensus: 'The unanimity test is, in fact, identical to the compensation test if compensation is interpreted as that payment, negative or positive, which is required to secure agreement.'[42] External costs fall to zero since each loser is offered (and accepts) compensation equal to the marginal disutility to him of the outcome in question – but decision-making costs are far from negligible, since no two actors are likely to experience identical marginal disutility, since each will therefore insist on a separate bargain, and since some will be tempted to exaggerate their misery in such a way as to abuse a system committed to the physician's principle that only the patient knows what he feels:

> If there is potential money in it, individuals will find it to their interest to be recalcitrant, not because this expresses their internal private preference but because it promises to yield valued returns. If the man who genuinely dislikes long-hairs so much that he is prompted to interfere in the absence of payment is 'bought off' by monetary reward, others who care not one whit for hair styles may also commence interfering, motivated by the promises of monetary reward.[43]

A system of unanimity of consent purchased by side-payments of variable amounts would thus seem to presuppose a high degree of honesty in the revelation of preference on the part of the population as a whole – any one of whom could, of course, hold out for the million-pound payoff falling like manna upon the venal beneath. Nor should it be forgotten that there might be authentic 'utility monsters' within the community in the form of a passionate minority which experiences more subjective harm when the dogs are killed or the pubs closed than the subjective benefit experienced by the whole of the majority from the taking of these steps: in such a case, clearly, the side-payments required to purchase consent (always assuming it is for sale at some price) are likely to be very high indeed. Bargains will have to be made with these 'utility-monsters' and transactions-costs will be incurred which would have been less had vote-selling not been coupled to a policy of universal compensation. The external costs will, however, not arise which would have existed had the dog-lovers and the chronic alcoholics been asked, being in a minority, to pay more tax for a diminished level of benefit:

'Redistribution elements must be a part of any collective decision reached by a less-than-unamity rule',[44] Buchanan and Tullock reflect, and evidently think that there is a case for combining side-payments with vote-selling – should the community decide, of course, to do something which Buchanan and Tullock merely elect to discuss, and to which Buchanan himself never subsequently devotes serious attention.

(b)　Vote-trading

A vote is a scarce commodity. A scarce commodity has a tendency to acquire a price. Where no market (official or illegal) exists such as might via variations in monetary payments resolve conflicts among competing bidders, some alternative mechanism must be found for rationing the scarce commodity. Vote-trading is such a mechanism.

In the case of vote-selling, I give you my vote today in exchange for cash on the table today. In the case of vote-trading, I give you my vote today in exchange for your vote tomorrow. In both cases the reason for the exchange is a difference in subjective valuations – since in the former case I rank the money above the vote while in the latter case I rank the outcome of the second election above the outcome of the first. In both cases we constitute that in some ways surprising political coalition which comes into being when the passionate join forces with the indifferent. The main differences between the two cases are less important than the similarities. The first difference is obviously that the one transaction is static and spot while the other is sequential and involves time (and therefore – unless a legally enforceable contract has been signed – trust as well). The second difference is that vote-selling permits some pecuniary measurement of inter-personal differences in intensity of desire (as picked up by the relative magnitude of the various prices and side-payments commanded) while vote-trading does not require each party to offer a precise monetary estimation of his own utility in his own terms (although the number of votes in a series is, of course, variable, and thus some indication of subjectivity in costs and benefits where the barter-ratio differs from '*one* today for *one* tomorrow').

One of the best-known instances of vote-trading is 'logrolling' such as is practised in representative democracies of the American but not the British type – in countries, in other words, where elected politicians have a relatively free hand in deciding how to vote on a given issue. This means that a Congressman from an industrial constituency has an incentive to vote today on farm-price support with a colleague from an agricultural constituency in exchange for a promise from that colleague to vote with him tomorrow in favour of a tariff to restrict imports of manufactured goods from abroad. Each exchanges his decision-making power in a matter about which he does not feel strongly for the other's support where such support is more highly valued, both by himself and by the constituents to whom he is accountable. If, of course, the representative feels equally strongly on all the issues on the agenda or order-paper, then there is no scope for trades and compromises and 'he will never rationally agree to exchange his vote for reciprocal favors'.[45] Intuitively, however, one would expect the nature and strength of preferences to vary with respect to collective as they do with respect to individual choice, and that there would be genuine differentiation as between constituencies and within a single constituency as between separate issues. It is this differentiation, needless to say, which means that the exchange of one vote now for one vote later is not a zero-sum game with the unusual characteristic of an identical transfer-payment going in each direction: the exchange is positive-sum since there are mutual utility-gains from trade, and this even after the costs of actually negotiating the agreement are taken into account (as any rational political actor would naturally wish to do).

Vote-trading as illustrated by 'logrolling' raises perceived welfare, but only in the case where it is the minority (not the majority) which harbours the intensity of passions: given a decision-making rule of simple majority, it would be a waste of scarce resources for me to promise to support your swimming-pool if you support my road should I happen to know that my coalition already commands 51 per cent of the parliamentary vote. Just as my coalition does not need more than 51 per cent to carry the day, however, so it is doomed to failure if it ends up by commanding less; and it is in the case where it expects to command less that such a coalition will strive to make bargains with proprietors of votes whose opinions are less strongly held on the issue in question than they are on another issue with respect to which my own coalition is prepared to negotiate. In such circumstances 51 per cent of the parliamentary vote on a given issue does not, admittedly, mean that 51 per cent of the enfranchised parliamentarians acknowledge the genuine merits of the scheme, but what it does mean is no less important: 'Without some form of vote-trading, even those voters who are completely indifferent on a given issue will find their preferences given as much weight as those of the most concerned individuals',[46] while with a system of vote-trading outcomes reflect more accurately the relative strength of desires. Passionate minorities threatened by discriminatory legislation introduced by casual majorities are bound to welcome the freedom of choice which such an option represents. The suggestion that 26 per cent support can actually embody more subjective utility than might 51 per cent is nonetheless certain to cause some raising of the eyebrows on the part of commentators accustomed to theorising in terms of single-issue (not serial or sequential) politics and more comfortable with the *how many* of head-counting than they are with the *how much* of vote-trading at exchange rates in line with supply and demand. Such commentators should be reminded that a market for votes has long existed in the form of 'logrolling' and apparently not undermined democratic processes in the countries where it has been practised; and that exchanging something which I do not much want for something with matters a great deal to me is *a priori* not necessarily antithetical to democratic values.

Vote-trading more commonly takes the form of 'logrolling' than it does any other form – partly because the transactions costs of negotiating agreements are not prohibitive where the group-size is that of the legislature rather than the whole nation, partly because one individual vote is more likely to reverse a decision in a Congress than in a country, partly because balloting in a nation is secret while in an assembly it is open (thereby providing a means of verifying that both favour and return favour were forthcoming as agreed), and partly because of the tempting opportunities that exist within parliaments continuously to shop around for new trading partners willing to supply the same vote for a lesser value of one's own in exchange. Even so, however, even now, even those of us who are not elected representatives do become involved to some extent in vote-trading (albeit implicit rather than explicit) for the simple reason that parties in an election offer not a single policy but a package of policies to the voters. In making up the mix, party leaders try to maximise support and hence 'keep firmly in mind the fact that the single voter may be so interested in the outcome of a particular issue that he will vote for the one party that supports this issue, although he may be opposed to the party stand on all other issues'.[47] Unlike 'logrolling', all issues in the case of the manifesto are presented to the voter simultaneously rather than sequentially, but otherwise the underlying principle is the same: he is asked to support a complex because of his strong commitment to the particular. His fellow-citizens are asked to make a similar choice and, similarly, made aware of the unique extent to which a given package contains provisions eminently conducive to the furtherance of their own respective minority interests. Just as in the 'logrolling' case one politican votes for farm-price supports in exchange for another's vote on the tariff, so, in the direct democracy case, I vote for incremental taxation to finance your access road if you vote for incremental taxation to finance mine. All of which is intensely democratic, participative and consultative – phenomena, in short, which would allow us to conclude our discussion of Buchanan's views on the decision-making rule, Pareto optimality and the microeconomics of consent in a mood of not inconsiderable optimism were there known to be no further costs associated with the benefits which we have examined. But that, sadly, is not the case.

4 Institutional Failure

Buchanan experienced student revolt at first hand in the 1960s, both at the LSE in 1967 and at UCLA (where a bomb exploded in the Economics Department) in 1968. Believing as he does that 'ingrained in Western tradition is a sense of respect for the rights of others, including property rights',[1] he was bound to regard the 'intolerance' of those troubled years as a serious threat to that tradition and to recognise in the 'chaos', the 'trespass', the 'violence', the 'social and political vandalism', the 'terrorist tactics', the 'class, race, and national hatred'[2] of those bad times nothing less than the embryo of the Hobbesian state of nature. Even so, Buchanan was quick to commit sociology in public and to declare that 'student activism is the result, rather than the cause, of social discontent'.[3] Student activism, Buchanan insisted, was more than an isolated and an *ad hoc* instance of spontaneous combustion. Rather, it was a sensitive social indicator of a deteriorating moral climate characterised by the 'now pervasive attitude which allows anarchist departures from constitutional procedures so long as the 'cause is good':[4]

> The student protest movement is to a large extent an expression of the social and political extremism with which we have increasingly come to live everywhere else in society. Much of it flows from the rapidly spreading taste for (and rising returns in) terror and myth-making, best developed among those addicted to a disregard of lawful conventions as a means of protest against the intrinsic nature of constitutional government.[5]

There is anarchy in the air and the turmoil and disruption caused by student revolt is but one index of it. Anarchy is a bad thing – as is the Leviathan of Fascism to which it all too often leads:

> Perhaps, and I emphasize the perhaps here, the excesses of student demands in the 1960's will have made the excesses of totalitarian democracy unnecessary. In miniature we may have seen the future, and there may still be time to change it. If this be the course of events, praise be to the student revolutionaries. If the intellectuals refuse to see and to make the proper inferences about their own behavior, our society will get the order that it deserves.[6]

Buchanan is concerned about the deteriorating moral climate which he sees around him, and of which the student activism of the 1960s, like the rising incidence of crime in the 1980s, is a sensitive social indicator. He is also concerned about the explosive growth of government expenditure: 'In the seven decades from 1900 to 1970, total government spending in real terms increased forty times over, attaining a share of one-third in national product. These basic facts are familiar and available for all to see. The point of emphasis is that this growth has occurred, almost exclusively, within the predictable workings of orderly democratic procedures.'[7] The growth has been rapid and is not sustainable; it has been accompanied by centralisation to the detriment of lower levels of government; it has been characterised by 'higher and higher taxes levied in support of governmental programs that become less and less efficient in providing benefits of real value';[8] and there is no end in sight. No end in sight – which means, as a simple matter of elementary logic buttressed by an understanding of internal pressures and the tyranny of small decisions, that 'democracy may become its own Leviathan unless constitutional limits are imposed and enforced'.[9]

Buchanan identifies an erosion in moral capital and an over-expansion of the public sector; and he clearly sees both problems as being closely linked with the lawlessness and the permissiveness, the eclecticism and the pragmatism, of our contemporary culture. The diagnosis he gives of the moral crisis in American society is that of a nation experiencing a normative vacuum: 'For several decades . . . our moral order has been in the process of erosion. Larger and larger numbers of persons seem to become moral anarchists; they seem to be losing a sense of mutual respect one for another along with any feeling to abide by generalizable rules and codes of conduct.'[10] His diagnosis of the contemporary crisis in polity and economy is in its essentials no different:

> Descriptively, we live in what might be called 'constitutional anarchy', where the range and extent of federal government influence over individual behavior depends largely on the accidental preferences of politicians in judicial, legislative, and executive positions of power. Increasingly, men feel themselves at the mercy of a faceless, irresponsible bureaucracy, subject to unpredictable twists and turns that destroy and distort personal expectations with little opportunity for redress or retribution.[11]

Whether for moral anarchy or for constitutional anarchy, his solution is legitimacy through law; and this we shall consider in the following chapter – the chapter entitled A Charter for Democrats. The title of this chapter is Institutional Failure, indicating that it is concerned with how we got *here* from *there*. The titles of the three sections are, respectively, The Over-Extended State, Decision-Making Rules and Keynesian Economics; and that must indicate something as well.

4.1   THE OVER-EXTENDED STATE

Once there was a time when the central value system eulogised 'experience, long-term learning processes, hard work, and responsible or rational behavior' and when younger members of the national moral community were prepared to be 'trained in the ways of conduct known to be "decent" by their elders'.[12] In those days American society, although composed of independent, autonomous and differentiated individuals in pursuit of their own self-interest, was nonetheless a viable and a united society, precisely because 'its citizens . . . adhered behaviourally to the precepts of a moral order'.[13]

Those days are to some extent our own days since that moral order has continued to some extent to constrain our own conduct: 'There has existed a tradition of respect for adherence to the rule of law, for general rules, for promise-keeping, for honesty in trading even of the most complex types. Voluntary adherence to the rules and regulations laid down by government remains widespread, including the voluntary payment of income taxes. With relatively few exceptions, government has not needed to become repressive.'[14] Even so, there are, in Buchanan's view, good grounds for thinking that his nation is finding it more and more difficult to live off those ethical resources, stored up in the past, which alone can provide an adequate structure for internal social stability and cohesion: 'We are living during a period of erosion of the "social capital" that provides the basic framework for our culture, our economy, and our polity – a framework within which the "free society" in the classically liberal ideal perhaps came closest to realization in all of history.'[15]

There are many causes of amorality, normlessness and rulelessness in our modern culture; and Buchanan himself would be the first to deny that he provides a comprehensive account of all the social facts that could possibly have given rise to the recrudescence of *anomie*. His objective, as a political economist who is also a fervent moralist, is more modest. He does not pretend to offer a complete explanation of all the various influences that have demonstrably undermined respect for rule-governed conduct, but he does entertain very strong convictions indeed concerning one of them, namely 'governmental intrusions into the lives of citizens':

> As laws and regulations have multiplied, competing group interests have been promoted. And persons selected for governmental office have exploited their positions to advance their own private interests under the guise of non-existent 'national purpose'. Observing this, citizens have become more disillusioned with governmental processes and are more and more attracted to assume roles as moral anarchists. Confronted with a government that imposes rules that seem to command little or no respect, individuals quite naturally come to question other long-standing rules that have traditionally solicited voluntary adherence.[16]

The over-expanded and over-intrusive State is not the only cause of moral decline. That the leadership of politicians and bureaucrats is *a* cause – and an *important* cause – is, however, in Buchanan's view, beyond question.

(a) Politicians

Citizens do not, even in a democracy, make decisions directly: the transactions-costs would be too high. Instead of the town meeting they opt for the elected representative. The representative is not, however, a robot, and he cannot but welcome the fact that he enjoys, once elected, considerable discretion with respect to matters such as the nature and incidence of taxation, the size and composition of public expenditure. Attracted to power he may be, but it is very frequently the case (and here Buchanan parts company with Downs) that it is power to do *something in particular* that the representative most craves. Even power-seekers, after all, can have a view of their own on the 'good life'; while persons who are genuinely indifferent as between alternative collective outcomes are, logically speaking, less likely to seek positions of specifically *political power* than are those with strong personal preferences on such matters. That being the case, there is no reason to think that government action will fully reflect voters' preferences: 'Within what he treats as his feasible set, the politician will choose that alternative or option which maximizes his own, not his constituents', utility. This opportunity offers one of the primary motivations to politicians. In a meaningful sense, this is "political income", and it must be reckoned as a part of the total rewards of office.'[17]

Politicans who substitute their own for the voters' preferences do, admittedly, run the risk of not being re-elected. For the genuine ideologue, however, this sacrifice might not be too high a price to pay for the pleasure of pushing through a favourite scheme. Nor is it certain (as is illustrated by the fact that only 55 per cent of eligible voters participated in the 1972 Presidential election) that the principals have any strong desire to monitor the performance of their agents: 'Information is poor, and citizens have relatively little private interest in securing more. As a result, almost any politician can, within rather wide limits, behave contrary to the interests of his constituents without suffering predictable harm.'[18] Citizens have a (for politicians) convenient propensity to treat free goods as free (neglecting the fact that someone must pay, even if not the consumer) and, if surveys are to be believed, are not much better on the true tax-costs of various projects: 'These costs are underestimated, sometimes by a factor of two-thirds. The people who pay taxes do not realize how much they pay, and they think that they secure government goods and services at bargain prices.'[19] It is easy enough to be ignorant when indirect taxes are contained in the price of the good; when income-tax is deducted at source via a pay-as-you-earn scheme; and when more than half of the annual increase in tax revenues results not from new taxes or higher rates of old but from natural growth in the economy. Easy or not, tax illusion and information deficiencies mean that citizens choose to put themselves in a position where they are unable to keep a watchful eye on the government which they employ to represent their interests.

Politicians can, in certain circumstances, clearly benefit from voters' ignorance. In other circumstances, however, it is on voters' knowledge that they most rely – as where they seek to mould voters' preferences through words (and 'if collective action is unbounded, the way is open for the political demagogue to appeal to the lowest common denominator among the rabble'[20]) or strive to purchase voters' support and allegiance through the deployment of well-calculated and well-publicised fiscal incentives. A general reduction in taxation is certainly one of the voter-pleasing strategems that politicians in government might wish to employ, perhaps in the run-up to a general election. Bribery through tax-cuts does, however, have the unpleasant side-effect of undermining civic morality by spreading cynicism wherever it goes: 'Nothing could do more towards promoting nonconstitutional attitudes than continued readjustment of basic income tax rates. Such readjustment surely furthers the view that the political process, as it operates, is after all little more than a complex profit-and-loss system.'[21] While some economic theorists of political democracy would no doubt say that such cynicism about politicians, such an apperception of the cost-benefit nature of politics, is a sad but true fact of life in democratic conditions, it is highly significant that one of the reasons why Buchanan opposes bribery through tax-cuts is that he simply cannot bring himself to share so cold and calculative a perspective. He believes in any case that a general reduction in taxation is likely to have less appeal to politicians than is the alternative voter-pleasing strategem of an increase in public expenditure. Being public expenditure, it can be more selective in its benefits than can any tax-cut, more finely-targeted on particular social groups whose latent demand politicial entrepreneurs particularly wish to tap. Being an increase, it is in keeping with the individual utility-functions both of power-seekers (who see in expanded budgets greater dominance for themselves over the lives of their fellow-citizens) and of ideologues (who want to 'do good' and feel they need increased resources for this purpose): 'Those persons who, ideologically, desire that the governmental role in society should be reduced to minimal levels are unlikely to be attracted to politics. Few natural anarchists or libertarians frequent capital cloakrooms.'[22] The upward bias in the budget that is so compatible with the personal preferences both of the power-seekers and of the ideologues is, needless to say, eminently compatible as well with the vested interests of those greedy profiteers who are to be found in politics just as they are to be found in any other area of social life:

> The prospect for profitable bribes, kickbacks, or by-product deals is directly related to the size and complexity of total government budgets, and, more generally, of the total governmental operation in the economy. With minimal governmental intrusion into the economy, with minimal and quasi-permanent spending components, the grasping politician may have little or no opportunities for graft. However, with a complex public sector, and one that involves new and expanding spending programs, there may be numerous opportunities.[23]

While the politician whose watchwords are cupidity and dishonesty is less likely to diffuse knowledge about his activities than is the committed ameliorationist who courts maximum publicity for his schemes, the truth is that information about the corrupt as well as the virtuous does tend to filter through – and to cause the ordinary citizen to question his own faith in morality.

A commitment to the reason of rules, moreover, which is likely to be still further shaken when decision-makers whose acknowledged role it is to act as referee in the social game and to take responsibility for the enforcement of agreed-upon standards decide instead to alter the constitutional contract by fiat, to 'modify and change the basic structure of rights without consent of citizens': 'Democracy can generate quite enough of its own excesses even if decision-makers adhere strictly to constitutional norms for behavior. When these norms are themselves subjected to arbitrary and unpredictable change by decision-makers who are not representative of the citizenry, the omnivorousness of the state becomes much more threatening'.[24] The problem is clearly more than simply one of a budget that has grown too large. It is also one of interfering decision-makers who irresponsibly ignore citizens' evaluations of the 'public interest' in order illegitimately to impose on the rest of us their own apperceptions of the 'good society'. Witness the role of the executive arm of the American government in escalating the Vietnam involvement without taking prior advice from the principals to whom the agents report (to say nothing of the haphazard and arguably inequitable way in which the tax of military conscription was subsequently levied in the course of that involvement). Witness the role of the activist judiciary of the 1960s in making law rather than merely enforcing it when confronted with the challenge of unquestionably illegal behaviour: 'Initially motivated by wholly admirable precepts for achieving racial justice, unlawful demonstrations were mounted against the operation of "bad laws" generally, demonstrations that were condoned ex post by judicial failure to enforce existing legal norms.'[25] The bungled attempt of the executive to employ discretion with respect to Vietnam promoted an 'antigovernmental attitude';[26] the *ad hoc* approach of the courts to right and wrong suggests that 'the existing legal order may have lost its claim to efficiency, or, in a somewhat different sense, to legitimacy';[27] and the overall result has been that citizens, witnessing the extent to which the protective State has itself become the principal lawbreaker with respect to the constitutional contract, then want themselves to have the opportunity to break the laws. After all, they will reason, 'if judges lose respect for law, why must citizens respect judges? If personal rights are subject to arbitrary confiscation at the hands of the state, why must individuals refrain from questioning the legitimacy of government?'[28] And thus it happens that an over-expanded and over-intrusive State comes to be a not insignificant cause of the moral decline which we increasingly observe around us.

(b) Bureaucrats

In order both to administer policies and to supply goods and services, politicians normally employ a staff of civil servants. The reader ignores at his own peril the extent to which the tail wags the dog where the privileges of those civil servants are concerned: 'As students of political economy have long recognized, producer interests tend to dominate consumer interests, and the producer interests of government employees are no different from those of any other group in society.'[29] The directives of legislators, naturally, do tend to impose limits on the range within which the bureaucrat can pursue his own objectives – but, 'within the constraints that he faces, the bureaucrat tends to maximize his own utility. He is no different from anyone else in this respect. He can hardly be expected to further some vaguely defined "public interest" unless this is consistent with his own, as he defines the latter.'[30] Already, then, the danger of distortion; for *even if* a benevolent despot could in some way uncover (like the scientist or the juryman) that which is 'the truth', still he could not rely on self-interested subordinates selflessly to carry out his precise instructions. No instruction is ever so crystal-clear that it leaves no room for freedom and discretion in the area of interpretation. And the master's eye cannot be everywhere.

Bureaucrats value privileges such as security of tenure, promotion by seniority, administered pay-scales and super-competitive remuneration. They also value expansion in the budgets of their bureaus, both because aggrandisement fosters a successful career while contraction does the opposite and because, 'as with elected politicians, those who are attracted to governmental employment are likely to exhibit personal preferences for collective action, at least by comparison with those who are employed in the private sector'.[31] Should that expansion generate discontent and frustration, the remedy is likely to be still further expansion: 'Reactions against the excesses of bureaucracy provide the source for bureaucratic expansion . . . Proposals come forward for resolving "social problems", almost on an assembly-line schedule, proposals that necessarily require expansion rather than contraction in elements of structure that generate the evils.'[32] A great number of those proposals originate in-house with government officials who are fond of treating social need, social progress and State expenditure virtually as synonymous; and who are prepared to back their pragmatic response to observed rents in the social fabric – 'If something is wrong, have government regulate it. If the regulators fail, regulate them'[33] – with their own vote in favour of a solution to a problem both of which they themselves may have either manufactured or exaggerated. In the United States one in five employees is in the public service. Government employees are more likely than are average citizens to exercise their right to vote. Understandably so, since their own personal well-being is so significantly dependent upon the outcome of elections.

This is not to say that the whole of twentieth-century expansion in public sector spending programmes (and in the public finance needed to make them possible) is to be explained on the supply side: 'Without doubt, some considerable part of the observed growth in the public sector, at all levels, is directly traceable to the demands of the citizenry, genuine demands for more services accompanied by an increased willingness to shoulder the tax burdens required for financing.'[34] The point is simply that, over and above that part of growth in public expenditure which is to be accounted for by reference to demand under democracy, there is a large gap that 'remains after we have exhausted all of the economic elements that might reflect genuine demands of the people for expanded governmental services',[35] a significant share which 'can be explained only by looking at the motivations of those who secure direct personal gains from government expansion'.[36] The citizen is hardly likely to be attracted to the path of rule-following self-denial by the spectacle of self-seeking public servants who display the gamester's fixation with strategy and cunning in their attempt to insulate their use of resources from the discipline of the electorate: the bureaucrat's well-known trick of responding to a request for savings by cutting *first* essential services most in demand, accurately recognised (as is nowadays frequently the case) as the clumsy attempt of a vested interest to mobilise popular opposition to further reductions in programmes, has the undesirable by-product of sowing cynicism among the manipulated and causing them to think of tricks of their own to play at the expense of their fellow-citizens. The society which results in such a climate of trickery and counter-trickery is far from ideal, even if undeniably not the full Hobbesian state of nature: 'Life in the here and now may be more brutish than need be, and certainly more nasty.'[37] And for that climate bureaucrats, like politicians, must accept some of the blame.

4.2 DECISION-MAKING RULES

An obsession with cream cakes or with gin is unhealthy. So too is an obsession with 51 per cent: 'We have witnessed an inversion whereby . . .

majority rule has been elevated to the status which the unanimity rule should occupy. At best, majority rule should be viewed as one among many practical expedients made necessary by the costs of securing widespread agreement on political issues when individual and group interests diverge.'[38] Majority rule is one among many possible proportions, each involving on each issue a different mix of external and decision-making costs. Simple majority is entirely appropriate in some cases. It is a cause of personal frustration and social disruption if applied in others. All cases of collective action do not suggest the same decision-making rule – there is no reason why they should. Government officials have consistently failed to recognise this fundamental truth – a failure which then makes its own small contribution to the moral and constitutional anarchy which increasingly characterises our times.

Where the external costs are low and the decision-making costs high, the rational citizen will opt for a less-inclusive rule. Where, however, 'significant damage may be imposed on the individual, he will not find it advantageous to agree to any decision-making rule other than one which will approach the results of the unanimity rule in its actual operation.'[39] Clearly, 'the individual will anticipate greater possible damage from collective action the more closely this action amounts to the creation and confiscation of human and property rights';[40] and it is in cases such as these – cases where public decisions threaten to 'modify or restrict the structure of individual human or property rights after these have once been defined and generally accepted by the community'[41] – that each and every rational citizen will want maximal defence against external costs even if maximal decision-making costs must be incurred in the process. The need for a more restrictive rule at the constitutional than at the operational stage is, arguably, self-evident to anyone who has ever reflected seriously on the difference between confiscating a man's home and charging a toll for a public motorway, between executing a troublesome neighbour and putting down a mad dog. Nor has the distinction between large and little entirely escaped the attention of legislators, as is illustrated by numerous instances – municipal zoning in the United States is one – where a change in rights is made contingent on the securing of a very high level of consent on the part of those likely to be affected by the scheme: 'If, due to the desires of a particular owner or prospective owner, the zoning board wants to change the designated usage for a piece of property, attainment of near-consensus of all the owners of nearby property may be required.'[42]

Despite such instances, however, where constitutional issues are quite properly resolved by consensual means, it is increasingly the practice,

Buchanan and Tullock warned in 1962, for constitutional issues to be settled under operational rules. This practice is deeply to be regretted. At the level of commission, it has led to a widespread sense of felt loss where 51 Pauls are seen legally to rob 49 Peters: 'Constitutional prohibitions against many forms of collective intervention in the market economy have been abolished within the last three decades. As a result, legislative action may now produce severe capital losses or lucrative capital gains to separate individuals and groups.'[43] Not merely unjustifiable capital losses and gains but excessive redistribution of income as well, where excessive is defined as being too much 'relative to the amount that the individual, in the role of constitution-maker, could choose to be rational on the basis of long-run utility-maximising considerations': 'The amount of redistribution that unrestrained majority voting will generate will tend to be greater than that which the whole group of individuals could conceptually agree on as "desirable" at the time of constitutional choice.'[44] Not merely excessive redistribution of income but taxation of the minority without representation and a public sector deplorably over-expanded as a result: 'Majority rule allows members of the decisive coalition to impose external costs on other individuals in the group, costs that are not adequately taken into account in the effective decisions. Aggregate marginal costs exceed the aggregate marginal benefits from public investment. Relatively too many resources are invested in the type of public projects analyzed in the model.'[45] Given the unjustifiable capital losses and gains, the excessive redistribution of income, the taxation of the minority without representation, the over-expansion of the public sector – all of these at the level of commission – it comes as no surprise that so many cautious risk-averters become *laissez-faire* liberals as a form of insurance against being the victims of (rather than the beneficiaries from) unpleasant spillovers. It comes as no surprise, in other words, that a rational citizen, even one who is *ceteris paribus* not unattracted by collective action, might, at the level of omission, strongly oppose any extension of State intervention: 'Unless the protection of something approaching the unanimity rule is granted him, he may rationally choose to bear the continued costs of private decision-making. He may fear that collective action, taken contrary to his interest, will be more harmful than the costs imposed on him by private organization of the activity.'[46] Private agreements, he will acknowledge, are typically more costly to negotiate than is State-coordinated consent – one reason why so many schemes to deal with public bads such as environmental pollution by means of compensation paid on a voluntary basis fail to get off the ground: 'The bargaining costs that are involved in organizing such arrangements may be prohibitively high in many cases, with the result that, if left in the private sector, the externalities will be allowed to continue.'[47] The decision-making costs associated with collective action under less-than-unanimity rules are likely to be less – but the danger that an exploitative majority might succeed in imposing its will on an exploited minority could well be enough to cause rational risk-averters to choose to live with the negative externality in preference to the external costs. Disgusted by the smoke and the filth but terrified nonetheless of that kind of collective measure under which I pay for your rubbish to be tipped into my garden, the thinking citizen cannot fail to experience some loss of confidence in the social and the democratic order.

Whether that confidence will be restored by vote-trading is debatable. Logrolling and package-deals do ensure that there is something on offer for everyone; and in the limiting case full side payments from the majority to the minority do produce the same level of self-specified utility as would a voting rule of unanimous consent. On the negative side, however, the spectacle of elected representatives bartering support on consecutive issues in a series of votes is bound to lead to accusations of cynical rulelessness in view of the fact that they are undeniably compromising on morality with respect to the lesser-valued matter so as to insure their pay-off with respect to the higher-valued – an argument more likely to appeal to the shoplifter who is proud not to be a murderer than to the ethically-minded citizen who objects strongly to corners being cut where duties and obligations are concerned. Besides that, exchanges often reflect the will not of isolated individuals but of individuals united in pressure-groups due to the intensity of their passions and preferences on a given project. Logrolling coalitions frequently mean in such a case that one lobby gets a road, a second minority gets space-exploration, a third pressure-group gets an irrigation scheme, and the community as a whole gets a larger State budget and higher taxation than any of us, taken individually, could possibly have predicted. Greedy politicking accompanied by expense is no more likely to endear the social and the democratic order to the thinking citizen than are the excrescences of commission and omission that result from the application of inappropriate decision-making rules: 'He is forced to abide by choices made for him by others, which may involve a net reduction in his own command over material goods. Taxes are levied on him, without his consent, to finance goods and services that he may value less highly than the foregone private-goods alternatives.'[48] Nowadays, Buchanan argues, 'the individual suffers alienation, social claustrophobia, and frustration in a congested, collectivized civilization that he feels powerless to control.'[49] The individual's *malaise* and estrangement from the moral and the constitutional order are deeply to be regretted by every believer in the value of constitutional individualism and liberal democracy.

4.3   KEYNESIAN ECONOMICS

Looking back on post-war developments from the vantage-point of the American bicentennial, Buchanan, together with Richard Wagner, had to report 'a generalized erosion in public and private manners, increasingly liberalized attitudes towards sexual activities, a declining vitality of the Puritan work ethic, deterioration in product quality, explosion of the welfare rolls, widespread corruption in both the private and the governmental sector, and, finally, observed increases in the alienation of voters from the political process'.[50] The conversion of the public and the politicians to Keynesian economics is, they suggested, a not insignificant cause of this observed deterioration in the moral climate. It is a cause which has this in common with the other causes of moral anarchy which we have examined, that it is a topic in the theory of constitutional anarchy as well:

> Budget balance was a part of the existing fiscal constitution of the United States prior to the Keynesian revolution in the theory of economic policy. Even if the constitution did not contain a formal, written requirement for budget balance, governmental decision makers acted as if such a constraint did limit their fiscal behavior. The effect of the Keynesian revolution was to repeal this part of the fiscal constitution.[51]

Permissiveness feeds upon permissiveness, and the title of Buchanan and Wagner's book – *Democracy in Deficit* – clearly refers not only to a polity that is recklessly spending more than it earns but also to a culture that is irresponsibily living off depletable moral resources inherited from the past. Neither the polity nor the culture can reasonably expect that the binge will last forever.

The Victorian fiscal morality was one which assimilated public to family finance in that it eulogised prudence and frugality while stigmatising prodigality and profligacy. Its precepts were particularly strict with respect to planned balance in the State budget as between tax revenues on the one hand, public spending on the other. Keynes, writing in the 1930s and deeply concerned about under-employment equilibrium, reacted against the older norms and put forward a case for public spending in excess of tax revenues in order to boost total demand and thereby to restore national prosperity. Buchanan and his colleagues, looking back on the moral and constitutional anarchy of the post-war period, are somewhat less willing to put their trust in an intellectual aristocracy of wise experts and enlightened leaders exercising the paternalistic discretion of the benevolent despot. Keynes, they point out, was only able to focus on the correction of market failure without taking into account the possibility of government failure because he himself had little faith in democratic structures: 'Keynes was not a democrat, but, rather, looked upon himself as a potential member of an enlightened ruling elite. Political institutions were largely irrelevant for the formulation of his policy presumptions.'[52] Being realistic, however, and whether he liked it or not, the sage of Harvey Road ought to have realised that 'the economy is not controlled by the sages of Harvey Road, but by politicians engaged in a continuing competition for office'.[53] He did not appreciate this fact, and that is why his revolution against the Victorian fiscal constitution was inadequate and one-dimensional: 'Keynesian economics has turned the politicians loose; it has destroyed the effective constraint on politicians' ordinary appetites . . . The academic scribbler of the past who must bear substantial responsibility is Lord Keynes himself.'[54] Inadequate and one-dimensional *and* a threat to the survival of the democratic order: 'Sober assessment suggests that, politically, Keynesianism may represent a substantial disease, one that can, over the long run, prove fatal for a functioning democracy.'[55] No contemporary sage of Harvey Road should assume that he will neccessarily be the beneficiary of such a collapse of the constitutional order. Yet that collapse must eventually occur, given the potentially lethal mixture of Keynesian economics and democratic government.

The *first* dimension of the problem is debt finance, where public spending not only exceeds tax revenues (hardly a good example for the ordinary household on a budget) but where the deficit is covered by claims to be repaid by future generations of taxpayers (men and women who are saddled with a liability despite the absence of consultation and representation such as should distinguish a democracy from a dictatorship). In the case of public finance through current taxation, both the costs and the benefits of current public spending are those of the current citizenry; whereas in the case of public finance through debt creation the benefits are enjoyed now while the costs are passed on to later generations who only learn of the contract when they receive the bill.

Such a spend now/pay later attitude is familiar to everyone with a credit card – the difference being that a private citizen who imposes burdens and sacrifices on others by using their credit without their consent is committing an offence whereas no offence is said to have occurred when the inter-temporal transfer of purchasing power is organised through a legitimately-elected government. The older that one is now, the greater the likelihood that one will be able to benefit without ever being asked to pay: 'A taxpayer is not required to purchase an exit visa before he can die. He does not have to undergo a final reckoning for his debt choices.'[56] The greater the likelihood, therefore, that the taxpayer (unless he should 'regard his heirs as lineal extensions of himself') will seek to run up a greater account than he would if he expected himself to have to settle: 'The nontransferable character of the encumbrances represented by public debt, then, creates incentives for increased public spending under debt finance.'[57] A phenomenon, needless to say, which is bound to please vote-buying politicians and bureau-expanding officials. These groups have long known that it is more nearly in their self-interest to rely on debt than on taxation for public finance; and, conveniently for them, 'what happened in this century was that debt financing ceased to be immoral'.[58] Keynes's contribution for them was not the discovery of new techniques but rather a licence to employ old ones without a guilty conscience or a spoiled reputation; since Keynesianism to them meant nothing so much as the ranking of present consumption above thrift and the goal-directed life. Constituents enjoy public outlays but disdain private abstinence. Debt finance permits the separation of spending and paying. Keynesianism was the long-awaited gospel that set the seal of approval on patterns of conduct which earlier and wiser generations of politicians, officials and constituents would have had no difficulty in recognising to be unethical: 'The human animal, as he behaves in modern political structures, has chosen to "eat up" the capital stock of his nation . . . This choice has been taken because of the shift in moral standards that the Keynesian revolution embodied. It is no longer immoral to mortgage the future flow of the national income.'[59]

The *second* dimension of the problem is asymmetry over the cycle, where a budget deficit is engineered by macroeconomic policy-makers in the downswing but a budget surplus is deliberately eschewed in an over-heated economy experiencing intolerable inflation rather than involuntary unemployment. The reason is to be found not in economics but in political economy: 'The prescriptive diagnosis that emerges suggests disease in the political structure as it responds to the Keynesian teachings about economic policy.'[60] It is not the ideas but the institutions that produce the bias, and this for an obvious reason: voters are pleased by a reduction in taxation and/or an increase in public spending but are unhappy when asked to make sacrifices now in order to enjoy rewards later. The fault is in a sense that of the voters themselves, who seem to be singularly lacking both in imagination (to look beyond present austerity to future price-stability) and in self-denial (to accept short-run cuts in private pleasures in order to secure long-run supplies of a valued public good); but it is in the circumstances only to be expected that elected politicians in democratic conditions will not have the courage to move in the direction of budgetary balance over the cycle by engineering surpluses in the upswing analogous to those deficits which they seek to bring about when priming the pump. Clearly, 'budget surpluses would seem to have weaker survival prospects in a political democracy than in a social order controlled by "wise men".'[61] What does happen is that there exists a fiscal ratchet-effect whereby there is in each downswing an upward displacement in the share of the State in the national income – a displacement that is not subsequently reversed.

The *third* dimension of the problem is inflation, where self-seeking politicians opt not only for a budget deficit but also elect to finance at least part of that excess of public spending over public earning by means of an expansion in the money supply. The issuing of interest-bearing government debt to the private sector can be unpopular, should it be seen to push up interest rates in the nation as a whole and/or crowd out firms' investment in order to support government consumption: 'Ploughs, generating plants, and fertilizer would be sacrificed for TV dinners purchased by food stamps.'[62] The issuing of non-interest-bearing government debt is obviously a tempting alternative in the face of such discontent, and not least because few citizens indeed actually appreciate the link between the monetisation of the debt and the continuous upward trend in the price-index:

The decline in real wealth is attributed to failings in the market economy, not to governmental money creation. It is a rare individual (not one in a million, according to Keynes) who is able to cut through the inflation veil and to attribute the price increases to government-induced inflation produced by the monetary financing of budget deficits. Inflationary finance, then, will generally produce an underestimation of the opportunity cost of public services, in addition to promoting a false attribution in the minds of citizens as to the reason for the decline in their real wealth.[63]

Underestimation of the cost leads *ceteris paribus* to an increase in the quantity demanded of public services, and this is only one way in which inflation is congenial to the personal objectives of self-seeking politicians. Another has to do with the fact that inflation tends to redistribute real income from lenders to borrowers (the State being the principal debtor in the modern economy) and automatically to shift taxpayers with constant purchasing power but higher incomes from lower into higher tax bands (the public revenues thereby expanding in real terms in consequence of 'fiscal drag') – a further illustration of the proposition that non-rationality in revenue matters leads to greater expansion in public spending than would have occurred in the absence of ignorance: 'Complex and indirect payment structures create a fiscal illusion that will systematically produce higher levels of public outlay than those that would be observed under simple-payments structures.'[64]

Inflation is also congenial to the personal objectives of self-seeking politicans precisely because of the extent to which it discredits markets (which are seen to be characterised by distorted signals, confusion and misinformation in the area of inter-temporal decision-making, and wasteful over-investment in consequence in the non-productive activities of forecasting and speculating) and engenders anti-business, anti-union attitudes on the part of households (who mistakenly blame the private sector for the malfunctioning of the allocative mechanism) such as inevitably lead to price-restraints and governmental pay-policies. The well-informed spectator who sees what is happening will, of course, be somewhat less sanguine about appointing the cat to watch over the mice, and will point with some concern to what he sees as being the real origins of the hidden tax: 'History provides more than sufficient evidence to suggest that governments find it relatively easy to default on their real-valued debt obligations through inflation. With access to money-creation powers, governments find it almost irresistible to destroy capital values of debt holders. Nominal obligations are honoured; real-valued obligations are ignored and capital values confiscated.'[65] Creeping default and partial confiscation are in themselves sensitive social indicators of moral erosion on the part of an irresponsible government bent on tricking its subjects. Should those subjects come to recognise that that government has no intention of honouring its promises in claims of constant value, they would have some grounds for fearing 'potential government seizure of other forms of capital' and thus for spending now resources that they would otherwise have saved: 'Individuals will tend to put aside relatively fewer resources for investment than they would in a regime characterized by government dedication to honour its own debt obligations.'[66] Even where the sinister hand of the government in papering over the deficit is not generally recognised, however, inflation *per se* is itself likely to produce broadly similar behaviour patterns: 'Inflation destroys expectations and creates uncertainty; it increases the sense of felt injustice and causes alienation. It prompts behavioral responses that reflect a generalized shortening of time horizons. 'Enjoy, enjoy' – the imperative of our time – becomes a rational response in a setting where tomorrow remains insecure and where the plans made yesterday seem to have been made in folly.'[67] Inflation, in sum, is both proof of past moral erosion and the cause of future, and for all of this the blame must be placed squarely where it belongs – on 'Keynesian-inspired budgetary anarchy'[68] and its premise that 'anything goes'.

The *fourth* dimension of the problem is frustration, where citizens demand too much of their government and end up feeling that, somehow, their leaders have let them down. Such disappointment is inevitable, for the sad fact is that the Keynesian tool-kit is empty and the Keynesian economist rather like a dentist who hasn't a drill: 'Even if wise persons of Whitehall or Washington, as envisaged by Keynes and the Keynesians, should be empowered to make macroeconomic policy without influence from the grubby world of everyday politics, they could scarcely attain satisfactorily full employment simultaneously with an acceptable rate of inflation.'[69] Politicians have, however, been among the last to recognise the intrinsic impotence of discretionary macroeconomic policy, not least because of wishful thinking on their part in the face of constituents' pressures and the competitive promising without delivering which characterises the democratic polity. Nowadays, 'any politicians who want to appear responsive to the needs of the unemployed must support expansionary fiscal measures',[70] even if those measures then lead to so high a level of inflation that the long-term interests of the market economy would seem to suggest contraction instead: politicians are fully aware that the next election is just around the corner and greatly fear the consequences of the key question which they think will be uppermost in the voters' minds, namely 'what decent politician could countenance greater unemployment simply to attain price-level stability?'[71] The late 1950s and the 1960s, being the hey-day of the Phillips Curve, were a period of particular stress for responsible but electorally-sensitive leadership; for it was then that the rate of inflation and the level of unemployment (and the allegedly-stable trade-off between them) 'became matters of political choice, and a politician who assigned weight to stability in the purchasing power of money was automatically branded by popular opinion as someone who favored higher rates of unemployment, as someone who would deliberately create food-stamp lines.'[72]

The increasing acceptance of Friedmanite monetarism in the 1970s and the 1980s at least strengthened the hand of the anti-inflationists, for the new doctrines emphasized the essentially *short-run* nature of the trade-off: unemployment can be made to fall by the use of Keynesian-type expansionary measures, Friedman sought to show, but only so long as the unanticipated rise in prices also occasioned by demand-expansion remains unperceived. To keep unemployment permanently below the natural level determined by real variables and the structure of the economy, Friedman warned, it would therefore be necessary contin-uously to reflate the economy so as to keep economic actors in a permanent state of error as to what money will buy – and the high price of such a policy must then be an accelerating rate of inflation.[73] Buchanan, as a political economist, goes further still and draws attention to the extreme frustration and disappointment which the spectacle of increasing doses of (hyper-) inflation associated with a by-no-means satisfactory level of unemployment is likely to provoke among ordinary citizens: 'The inflation-unemployment spiral that results from short-sighted efforts at demand stimulation will simply increase the dissonance between people's aspirations and their realizations. As a result, democratic institutions become more fragile.'[74] Even were there to exist a stable, fixed, expectations-unaugmented Phillips-type trade-off, still only one point among many on a continuous curve can be selected; and 'as such, there is no demonstrably unique point that dominates all others . . . Reasonable persons may differ concerning the relative weights to be assigned to the two conflicting objectives, increased employment and reduced inflation.'[75] Such differences of opinion concerning the optimum mix are bound to generate discontent with whatever social indifference curve politicians pluck out of the air; while any outward shift in the Phillips Curve over time is likely to produce still further disillusionment due to the demonstrated inability of democratic structures to deliver full employment at stable prices. Thence the call for a 'leader' (as in 'Britain in the late 1970s'[76]), reflecting 'a yearning that emerges when people lose their faith in the ability of ordinary democratic process to produce meaningful patterns of econ-omic and social existence.'[77] Given that 'the political system is burdened with claims on which it cannot possibly deliver, at least within the context of a nonregimented society',[78] such a call is in effect the expression of a preference for claims with regimentation to be ranked above no claims with no regimentation. The limping democrat with a predilection for order should, however, be reminded that regimentation is likely to produce new forms of frustration and disillusionment all its own: 'The costs of controls both in terms of economic value and in terms of restrictions on personal liberty, should, therefore, be reckoned as major components of the inclusive costs of inflation.'[79] Nor does the exchange of freedom for order produce significantly more than merely cosmetic gains from trade; for, when all is said and done, they may conceal but cannot repeal the fundamental economic law of supply and demand. Yet 'it is simply impossible to promise more to one person without reducing that which is promised to others.'[80] Keynesian economics makes such bogus promises, and therewith, in the political economy of James Buchanan, a not unimportant contribution to the moral and constitutional anarchy which characterises our times.

5 A Charter for Democrats

Institutions exist which encourage rather than repress moral and constitutional anarchy. Politicians and bureaucrats neither possess nor are seen to possess much sense of the 'national interest', decision-making rules open the door to vested interests while reinforcing popular perceptions of powerlessness, and Keynesian economics is an unhealthy combination of irresponsible attitudes and unenforceable contracts. Clearly, institutions can and do evolve which no convinced democrat ought to regard with equanimity: 'I have no faith in the efficacy of social evolutionary process. The institutions that survive and prosper need not be those that maximize man's potential. Evolution may produce social dilemma as readily as social paradise.'[1] Economists such as Hayek have argued in effect that 'basic institutional change will somehow spontaneously evolve in the direction of structural efficiency'.[2] They have done, in Buchanan's words, 'great damage':

> My basic criticism of F.A. Hayek's profound interpretation of modern history and his diagnosis for improvement is directed at his apparent belief or faith that social evolution will, in fact, insure the survival of efficient institutional forms. Hayek is so distrustful of man's explicit attempts at reforming institutions that he accepts uncritically the evolutionary alternative. We may share much of Hayek's skepticism about social and institutional reform, however, without elevating the evolutionary process to an ideal role. Reform may, indeed, be difficult, but this is no argument that its alternative is ideal.[3]

Evolution must be in some measure responsible for the emergence of those present-day institutions which encourage rather than repress moral and constitutional anarchy. Conscious action may thus be in some measure legitimate if the long-overdue task of institutional overhaul is now to be accomplished.

It is with conscious action to repress rather than to encourage the moral and constitutional anarchy of our times that we shall be concerned in this chapter; and the first section, putting to one side all talk of automaticity and evolution, is accordingly entitled Constitutional Reform. The second section, The Role of the State, deals with the protective and the productive functions. The final section, Macroeconomic Policy, is concerned with the fiscal and the monetary.

5.1 CONSTITUTIONAL REFORM

The political economy of James Buchanan takes as its point of departure the perceived importance to individuals of personal involvement in collective processes: 'Viable society is impossible unless most people conceive political order in the consent paradigm.'[4] Bombs placed in university offices are only one indicator among many that this condition is not being met. It ought to be. Institutional overhaul is eminently desirable in the light of the widespread 'alienation from the enforcer state'[5] which is so characteristic of attitudes in the modern community: citizens, expected to honour the existing social contract, evidently find its contents so much at variance with their own interests, that they demonstrably refuse, and on an increasing scale, to give their implicit consent to an agreement which they inherited and did not negotiate. This does not mean that citizens are coming increasingly to adopt the anti-constitutionalist posture of the selfish libertine or the political illiterate, only that 'the effective constitutional status quo is dynamic',[6] that real-world rules are far too static, and that even the most committed of contractarians will feel tempted to violate regulations which he regards as genuinely coercive. If perceived other-directedness is not to degenerate into anarchy, then conscious action must be taken – and taken continuously – to ensure that the precise content of the constitutional contract is up-to-date and capable of commanding voluntary allegiance on a fully consensual basis: 'The "social contract" is best conceived as subject to continual revision and change, and the consent that is given must be thought of as being continuous. However, the relevant point is that change in this "contract", if it is desirable at all, can always find unanimous support, given the appropriate time for compromise.'[7] Evolution by itself is incapable of ensuring that the terms of the social contract move in step with the demands of the times. If adjustment process is truly to triumph over equilibrium construct, in political economy as in economics, then there is simply no substitute for conscious action.

The fact that there is a need for conscious action in the area of constitutional reform does not, however, mean that either the action or the reform will in practice be forthcoming. An up-to-date code is, after all, a public good; and, precisely because each of us is capable in such circumstances of acting the free rider with respect to the benefits, none of us will have any particular incentive to act the initiator and pay the costs. Even where there is considerable dissatisfaction with the *status quo*, it would appear, nonetheless conscious action to initiate reform simply cannot be expected given the returns-maximising orientation of public choice theory: 'The basis analytics of "positive public choice" cannot be readily extended to explain changes in the basic rules of political order that are necessarily "public" in scope.'[8] And yet such changes do occur, of which the budget-limiting Proposition 13 in 1978 provides a dramatic illustration. Admittedly it originated in populist pressures outside the standard political channels; and in that sense 'the enormous success of Proposition 13 in California in the face of indifference and even opposition from most of the political establishment must surely raise some doubts about the extent to which normal political processes reflect the popular will'.[9] Doubts there are bound to be, but the fact remains that, in the case of Proposition 13, individuals clearly – and successfully – sought out, designed, and supported changes in the socio-political order despite the fact that such behaviour is contrary to private interest, narrowly defined. As Brennan and Buchanan put it: 'To hold out hope for reform in the basic rules describing the sociopolitical game, we must introduce elements that violate the self-interest postulate.'[10] Collective action on the part of many who share a common perception and wish to persuade still more – the Proposition 13 case – is evidently fully compatible with the overall Virginia School perspective: 'Persons must be alleged to place positive private value on "public good" for the whole community of persons, over and beyond the value placed on their own individualized or partitioned shares.'[11] *Homo economicus* moves in strange ways, but at least he does move – and move in such a way as to play his part in ensuring that the social contract is kept up to date.

Constitutions and institutions ought to change with the times, Buchanan stresses, and an 'unthinking conservative stance'[12] should therefore be avoided: whatever *is* need not be good, whatever *is good* need not spontaneously evolve, and natural conservatives should be warned that it would be foolish and irresponsible to treat the *status quo* as if it were the social optimum. *Natura*, however, *non facit saltum*, and natural revolutionaries should not take Buchanan's support for flexibility and reform, for deliberation and discussion, for normative changes legitimated by democratic decision-making mechanisms, as being proof of any great leaning in the direction of permissiveness. Far from it: 'Indeed, the meaning of "rule" implies quasi-permanence: a game whose rules were changed with every round of play would be little different from a game without any rules.'[13] Rules provide the bed-rock for social stability and predictability, but only if they themselves are stable and predictable over reasonable periods of time. Besides which, the outcomes that are to be regarded as fair and just in Buchanan's system are precisely those that emerge from rules drafted when 'the thick

Rawlsian veil of ignorance is drawn and individuals are totally uncertain as to their future positions'[14] – a very good reason indeed for eschewing alterations so frequent (with respect, say, to taxation) that decisions come to be made in the light of interests to be defended: 'Once chosen, the fiscal structure should not be subject to year-to-year manipulation and change by shifting coalitions in democratic legislative assemblies.'[15] Nor should it be forgotten that change *per se* always bears a positive marginal cost whereas preservation of the *status quo* does not, for the well-known reason that by-gones and sunk costs are forever by-gone and sunk: 'The cost of making any change in structure from what was to what is has been borne *in past periods*. The cost involved in making a change to something different must be borne *at the time of decision*. There is always a bias toward the status quo, toward continuing in existence the set of organizational rules that exist.'[16] This is not to say that regets cannot well up to such an extent as to drown out the fixed costs – sometimes on a massive scale: 'Quantum changes in organization, derived from the behavioral choices of individual participants, are not inconsistent with our model. The results of choices made over a whole sequence of time periods may be reversed at one fell swoop.'[17] Buchanan's point is simply that change *per se* is not a free good and that the social reformer who is also a prudent economist should think twice before opting to replace old rules not yet fully used up.

Where changes are to be made in the rules, then those changes must be made by democratic means – a not entirely reassuring recommendation when one recalls Buchanan's diagnosis that periodic competition between parties and rotation of governments is not sufficient to protect the median voter against the depredations of self-seeking politicians (supported by influential bureaucrats) with a monopoly of power for a fixed term of office and an unenforceable contract of service with respect to the actual product ultimately supplied: 'The move from unanimity to majority rule involves a drastic weakening of the power of purely electoral constraints. Indeed, it may be suggested that commonly observed majoritarian rule can best be modeled as if it embodies *no effective constraint on the exercise of government powers at all.*'[18] From which follow three important considerations that must at all times be kept in mind by every friend of participation, consultation and individual autonomy.

First, constitutional rules must constrain the leadership as well as the citizenry – as in the case, say, of a constitutional ceiling on public spending: 'Budgets cannot be left adrift in the sea of democratic politics . . The elected politicians, who must be responsive to their constituents, the governmental bureaucracy as well as the electorate, need something by way of an external and 'superior' rule that will allow them to forestall the persistent demands for an increased flow of public-spending benefits along with reduced levels of taxation.'[19] The rule should be simple, straightforward, and comprehensible to all members of the public; it should offer clear criteria for conformity and violation; and 'finally, and most importantly, the fiscal rule must reflect and express values held by the citizenry, for then adherence to the precepts of the rule may, to some extent, be regarded as sacrosanct'.[20] Whatever changes are to be made in the rules, the first consideration must be to limit the discretionary powers of the voter-pleasers and the logrollers, not to regard them as philosopher-rulers and look to them for new ideas.

Second, constitutional rules must be altered in the same way that they were originally conceived: 'The process involved in choosing an "optimal" set of decision rules, starting *de novo*, can be extended without difficulty to the discussion of improvements in existing rules.'[21] That process, needless to say, involves unanimity of consensus, the only real indicator of the public interest and of the overall gains from trade. Our present-day choices are situated, admittedly, within the framework of an existing decision-making structure, and for that reason the calculus of consent would seem to be inseparable from the problem of 'infinite regression': 'For individual decisions on constitutional questions to be combined, some rules must be laid down; but, if so, who chooses these rules? And so on.'[22] It is easy enough to accuse Buchanan and his associates of evasiveness on this matter, as when they make declarations such as the following: 'We prefer to put this issue aside and to assume, without elaboration, that at this ultimate stage, which we shall call the constitutional, the rule of unanimity holds.'[23] Nor do they entirely win the reader's confidence when they state that unanimity of support leads to the adoption of a rule irrespective of the rules-adopting rule currently in force: 'It is clear that if all members of a social group desire something done that is within their power, action will be taken regardless of the decision rule in operation.'[24] But the main point is unambiguous, that for a change in a constitutional rule to be legitimate, 100 per cent of support is ideal and 51 per cent too low. In practice Wicksell was willing to countenance a five-sixths majority in the legislative assembly and Proposition 13 (when referring specifically to the enactment of new taxes) envisaged the compromise figure of two-thirds.[25] It is also the figure of two-thirds which appears to have the greatest attraction for Buchanan (particularly where it is applied in each of the two houses of a bi-cameral legislature as an additional safeguard);

but he and his colleagues accept that it could create problems in a country such as Britain, partly because of the *de facto* dominance of one House over the other, partly because individual representatives do not enjoy an independent vote free from Cabinet guidance. In fact, no majority party in Britain in the post-war period has ever controlled as many as two-thirds of the seats in the House of Commons; but, if one ever did, then, clearly, a waiver clause would have to be introduced in respect of constitutional issues such as a potential balanced budget rule in order to 'restrain the potential manipulation of the economy by the Executive for political profit. Our specific proposal is that, if the governing party or coalition holds more than two-thirds of parliamentary seats, the balanced-budget rule may be waived only if a third or more of the remaining non-governing-party MPs do vote with government-party MPs'.[26] No one can deny that two-thirds support in a legislature is significantly less than 100 per cent consent in the nation. To that extent, Buchanan's approach to constitutional change relies on second-best constructs – preferable nonetheless, he would reply, to no change or to change based on the illegitimately-small proportion of 51 per cent. Given that 'property rights especially can never be defined once and for all',[27] no rational citizen would give his consent to a system under which his house could legally be taken from him despite the objections of 49 per cent of the electorate. He would no doubt feel less strongly about external costs in the case of non-constitutional issues such as whether or not to allow Sunday trading or to encourage greater competition on the cross-Channel routes.

Third, constitutional rules should be changed with a view to overall improvement, the non-zero sum game, and Pareto optimality. Pragmatism under democracy has over time produced an illogical mix of sequential inconsistencies, precisely the 'cumulation of distortions that piecemeal policy making generates'.[28] Reversing the trend in the Pareto optimal manner calls for greater breadth of vision. It would be against the self-interest of a single group of beneficiaries unilaterally to renounce their privileges (even if they are fully aware that similar privileges granted to a multitude of other groups actually leave them on balance significantly in the red). It would, however, be very much in the self-interest of such a group to support a government which tried to alter the constitution so as to produce an across-the-board reduction in external costs. The real hope for the future, it would appear, lies in coordinated multilateral disarmament (my tariff for your subsidy, my tax-deduction for your selective exemption) and thus in 'the mutual consent of the special interests themselves for constitutional changes which will so act as to reduce the excessive costs that discriminatory legislation imposes on all groups over time. It is in seeking such changes in the organizational rules themselves that genuinely enlightened self-interests of these groups may be expressed.'[29]

Buchanan, in looking to the future, and in seeking to design institutions which will repress rather than encourage moral and constitutional anarchy, clearly reveals himself to be an advocate of conscious action and constitutional reform. There is no reason to think, he stresses, that the genuine constitutionalist need be a conservative, neither with respect to the rules nor to the direction of social reform pursued within the rules. Simply, he argues, the genuine constitutionalist must retain a strong belief in the reason of rules:

> The constitutionalist seeks to reform the social structure by modifying the general rules of order, and by doing so in a process that preserves orderly measures for making further changes which are now unpredictable but which may be desired in the future. He places 'preserving the means for change' high on his scale of valuation relative to 'securing the specific objectives of change'. He values 'process' above 'social priorities.'[30]

The genuine constitutionalist must concern himself with the way in which rules emerge, not spontaneously (as if guided by an invisible hand) but in consequence of deliberate action legitimated by agreement, consent and contract; but 'beyond agreement there is simply no place for the contractarian to go'.[31] That is why the genuine constitutionalist must not concern himself in his professional capacity with the content of the rules, with precise end states, with particular patterns of behaviour such as might arise within the rules. Beyond agreement, the genuine constitutionalist will say, the rest is silence: 'We do not want to make the mistake of suggesting that a unique constitutional solution will necessarily emerge even from the most idealized modeling of constitutional choice.'[32] Inevitably, however, even the most genuine of constitutionalists will feel tempted to make proposals and predictions in his purely personal capacity; and Buchanan, self-appointed prophet as well as self-avowed scientist, is no exception to the rule.

5.2 THE ROLE OF THE STATE

Adam Smith assigned to the State the duty of 'establishing an exact administration of justice'[33] and joined to it the complementary duty of 'protecting the society from the violence and invasion of other independent societies'.[34] It is this dual function – law and order in domestic affairs, national defence in the wider world – which constitutes the essence of Buchanan's protective State. There is more to Smith than simply the night-watchman, however; and the fact is that the eternal eclectic was also prepared to assign to the State an active role in the furtherance of the wealth of nations by means of 'erecting and maintaining certain public works and certain public institutions, which it can never be for the interest of any individual, or small number of individuals, to erect and maintain'.[35] It is this duty to be participant as well as policeman which is at the heart of Buchanan's productive State. The protective State and the productive State are examined in the two sub-sections which follow.

(a) The protective state

Buchanan, as we have noted, advocates a framework of law within which individuals with divergent values and interests are protected both from one another (anarchy) and from the State (Leviathan). Within that framework each accepts that his own liberty will be limited (a cost) but sees that, because of that framework, he himself enjoys protection from the aggressive depredations of others (a benefit): 'Each man's freedom to do his own thing implies the principle of equal freedom upon which constitutional order is based. One man's thing differs from another's, and this principle, in turn, implies that no man can act out of his own commitment so that it prevents others from acting.'[36] Tolerance is here derived from interest, but the effect is the same as if it were taken as an absolute value: 'harmony and mutual respect' and a 'prospect for dialogue'[37] not unlike that which exists in a university seminar or common-room discussion. The idea being in so many ways similar to the academic freedom of the idealised community of scholars, it is no surprise that Buchanan was so disturbed by the conflicts and clashes of the 1960s: 'I criticize the student revolutionary not because he is "wrong", but because his behavior tends often to deny similar behavior on the part of others.'[38]

Buchanan believes that 'individual freedom, in any meaningful sense, is possible only under law';[39] and he criticises anarchists for having an overly-rosy view of human nature and social reality in the harsh world of scarcity. Given things as they are, Buchanan argues, and without wishing to deny the very great attractions of spontaneous cooperation in a ruler-less order, the fact is that law and law-enforcement are indispensable. The formulation of the rules is the task of society. Their enforcement is the task of the State. The danger is that such enforcement can well mean coercion of the lawful as well as the lawless: 'The voluntary limits on behaviour that have worked in the past but which now seem to fail must be replaced by governmentally imposed restrictions. Government necessarily will move towards repression in the society as moral anarchy becomes more and more descriptive of the relationships among persons.'[40] Growing moral anarchy leads to a demand for improved enforcement, for 'an increase in governmental coercion on all persons, the lawful and unlawful alike',[41] for an expanded governmental role in maintaining social stability. Thus emerges the curious phenomenon that an increasingly over-governed society is an increasingly ungovernable one as well. Other-directedness and political interference are probably not the principal causes of crime – Buchanan as a political economist does not see it as his task to provide a full account of what those causes might be – but they certainly play their part in reinforcing the perceived estrangement of the unconsulted individual from the purposes and standards of the community. Nowadays, even the 'ordinary man' is discontented: 'He has lost his faith in government as it operates, but he remains unwilling to jettison the governmental crutch.'[42] Given rising crime-rates, he is naturally keen to ensure that the rules of the game with respect to property-rights in human and non-human resource endowments will be enforced; but he is anxious nonetheless to see that some constitutional limits should be imposed *ex ante* on the protective State lest it take advantage of its considerable power to present illegitimate claims of its own.

It is the duty of the protective State to enforce property-rights; but it can, clearly, only do this when these rights exist and are clearly defined. It is in the circumstances incumbent upon a responsible community to ensure that a proper network of rights is specified, and that new rights are created where the Hobbesian state of nature is still to be observed. The standard textbook illustration of such definition, specification and creation involves the assignment of property-rights in a public good, in a river or a common, for example, which in advance of privatisation was neglected precisely what is the property of all is all too often regarded as the property of none. Buchanan's own most interesting illustration of the potential assignment of property-rights as a preferred alternative to State injunctions and governmental regulations involves free public education and its relationship to the state of moral anarchy experienced by the student activist: 'There is no incentive for the student to avoid wastage of scarce resources. He has no conception, individually, that costs are involved at all. Is it to be wondered that he treats the whole university setting with disrespect or even with contempt?'[43]

The activist's intolerance cannot be condoned but it can be explained, and explained in terms of an institutional environment which the student-consumer quite correctly regards as alienating, unfriendly and unresponsive. In a private market, paying customers have the opportunity to shop around and choose between a number of differentiated products offered in direct competition with one another; while in the case of public education the very fact that the consumer pays no fees means that he possesses no economic sanctions to back up his preferences. In a private corporation, moreover, managers and other employees are ultimately responsible to the shareholders for the effective discharge of their duties (and stand to lose their jobs if owners' profits fall in consequence of boycotts and disruptions); while in the case of a public university, lecturers and administrators are only nominally responsible to the taxpayer[44] (and thus have little incentive either to carry out proper market research or – once disruption has occurred – to defend private property which is not their own). The situation is a sad one, but no more than could have been predicted from a knowledge of the institutions in question. If students had had economic sanctions to apply, they would have had less of a need for violent demonstrations. If lecturers and administrators had had property rights in their organisations (or at least been accountable to owners with an eye to the audit of performance), they would have had less of an incentive spinelessly to meet civil disobedience with concession and appeasement. As things stood in the 1960s, however, the institutional environment was unsuited to peaceful resolution of conflict: 'Constitutional authority is everywhere massively retreating',[45] Buchanan said, and one reason was that, in educational institutions at least, property rights were nebulous and communal, 'hazy and ill-defined'.[46] The fault lay not with the students and the faculty but with the impossible demands of the economic environment with which they were confronted. Adam Smith had made the same point when reflecting on the 'wasting', the 'embezzling', the 'disorderly conduct' which he found so common among corporate bureaucrats on a salary not proportioned to performance: 'It is the system of government, the situation in which they are placed, that I mean to censure; not the character of those who have acted in it. They acted as their situation naturally directed.'[47] Smith could not condone the negligent profusion of the organisation man but he could explain it. He also sought to reform attitudes which he regarded as uneconomic and irresponsible not by preaching ethical values to the unconverted but by first reforming the institutions which had produced the values. Buchanan's approach to the intolerance of the activist is in essence no different.

Thus, Buchanan points out that the student militant is likely to feel less frustrated if converted from being a passive client into being a powerful consumer – as he would be if education were not free but priced and the rational actor were able to back up his choices with money (his own or from a loan): 'The property rights that students would so develop in their universities would contribute toward the elimination of the physical and intellectual vandalism we observe around us.'[48] Again, Buchanan calls for institutions which boost the accountability of the agent to the principal who provides his income. Such institutions, he says, would negate the present negation whereby tenured academics can support student disruption at little personal cost to themselves, whereby the authorities have little personal incentive not to meet threats of violence with appeasement and concession despite the fact that such conspicuous cowardice and cumulative capitulation themselves breed still further anarchy: 'Is it to be wondered that this growing civil disobedience should have so dramatically weakened, and in many cases ridiculed, the respect for the rule of law which guarantees the rights and the safety of all persons in all universities?'[49] Buchanan does not state precisely what institutions would stimulate the proper attention of the employee to the interests of his employer, but privatisation accompanied by the abolition of tenure are clearly proposals that are not incompatible with his general perspective. Denationalisation to promote employee accountability is an *economic* solution to a social problem, and thus entirely symmetrical with the previous proposal to secure consumer consultation not via committees and assessment-forms but through the pecuniary process of voting with the fees. Nor should it be forgotten to how great an extent the *political* solution to the problem of student discontent is no solution at all but nothing less than a cause of resentment in its own right: 'Consider the potential student who is denied admission because he fails to meet a specific test score or because he fails to obtain the required decile ranking in his high school performance. Relatively complacent when he is refused a university place, he will naturally become aroused when he recognizes that other students, who do no better and perhaps worse on these same criteria, are awarded places.'[50] Most of us would question the legitimacy of a tax system which discriminated between black and white. In Buchanan's view the legitimacy of a benefits-system which violated the principle of equality of treatment of equals is no less questionable: 'Special-benefit and discriminatory spending has no more place in a system reflecting democratic values than does discriminatory taxation.'[51] Students and would-be students are bound to feel alienated from democratic procedures when these so flagrantly skew resources towards groups defined by characteristics (sex and race being the two most common) other than merit and ability to benefit. No student or would-be student is likely to feel a genuine sense of moral commitment to a system which adopts so permissive an attitude to rules and regulations; and if asked to sign a 'solemn promise'[52] or pledge as the price of a place, he might do so but only out of fear and not out of conviction. A system of user-charges, competing producers, and non-specific criteria would, Buchanan clearly feels, do more to combat frustration and foster conviction – and in that way make its own not insignificant contribution towards combatting the moral and constitutional anarchy of our times.

(b) The productive state

Whenever a productive activity is transferred from the private to the State sector, the subsequent concentration and centralisation of decision-making is likely to occasion a rise in external but a fall in decision-making costs. The rational individual, perceiving this, will refuse to make a categorical statement about the optimally-mixed economy until he knows something of the voting-rule under which the decision about nationalisation is to be taken:

> Whether or not the individual will or will not support a shift of an activity from the public to the private sector . . . will depend, as we have repeatedly stated, on the decision-making rule that is to prevail in collective choice-making . . . Our analysis clearly suggests that the individual will choose to shift *more* activities to the public sector the more inclusive is the decision-making rule . . . Much state action, which could be rationally supported under *some* decision-making rules, cannot be rationally supported under *all* decision-making rules.[53]

The believer in self-interest, *laissez-faire* and private organisation of economic activity should accordingly learn and remember this fundamental lesson of constitutional political economy, that 'an independent criterion for determining the appropriate allocation of resources between the public sector and the private sector does not exist'[54] and relative costs is all.

The unanimity rule is, here as elsewhere, a useful benchmark (and not least because nationalisation involves the clearly-constitutional issue of property-rights). In the case of the 100 per cent rule, the spillover costs associated with the scheme fall to zero – but the costs of securing consent do not. Those costs, indeed, are likely to be extremely high save in that genuinely exceptional community where the degree of dissensus happens to be extremely low. Given such costs, the rule of cost-minimisation is likely to point to a proportion of something less than 100 per cent agreement – to a proportion, in other words, in the case of which both external and decision-making costs must be assumed to be present and non-zero. But what that precise proportion will turn out to be will vary from issue to issue and cannot therefore be established *a priori*. That means in turn, that no general statement can be made *a priori* as to whether or not any given activity should be collectivised or left in the private sector:

> In one sense . . . we can quite properly say that all decision-making rules embodying less than full consensus will tend to cause relatively too many resources to be devoted to the public sector – too many relative to that idealized allocation of resources that the omniscient observer, knowing all utility functions over time, might be able to describe. In another sense, however, if we leave such omniscience out of account, no such conclusion can be reached . . . The only meaningful overextension of the public sector must refer to realizable alternatives, and unless interdependence costs can be shown to be reduced under these alternatives, normative statements cannot be made.[55]

There is, in other words, no clear statement to be made, no ideal solution to be advocated. Instead there is caution, hesitation and doubt.

Buchanan at his most agnostic is capable of writing as follows about the desirability or otherwise of the productive State: 'While the absence of the unanimity rule in politics does give some basis for the generalized hypothesis that where they are substitutes, individuals would agree to replace politicized arrangements with market-like arrangements this must remain strictly a hypothesis subject to the agreement test.'[56] The *multi-period* agreement test, of course. Property-rights are far too important to be left to the vagaries of in-period negotiation. Instead Buchanan maintains, 'some restrictions on the type of goods to be provided and financed collectively' must be included at the original, constitutional stage: 'At least in some rough sense, the dividing line between the private and the public or governmental sector of the economy should be settled in the basic constitution.'[57] Wherever the actual line is ultimately drawn, however, the crucial point is that Buchanan's focus is on the *rules* governing the collectivisation or privatisation of the activities. It is not on the nature of the *activities* themselves. Individuals and individuals alone can say which activities are properly public and which properly private. Buchanan's sole recommendation is that in making their choice they should pay due attention to due process: 'To the external observer, *any* result reached by the procedure of voluntary contract among persons is equally desirable, provided only that the procedural norms are followed, that the process itself is efficient, and that the interests of the parties in contract are the only ones to be counted.'[58] Where due process is neglected, the protective State must all too frequently be called upon to impose the illegitimate and unconstitutional decisions of the productive State. Where due process is respected, private gas, nationalised gas, collectivised rail, free enterprise rail – *a priori* there is nothing in it, and the consumer-citizen remains the sovereign.

5.3   MACROECONOMIC POLICY

Total demand bulks large in Buchanan's writings. One would expect nothing less; for an author strongly committed to the reason of rules and the stability of multi-period institutions is bound to be anxious, here as elsewhere, about the wisdom of the pragmatic and the discretionary, the rule-of-thumb and the day-to-day. It is with one eye on the interventionism of the past as well as with one eye on the constitutionalism of the future that Buchanan proceeds when he advances the specific proposals for the reform of fiscal and monetary policy that form the subject-matter of this section.

(a)   Fiscal policy

The term fiscal policy refers to public finance, public expenditure and the budget – three closely-related constructs which it will be useful nonetheless to examine sequentially.

(i)   Public finance

Deficit-spending and money-creation will be examined later. Our present concern is Buchanan's attitude to taxation. Specifically, he argues that absolute levels of taxation should be limited at the constitutional stage for the reason that such limitation enjoys consensual support: widely-shared perceptions of 'justice' dictate that the maximum proportion of national income that can be taxed away for collective purposes be specified in advance, and it is precisely these pressures that lead to the constitutional ceiling.

Constitutions mean prospectiveness, prospectiveness means ignorance of outcome; and it is behind the thick veil of uncertainty, where no individual can identify his own future position in subsequent time-periods, that rates as well as ceilings are to be established. Due process dictates the extensive horizon – not just one 'play' but a series. Due process says nothing about uniformity. Uncertainty could, of course, generate support for a proportional income tax such as was advocated so strongly by Hayek in *The Constitution of Liberty* and by Friedman in *Capitalism and Freedom*, and to which the Virginia approach is not antithetical *a priori*: 'The proportionality restriction might well serve to constrain discrimination among different groups of taxpayers.'[59] Uncertainty could, however, produce other rate-structures as well: 'In this approach it matters relatively little whether a tax system is regressive or progressive. What does matter is whether or not the tax structure, along with the pattern of budgetary outlays, is generated through a decision-making process that reflects, even if imperfectly, individual values in a regime where all persons are given roughly equal weights.'[60]

The crucial proviso is, naturally, that whatever rate-structure is adopted, the choice should be constitutional rather than operational, multi-period rather than in-period, lest transient coalitions of the disgruntled and the greedy exploit the fiscal process to secure redistribution in favour of their own known interest-groups. Redistribution through the tax-system is fully legitimate if the proposals are adopted at the constitutional stage when uncertainty reigns as to future income and wealth positions; but only if the rules of the game then introduced are not subsequently dropped by legislative majorities which substitute the expedient for the quasi-permanent. Preannouncement and constitutionalisation of tax-structures will put an end to such abominations. And, apart from everything else, the *ex ante facto* declaration of rates (together with the precise specification of the earnings and assets with respect to which those rates are to be applied) allows taxpayers to plan ahead without fear of unexpected changes such as might cause them later on to regret how little leisure they actually enjoyed, how much capital they in fact built up: 'At the constitutional stage of decision, the potential taxpayer will prefer that governments be required to announce tax rates before the appropriate behavioral adjustments take place. The generalization of the legal precept against *ex post facto* legislation becomes especially significant under capital taxation, although it is by no means absent from income tax considerations.'[61] If individuals are to make rational decisions, then the relevant information must be available. Preannouncement ensures that at least some of that information will be available, and thus makes a contribution to predictability as well as to justice.

(ii)   Public expenditure

The concomitant of the constitutional ceiling on taxing is the constitutional ceiling on spending, *as if* decided behind the well-known thick veil – where, 'since the individual remains ignorant concerning his own predicted income or tastes, he cannot identify a cost share for himself under any particular tax system. He cannot, therefore, predict whether, post-constitutionally, he might prefer a larger or a smaller public-goods quantity than that which he predicts would be "efficient" for the whole community.'[62] Behind the thick veil, in other words, the perception of each is likely to converge on that which is optimal for all; and this optimum then becomes embodied in a constitutional constraint intended to be operative for the foreseeable future. But the precise amount of money represented by that optimum cannot be specified *a priori* (either in absolute terms or as a proportion of the national product). The voters of California, in the case of Proposition 13, called for cuts, not once-for-all but quasi-permanent, in the funds to be made available to democratically-elected leadership: 'The avowed intention was to constrain the size of government below the level that would prevail under normal electoral processes.'[63] In so doing they were expressing their discontent with the relentless incrementalism, the piecemeal something-for-everyoneism, the 'pragmatic drift' of modern spending policies, which must inevitably generate a State that is little short of an 'insatiable Leviathan': 'Indeed, my primary critique of those philosophers who hold up the evolutionary process as ideal is based on my reading of what this process has now produced.'[64] Buchanan himself is clearly on the side of those who believe that *ad hoc* choices of individual decision-makers add up to over-expanded budgets; and he would, it is clear, expect the introduction of a constitutional ceiling to involve cuts rather than growth. That growth rather than cuts could result, however, he never denies, as is illustrated by the observation of Brennan and Buchanan that the expansion in the United States in public spending from 7 per cent of GNP in 1902 to over 30 per cent in 1970 by itself proves nothing: 'There is no presumption that government was the "right size" in 1902, or that increases in size do not accurately reflect electoral wishes.'[65] What matters most, Buchanan stresses, is that there should be a constitutional ceiling and that it should be established (and, where necessary, altered) by the proper procedures. The precise height of the ceiling, he would add, is, like all end states, not his to prescribe.

Once the ceiling has been established, the next step must be to reach agreement on the allocation of the benefits within the whole. Pragmatists tend to proceed policy by policy and programme by programme. Constitutionalists, Buchanan recommends, should look at proposals in a bundle, not in isolation, and should never neglect the interconnection and interdependence of issues. Not only should they look at the whole of the governmental package, he argues, but they should remember as well that the benchmark is unanimity and the ideal test that of Pareto optimality: thus 'constitutional restrictions might be imposed which dictate that only spending proposals that promise *general* benefits to the whole membership of the community can be considered.'[66] The present-day rule of simple majority leads to a situation in which the minority is exploited by fiscal means – a situation in which some pay while others benefit – and the constitutional rule which Buchanan proposes is intended to deal democratically with the problem of such unwarranted gains.

Existing contracts, however, must be honoured; for we start from here and nowhere else. Even so, the honouring of contracts does not preclude their being renegotiated, so long as the renegotiation is entirely voluntary and gains from trade are believed by all parties to have arisen. Thus a poor man (who perceives that he has a vested interest in a given benefit) and a rich man (who happens to 'desire that the range of collective or state action be restricted') might enter into an arrangement whereby the rich man offers 'a once-for-all or quasi-permanent transfer of wealth to the poor man' in exchange for the poor man's 'agreement to a genuinely new constitution that will overtly limit governmentally directed fiscal transfers':[67] both parties gain from this negotiated running down of the State, neither loses, and neither feels resentful or vulnerable when he looks to the future. Again, should the present tax-transfer approach to old age pensions be abandoned (on the grounds that it involves an inter-generational transfer which commits the unborn and the unconsulted) and replaced by an insurance-based system (under which each person pays in over time the full cost of his own pension, whether that pension is subsequently provided by government or by the private sector), then existing contracts must not be violated — but they may be bought back subject to adequate compensation or side payments being offered to win the requisite Wicksellian unanimity of consent: 'The welfare state should be dismantled if those who gain from the change can pay off those who have positive claims and still have some surplus left over.'[68]

Should those who gain fail to compensate those who lose, their self-seeking behaviour would be widely regarded as immoral and unethical. Few of us would want to continue to trade with a butcher, a brewer or a baker who did not keep his word and pay his debts. We would instead strive to shift our business to his more responsible competitor. Our attitude to our government is essentially the same in that few of us could continue to regard as legitimate a ruling party which consistently ignored consensual standards of fairness and justice. This is not to say that reformers should not dismantle the welfare state: they are, on the contrary, honour-bound to do so should that be part of the contract which they concluded with the electorate. Simply, in concluding a new contract they should not default on an old one to which they are honour-bound already. Instead of default they should renegotiate, and it is here that the sound counsels of the economist will prove of exceptional value indeed: 'Political economists fulfill their proper role when they can show politicians that there do exist ways to close down the excesses of the welfare state *without* involving default on the contracts that this State has obligated itself to.'[69] The shopper who pays is morally superior to the shoplifter who steals. The man who divorces with maintenance is morally superior to the man who deserts his wife and children. The State which buys its way out of an initial mistake is morally superior to the State which disestablishes institutions without compensating victims. Morality is morality, contracts are contracts – and anarchy in great ones will not unattended go.

(iii)   The budget

Once upon a time governments observed an unwritten 'fiscal constitution' which prescribed that public spending be financed from tax revenues, not budget deficits and not money-creation. Sadly, Keynesian economics since the 1930s has caused the old norms of fiscal prudence to be dropped and thereby destroyed 'a valuable portion of our public capital stock'.[70] Politicians welcomed the change, given that spending without taxing yields rich dividends in votes whereas 'fiscal prudence simply cannot be made to pay off in democracy'.[71] Buchanan does not welcome it, regarding it as the mother and father of irresponsible attitudes, an over-expanded public sector, extensive fiscal illusion and excessive inflation. Buchanan does not say that the old cultural norms should be revived: norms are a growth, not a manufacture, and cannot be re-created at will. What he does say is that an equivalent must be found – since in the absence of external constraint 'rational behaviour on the part of public choosers ensures the regime of continuing and accelerating budget deficits'.[72] That equivalent must be a written constitutional rule to pre-commit and pre-constrain the spending proclivities of elected politicians: 'Having lived through the destruction of the fiscal morality by the Keynesian mind-set, we must make every effort to replace this morality with deliberately chosen constraints that will produce substantially the pre-Keynesian patterns of results.'[73] Just as the police and prisons of the protective State are a poor second-best for personal commitment to the social contract, so, Buchanan clearly believes, 'our previously informal fiscal constitution' is morally superior to that which must now fulfil its function – 'a constitutional rule that will become legally as well as morally binding, a rule that is explicitly written into the constitutional document of the United States'.[74] The 'previously unwritten fiscal constitution' is, however, no longer on offer in an era when spending has become open-ended and thrift has become a paradox. Keynesian economics has turned the politicians loose and destroyed the old attitudes; and we start from here.

Hence the case for the balanced budget amendment – *ex ante* (planned), not *ex post* (realised), possibly complemented by a residual or back-up proviso that an unintended deficit must be corrected within three months through a reduction in public spending while an unexpected surplus in public revenues must be employed to retire existing national debt. The amendment should not specify either the size of the budget or its allocation as between alternative projects: those choices must be made, but they must be made separately. The amendment should specify, simply, that the national budget must balance and that if the electorate wants more aggregate spending it must pay more aggregate tax. It thus has an educational function with respect to the electorate which is the counterpart of the constraining function which it exercises with respect to elected politicians. Our present fiscal practices are on both accounts to be found wanting: 'Debt financing reduces the perceived price of publicly provided goods and services. In response, citizen-taxpayers increase their demands for such goods and services. Preferred budget levels will be higher, and these preferences will be sensed by politicians and translated into political outcomes.'[75] Budgetary balance terminates the abuse and makes public provision a matter of rational choice. It makes the electorate aware of real costs and helps to dispel the something-for-nothing mentality that has been sedulously fostered by politicians acting in the darkness of the shadow cast by Keynes. It does no more than that; for, here again, it is process and not outcome which enjoys pride of place in Buchanan's social philosophy.

(b) Monetary Policy

Elected politicians are strongly tempted to finance new spending out of new money: taxation is unpopular because it reduces private sector purchasing power, debt-issue is unpopular because it causes the crowding-up of interest-rates, and inflation is not widely understood to be a political phenomenon. Obviously there are limits, since citizens will rapidly run down their holdings of cash in a period of hyper-inflation; and for that reason even Leviathan 'needs to play a strategy of restraint'.[76] Within those limits, however, elected politicians have considerable opportunity indeed to expand the money-supply to an extent that is detrimental to the effective functioning of the price-system. They also have the incentive to do so.

Nor can central bankers be looked to for countervailing power. Both the Federal Reserve System and the Bank of England are nominally independent of political pressures, but political influence can be brought to bear nonetheless on their operations:

A monetary decision maker is in a position only one stage removed from that of the directly elected politician. He will normally have been appointed to office by a politician subject to electoral testing, and he may even serve at the pleasure of the latter. It is scarcely to be expected that persons who are chosen as monetary decision makers will be the sort that are likely to take policy stances sharply contrary to those desired by their political associates, especially since these stances would also run counter to strong public opinion and media pressures.[77]

Neither the central banker nor the politician wishes to be blamed for low investment and high unemployment, especially since neither can expect much in the way of a personal reward should the long-term result of tight money prove to be the desirable public good of price-stability.

Each, because his personal utility-function is such as, to bias his decision-making preferences in favour of short-term benefits, will be drawn instead to easy money. The fault is not his own and inheres in the institutional environment within which he operates. It is accordingly that structure which must be altered if genuine improvement is to be brought about – for, here as elsewhere, 'good games depend on good rules more than they depend on good players',[78] and even a highly moral man is in danger of becoming a rascal if expected successfully to adapt to the constraints of a highly immoral situation.

The problem of inflation is not one of economic technique – the doctors are not ignorant of the proper medicine to be prescribed. The problem is a political one – since it is via politics that economic ideas are translated into collective realities. The problem is compounded by the insularity of orthodox unidisciplinary economics – which seems unaware that 'the criteria for good theory are necessarily related to the political institutions of the society': 'The necessary linkage or interdependence between the basic political structure of society and the economic theory of policy has never been properly recognized by economists, despite its elementary logic and its overwhelming empirical apparency.'[79] The solution to the problem is precommitment through good laws that prevent irresponsible behaviour – and, specifically, through a further constitutional amendment 'that would direct the Federal Reserve Board to increase the monetary base at a rate roughly equivalent to the rate of growth in real output in the national economy'.[80] Buchanan could have recommended a free market in money, 100 per cent reserves, a return to a metallic (e.g. a gold) standard or the denationalisation of central banking; and in that sense his precise proposals are conspicuously moderate and cautious. He does not call for the abolition of the State monopoly, since it is the opportunity to exercise *discretionary* power which is the fundamental cause of the chronic abuse – as competition even without denationalisation serves to demonstrate: 'Given the same basic motivation for each of two governments, a continuing rotation in office of the two would be predicted to exploit the monopoly prospects of the money-creation franchise more fully than if either of the two were placed in permanent office.'[81] Buchanan wishes to combine economic stability with democratic conditions, and the solution he puts forward is the money supply rule – since decision-makers 'will behave in accordance with such a rule only if it exists', and 'otherwise, the ship may sink while we debate which lifeboat to use'.[82]

A well-publicised and legally-enforceable money-supply rule converts anarchy into order and ensures that 'the rational citizen's monetary expectations are stable';[83] whereas 'in the absence of a genuinely binding monetary constitution, any monetary equilibrium must be inherently precarious'.[84] The advantage of a rule is that it gives citizens some idea of what rate of inflation to anticipate. Anticipated inflation 'would seem to create some minor irritations – frequent changes in vending machines and more resort to long division – but little else'.[85] It is *unanticipated* inflation which confuses market signals, intensifies existing uncertainties, and tempts politicians to make promises concerning growth and employment which can only be honoured in the short-run. The money-supply rule is not, of course, a rate-of-inflation rule – partly because expectations are volatile enough to render the demand-for-money function difficult to estimate with absolute precision, partly because money-substitutes of various kinds do exist – but it is the conviction of the monetarist that there is a good correlation nonetheless; and that, with a multi-period money-supply rule, at least 'the rate of inflation is chosen constitutionally, as a rule to be enforced in government, rather than an announcement of intent by government'.[86]

The money-supply rule is the procedure, the rate of inflation the outcome – and recession in the transition from discretion to law is the price: 'There is no costless cure for a maladjusted economy . . . Recession is an inherent part of the recovery process; it is the economic analogue to a hangover for a nation that is drunk from Keynesian stimulation.'[87] These 'readjustment costs' are unavoidable. They are also discriminatory, in the sense that they are not a poll-tax levied, like the price of a cinema-ticket, on the whole population of those who expect to derive the benefit, but rather a selective tax levied, like the sniper's bullet, on those who happen to be in the wrong place at the wrong time. It can hardly be Pareto optimal, however, for the deintoxication of the many to be financed through the sacrifices of the few; and that is why one would have expected a theorist of social justice such as James Buchanan to have joined his voice to a theorist of social democracy such as Richard Titmuss in proposing generous compensation via the welfare state to the marginal and the expendable – to those unfortunates, in other words, who, in Titmuss's memorable phrase, would without such equitable treatment prove 'the social pathologies of other people's progress'.[88] Buchanan's monetarism is strangely silent as to the problem of whether it is morally right to allow the social costs of recession to lie where they fall, to allow the vulnerable to pay the bill for a public good which then becomes the property of all. Had he opted to reject *laissez-faire* in the case of the social costs of recession, of course, there would have been no alternative but to reject it in the case of the multiple analogous diswelfares such as technological displacement, and for that reason the counterpart benefit of Buchanan's remaining strangely silent on the question of compensation for the victims of a recession not of their own making is that he does not have to follow Titmuss in advancing proposals for State intervention such as could easily prove an endless list to be settled by means of a blank cheque. Besides that, and discriminatory or not, Buchanan takes the view that the 'readjustment costs' which inevitably accompany the recession are, fortunately, short-lived and transitory – and that the long-run state of the economy will be far healthier for *all* members of the community once macroeconomic sources of instability (the unbalanced budget, the escalating debt, the open-ended money supply) have been removed. There will, in that post-Keynesian era, be no full employment policy, but also no need for one: competition, flexibility and self-adjusting mechanisms will effectively see to that.

6 The Democratic State

Despite his strong personal commitment to political democracy, Buchanan nowhere provides a full and rigorous definition of the concept. He does not need to do so since he is a political *economist* whose model is the consensual agreement represented by voluntary trades and unregulated markets: 'The simple exchange of apples and oranges between two traders – this institutional model is the starting point for all that I have done.'[1] Exchanging rather than economising being the essential activity that most merits the investigation of the economist, it is no surprise that Buchanan should elect to assign pride of place to the catallactic perspective when it is as a *political* economist that he comes to write: 'The subject matter of economics has always seemed to me to be the institution of exchange, embodying agreement between or among choosing parties . . . Almost by definition, the economist who shifts his attention to political process while retaining his methodological individualism must be contractarian.'[2] It is contracting and mutually gaining through freely trading that constitute the core of the economic market – and of political democracy as well. We all know that the British people as individuals hold preferences with respect to the quantity and quality of their collectively-provided national health services, and it is therefore eminently reassuring to learn that those preferences are in fact taken into account by the State which is the supplier: 'The results suggest that the transmission of these preferences into outcomes does take place, quite independently of the particular way in which this process operates.'[3] This 'simple acknowledgement that individual preferences are influential in determining political outcomes'[4] is 'merely another way of stating that the British political order is assumed to be effectively "democratic"':[5]

The National Health Service in Great Britain is publicly financed, in large part from general taxes levied on the whole population, and the persons who receive benefits get these free or at very low cost to themselves individually. *The British people have apparently decided that the indivisible benefits to the community at large outweigh the disadvantages which arise due to the absence of direct user prices.*[6]

That which was demanded became that which was supplied. In the absence of a rigorous definition of the concept of political democracy, this evocative example is a more-than-serviceable second-best. More analytically, Buchanan's approach to political democracy can usefully be examined in three parts dealing, respectively, with Individualism, Unanimity, and Constitutionalism.

6.1 INDIVIDUALISM

Buchanan says: 'I do not offer a description of the "good society", even on my own terms.'[7] Such a declaration is so modest as to be misleading. If the 'good society' is to be defined in terms of outcomes and end states, then it is not to be denied that Buchanan's normal practice as a constitutional political economist is to treat the choice between planned communism and market capitalism with the same ethical neutrality that the well-trained microeconomist brings to the choice between apples and oranges. If the 'good society' is to be defined in terms of processes and rules, however, then the medium becomes the message and the ideal state becomes that of participative involvement *per se*:

> A 'good society' defined independently of the choices of its members, *all* members, is contradictory with a social order derived from individual values. In the postconstitutional stage of contract, those outcomes are 'good' that emerge from the choices of men, in both the private and the public sector. The 'goodness' of an outcome is evaluated on procedural criteria applied to the means of its attainment and not on substantive criteria intrinsic to such outcome.[8]

The denationalisation of the coal mines or the subsidisation of urban renewal in the inner city ghetto may well be matters of ethical indifference to the constitutional political economist speaking in his professional capacity, but not so the mechanisms through which normative decisions are taken on these and other matters of public policy. On the contrary; for it is central to the perspective of the constitutional political economist that mechanisms matter and matter very much. To that extent at least Buchanan, despite his contention that he offers no description of the 'good society' (even on his own terms), does in the last analysis admit to the value-laden nature of his enterprise and reveal his own personal preferences with respect to the decision-making structures of the 'good society' in which he would like to live.

If consent and agreement are good while coercion and other-directed-ness are bad, then the underlying reason is that 'effective political equality' ('the operative principle of democracy') is itself good: 'Stated in somewhat more concrete detail, my argument is that "democracy" assumes evaluative significance only under the presupposition that individual liberty is, itself, of value.'[9] Buchanan for his own part shares that presupposition: 'I consider the 'individualistic' assumptions to be the only appropriate ones for democratically-organized societies.'[10] Thence his consistent disenchantment with Keynesian macroeconomics not least because it couched its models in terms of composite statistical aggregates lacking behavioural content (although every citizen knows what no Keynesian seems to see, that the nation or community is *not* a sentient being)[11] and his consistent disparagement of Keynesian pedagogues not least because they failed properly to explain how it is that individuals make markets work: 'Micro-economics probably remained largely unknown to many of the post-1950s economists who were trained in the post-war years. They may have been compelled to take micro-economics courses, but both they and their instructors thought of this analysis as some rather tedious bit of the history of the discipline, more or less like Latin.'[12] This concern with national aggregates, this neglect of decentralised decision-making, is doubly to be regretted in view of the fact that it not only shunted the car of economic science on to a wrong line but also undermined the fundamental foundations of the democratic order by opening the door to State direction, the notion of the scientific shaping of the collective future, the conception of a public interest which omniscient and benevolent leaders could pluck out of the air as if guided by a well-tempered social welfare function. The dentistry model of fiduciary politics that is embodied in organicist and frequently paternalist words and phrases such as these is imbued with the conviction that individuals (or, at least, most individuals) prefer efficient government to participative government – whereas it is the essence of Buchanan's position that no meaningful model can begin elsewhere than with the consent and agreement of discrete and unique persons: 'I have been consistently reductionist in that I have insisted that analysis be factored down to the level of choices faced by individual actors.'[13] A model which begins with consent and agreement can, of course, quite easily end with something which a libertarian from Mars might choose to call coercion and other-directedness; and it is by no means entirely satisfying to say that the coercion cannot be coercion merely because it was voluntarily embraced and thus legitimated by consent. That fully rational citizens might convince themselves that there are gains from trade to be reaped through the division of labour in general, the delegation of political duties to political specialists in particular, is not to be denied, and it is here that the believer in individualism who is also a believer in the *survival* of individualism finds himself in the quandary of liberalism which is evoked as follows by Buchanan: 'The final choices is a free society rest with individuals who participate in that society. Men may choose to live primitively and to refuse to recognize the simple principles that economists continually repeat. If they so choose, they will so choose, and it is not the task of the economist, or anyone else, to say that they "should" necessarily choose differently.'[14] Free individuals in a free society retain the right to alienate their freedom of choice to wise dentists and other skilled employees (the only *caveat* being, presumably, that the burden of unfreedom not be passed, like that of the national debt, to generations as yet unconsulted); and it must inevitably be the study of those committed not merely to individualism but to the *survival* of individualism to show that the voluntary transfer of autonomy will not take place save within narrow limits. Such a demonstration Buchanan in the event does not provide; and his occasional references to perceived governmental failure (as, in the landmark year of 1976, to 'the current mistrust of governmental solutions'[15]) are hardly a reassuring reaffirmation of the secure hold upon the popular mind that he and many others would like to see enjoyed by the idea that the individual remains the best judge of his own best interests – a value-judgement, admittedly, but '*the* value judgement upon which Western liberal society has been founded'.[16]

Individualism and democracy are closely linked in Buchanan's conceptualisation of the political order. The bridge is provided by revealed preference, the sole source of information to which any outside observer can have access concerning the nature of non-ego perceptions: 'No social welfare function exists independently of the mutual adjustment process itself. Regardless of how they may be defined, 'equity' and 'efficiency' will characterize observed results only as they are embodied in the choices made by individual participants.'[17] It is thus impossible, in Buchanan's intellectual system, for there to emerge a conflict between justice and democracy in view of the simple fact that the former concept is logically derivative from the latter: 'My position might be interpreted as one that places democratic values above those of "justice" or "equity" . . . In my view, democratic values must be founded on the basic Kantian notion that individual human beings are the ultimate ethical units, that persons are to be treated strictly as ends and never as means, and that there are no transcendental, suprapersonal norms.'[18] Such a categorical assertion that individual persons are *qua* persons naturally equal leaves no doubt as to Buchanan's deep-seated conviction that there can exist no 'good' – save for the initial Kantian premise of respect for persons and their moral autonomy which serves as the ineluctable *a priori* and the inevitable *sine qua non* without which no further chain of reasoning can be possible – independently of that which individuals define as 'good'. Just as 'good' is preference, moreover, so 'truth' is perception, and that is why the absolutist or 'truth judgement' approach to political and social issues is 'fundamentally illiberal and intolerant': ' "Truth", in the final analysis, is tested by agreement. And if men disagree, there is no "truth". Acknowledgement of this test prompts an attitude of respect for and tolerance of the views of others, for dissenters, whoever they might be.'[19] He who has a hot line direct to God may reasonably formulate a conception of the 'public interest' without having to ask his fellow citizens to reveal their preferences. He who does not have a hot line direct to God and is unprepared to put his faith in the great book, be it *The Bible* or *Das Kapital*, has no choice but to listen and learn. Methodological individualism is evidently a second-best. Both Leviathan and anarchy are, however, infinitely worse.

6.2 UNANIMITY

The model is the economic market, where one rational, purposive, utility-orientated actor meets another of similar disposition and a mutually-beneficial exchange of apples for oranges at a freely-negotiated exchange ratio then results. The arrangement is satisfactory to both parties as otherwise the choice calculus of at least one individual would have ensured that the agreement was never concluded. Once the higgling and the bargaining, the strategic concealment and the competitive jockeying for advantage, have given way to the tranquil double-bed of consensual accord, the impartial spectator may justly have reason to regard himself as being in the presence of an equilibrium position of Paretian optimality – a position, as noted in Chapter 3, in which it would not be possible to make one person better off without making another person worse off. No inter-personal comparisons are required in order to isolate the meaning of 'better' and 'worse': each person is relied upon to define his own welfare and then to make his values known by means of revealed preference.

The model is the economic market, where the very existence of a sale that is also a purchase is living proof of unanimity of consent. It is a model which rapidly captured the commitment of the farm-boy from Tennessee when, after war-service in the Navy, he enrolled in late 1945 as a Ph.D. student in the University of Chicago: there, inpressed most of all by the teaching and teachings of Frank Knight, he apparently became within no more than six weeks 'a zealous advocate of the market order'.[20] Chicago contributed more than Knight to public choice, however: Buchanan, having learned German and not sure how better to spend the summer of 1948 than in the Harper Library, stumbled 'by sheer chance'[21] upon Wicksell's *Finanztheoretische Untersuchungen*. He wasted no time in recognising in the stress upon political unanimity that is laid in that volume the counterpart, for the theory of democracy, of the concept of Paretian optimality as applied to the economic market: 'Translated into political-choice terms, Pareto optimality becomes Wicksellian un-animity. The direct relationship between these two concepts is self-evident.'[22] Self-evident and quite obviously self-evident, since, unless *each and every* citizen gives his or her consent to a proposal for collective change, it is true by definition that dissenters will experience disutility as a direct consequence of having to pay taxes in support of public expenditures to which they are themselves opposed. The alternative to such disenchantment is the Wicksellian rule of full consensus:

> Although it was developed independently, it is evident that this criterion is the political counterpart of the Pareto criterion for optimality. If, from a given position, no change can be made through general agreement among all parties, the initial position may be classified as one belonging to the optimal or efficient set. On the other hand, if a change is proposed and all members of the group agree to this change, the initial position is nonoptimal.[23]

And, of course, if all members of the group but one agree to the change, then the resultant implications for social welfare are indeterminate. Utility can be quantified by means of consent and agreement. It cannot be quantified where the outsider is consigned to a neglected minority and never asked to reveal his marginal valuations. A consumer asked to consume apples when he wants oranges will feel that his tastes, preferences and expectations are being frustrated by others. A citizen committed to the indivisible benefits of national defence when his own inclinations and desires point in the direction of public parks will feel similarly excluded. The lesson of Pareto and Wicksell as interpreted by Buchanan is that no one, whether in the economic or the political market, should have to experience the painful other-directedness of the innocent citizen mugged by a thug, let alone a gang of thugs, when all he desires is that he be allowed to express the nature and intensity of his personal orientations and idiosyncrasies.

The emphasis on unanimity follows logically from Buchanan's Kantian *a priori* (namely the commitment to respect for persons) and from his methodological individualism (including his reliance on revealed subjectivity): 'Since there is no way of assessing the intensities of individual interests except through the revealed choice behavior of individuals themselves, a group decision rule of unanimity was suggested by Wicksell. If as much as one person in the community is harmed, there is no insurance that the damage he suffers may not outweigh the benefits or gains to all other persons in the group.'[24] Nor is Buchanan himself entirely without personal experience of minority status and the bitter taste of second-rate citizenship – a sensation to which he was exposed in his early 20s when the outbreak of war translated him from milking cows in the upper South to undergoing officer-training in New York: 'Along with many others, I was subjected to overt discrimination based on favoritism for products of the eastern establishment universities. This sobering experience made me forever sympathetic to those who suffer discriminatory treatment.'[25] Compared with the felt exclusion of minority-status, the Wicksellian ideal of unanimity of consent appears attractive indeed.

In some cases, fortunately, the requisite unanimity is non-problematic – most notably so, it must be stated, where there is a high degree of cultural consensus within the decision-making unit. Thus it is that most people in England would probably regard it more nearly as a simple codification of the *status quo* than as a *diktat* of the *dirigiste* that their income tax form should employ the English language; and it is likely in addition, always assuming that there is antecedent agreement on the concept of sumptuary taxation *per se*, that they would ultimately converge on the perception that alcohol is more nearly a luxury than a necessity. Wide divergences in popular attitudes would, needless to say, militate against a reliance on income-tax forms printed in one language only (a state of affairs hardly likely to endear the *petit flamand* to the *francophone peu sortable*), to say nothing of punitive taxation of a commodity such as wine which is frowned upon by some cults (the Moslems, the Methodists) while constituting an integral part of the religious practices of others (the Jews, the Catholics). Wide divergences in popular attitudes undeniably render the requisite unanimity that much more difficult to secure – but then, it is a reassuring fact that 'members of most political communities are culturally homogeneous to some degree', and one the significance of which is not lost on, let us say, the student of public finance. Such consensus, he will reason, 'suggests that substantial, if not total, agreement may be attainable on a relatively small set of specific commodities that might be subjected to excise duties.

To the extent that the required homogeneity holds, indirect taxation may emerge from the group decision process.'[26] To the extent that it does not, after all, indirect taxation may still emerge, but it will in this latter case carry with it the not insignificant external diswelfares that inevitably arise when a majority (perhaps of 51 per cent) legally imposes its will on a minority (perhaps of 49 per cent). No one could reasonably describe such a state of affairs as 'efficient', seeing that 49 human beings out of every 100 are there put in a position where they in effect reveal their preference for apples only to be told that the democratic choice is oranges.

A more 'efficient' outcome would clearly be the outcome that emerges from consensus, the shared behaviour-pattern that actualises the shared body of ideals, and it is in the circumstances somewhat of a disappointment to the reader that Buchanan's political economy, stronger on politics and economics than it is on sociology, has so little to say about the social origins of cultural attitudes and especially of cultural homogeneity. In some places Buchanan writes (and this despite his criticisms of Hayek on the evolution of rules and norms, tastes and preferences) as if the explanation is to be found in the non-thinking and the non-conscious – as where he states that the Victorian fiscal morality 'was neither rationally nor biologically derived. It was an outgrowth of a cultural evolutionary process that those who shared the morality did not understand.'[27] Culture, in that instance was evidently a growth and not a manufacture; but not, it would appear, a very robust growth in view of the exceptional ease with which the old standards were supplanted by the Keynesian innovations. In other places (there revealing himself to be a cross between the jurisprudential and the economic determinist) Buchanan seeks to explain values in terms of institutions – as where he suggests that unbalanced budgets discredit deferred gratification and thrift while fostering a present-orientated consumer culture of 'enjoy, enjoy' that then breeds sexual permissiveness; or where he says that lack of consultation of the public by governments who play God provides both a role-model and an incentive for the alienated to disobey laws which they perceive as being of dubious legitimacy; or where he states that nebulously-specified property-rights in universities and similar public facilities do not repress student revolt but rather encourage both the manifestation and the dissatisfaction which is the immediate cause of the rebellion. Culture in this second instance would seem to be a manufacture rather than being a growth; since, clearly, a society with a balanced budget, constitutionally-circumscribed political powers and unambiguously-specified property-rights in the field of higher education is very likely to throw up revealed preferences quite different from those one would expect to encounter in a society as yet unexposed to so radical an exercise in social engineering. In still other places Buchanan makes reference to the impact on the extent and content of consensus that is made by those well-known agencies of socialisation – the family, the neighbourhood, the school, the place of worship – which are not the less important for constituting the meat and potatoes of every social science student's first-year essay. What emerges from all of this is that Buchanan might usefully have enriched the stew of his system with more than a few more slices of good, wholesome sociology – the key to any proper understanding of the origins of those attitudes which, where convergent, render non-problematic the requisite unanimity of consent.

Even where cultural attitudes are disparate, however, unanimity of consent might nonetheless through a series of compromises over time be brought into being, always provided that there is initial acceptance of the one fundamental social value that exchanging is in and of itself a legitimate activity. That value accepted, catallactics may then be called upon to purchase agreement in cases where it is not costlessly given through consensus and where they tyranny of the majority is ruled out lest such coercion represent the thin end of the Hobbesian Leviathan. Costless or costly, after all, agreement there must be if there is to be true democracy: 'The ultimate test for institutional reform remains that of agreement among affected parties.'[28] Purchase of consent is hardly a new idea in the economics of welfare – it is the essence, to cite but one example, of Ronald Coase's important proposal in 1960 that compensation for external costs be freely negotiated between the affected parties in an attempt to allow the individuals themselves first to define and then to reap the maximal gains from trade. What is unusual is to see the purchase of *political* consent being treated in the same way as Coase treats the purchase of a permit to pollute.[29] Such an approach to the reconciliation of conflicts and the aggregation of preferences in the political arena ought not, however, to surprise the citizen of a democracy in which elections are conducted on the basis of the mixed-bag manifesto (the manifesto, in other words, that promises a deer to one minority, a beaver to the other, and thereby wins the support of both), to say nothing of vote-trading on the part of logrolling legislators (where one representative purchases the consent of another and pays in the currency of his own subsequent support). The political *quid pro quo* is, rationally considered, not all that dissimilar from the political *status quo*, even to the extent of using money itself as a counter.

Thus, and real-world economic experience supports Buchanan's conjecture, the citizens of a democracy are prone to feel so great a temperamental antipathy to the State seizure of private assets (even where the assets to be expropriated are those of an inefficient and/or a predatory natural monopoly) that they will press for the payment of compensation precisely because the Paretian optimality thereby secured appeals to their sense of fairness: 'At best the hypothesis may be advanced to the effect that consensus should emerge on a scheme to 'buy out' existing owners of such monopolized resources.'[30] A similar observation must be made concerning the protective tariff (or the closed shop), where the businessmen and the workers (or the doctors and the lawyers) must not simply be stripped of their entitlements without redress but rather offered compensation such as induces them voluntarily to sell their rights: whatever you and I might think of restrictive practices, after all, they do exist, 'we start from here', and respect for persons compels a search for agreement even where that unanimity of consent must be bought with money. Money is a great asset in the market place for tolerance – very great indeed, as it happens, since its property of divisibility permits it with a high degree of sensitivity to proportion exchange of privileges to intensity of desire: 'Strictly speaking, there is no assurance that the Pareto frontier will be attained under any rule short of full unanimity if side payments in money are not allowed.'[31]

Proposals for vote-selling, seen in that light, must be taken very seriously indeed. They ensure that every player has a prize. They allow a passionate minority to buy off an oppressive majority. They moderate the instabilities of the Arrow outcome, with its rotating coalitions and its cyclical majorities. They guarantee unanimity of consent – as much the antithesis of dictatorship as perfect competition is the antithesis of monopoly. Yet they are unlikely to be adopted. Buchanan himself draws attention to the decision-making costs involved in negotiating the bargains; to the strategic concealment and expensive blackmailing that must exist where a single vote is sufficient to block a decision (one reason why Wicksell substituted five-sixths for 100 per cent, lest a tiny minority effectively rule); to the widespread moral perception that a civil duty cannot legitimately be demoted to the status of a tradeable commodity; and to the not inconsiderable problem of present-day inequalities in the distribution of income that could potentially be employed to buy votes. These observations would seem to constitute a very strong case indeed (despite what one feels sure is Buchanan's own intellectual inclination in the opposite direction) against proposals aimed at extending the existing list of political trades and swaps (the mixed manifesto, legislative logrolling, financial compensation for felt diswelfares) to encompass vote-selling as well. And that *ceteris paribus* tends to suggest a more limited role for collective action than would be tolerable were property-rights to be redefined in such a way as to render political and pecuniary power more easily interchangeable: 'The society that is characterized by strong and effective ethical and moral restraints, which prevent vote-trading, will find it more essential to place constitutional curbs on the political decisions of the majority than will the society in which these restraints are less effective.'[32] Unless, of course, that society happened to be characterised by so high a degree of cultural consensus that the attainment of the requisite unanimity turned out to be non-problematic. But then, were that to be the case, vote-selling itself would have approximately the same attraction for the consumer as would central heating in the heat of the desert sun; since no rational shopper pays good money to rid himself of an external diswelfare which he does not seriously expect will arise.

Unanimity is an important topic in Buchanan's intellectual system, orientated as it is to individuals revealing preferences and making choices. The absence of unanimity is by the same token a significant threat to the personal autonomy of the individual burdened with an outcome to which he knows he denied his consent. Such an outcome might be the provision of an unwanted good or service, which the individual in question is bound to regard as an inefficient use of scarce resources: 'When we say that collective goods and services are not provided efficiently, we are saying that taxes and public expenditure benefits are not distinctly related in the decision making of the individual who participates in democratic choice institutions'.[33] Such an outcome might even be the 'constitutional anarchy' that all too easily arises when a legislative majority uses its power to modify the laws in its own favour: 'To the extent that majoritarian democracy uses governmental processes to modify the basic structure of individual rights, which are presumably defined in the legal structure, there is an encroachment on the domain of the protective state'.[34] No one would like to be on the receiving end of these external costs – and least of all so where his own particular minority stood little or no chance of ever being given a proper outlet for expression: 'Decisions made by voting majorities are acceptable, tolerably so, only to the extent that these majorities are shifting and unstable.'[35] To the extent that they are not, the position of blacks in a nation of whites is nasty, of academics in a nation of philistines brutish – and the list of political interventions in the absence of unanimity of consent is of necessity and as a safety-measure short.

6.3 CONSTITUTIONALISM

The intellectual system which builds upwards from individual perceptions (since 'national economies, as such, cannot enjoy gains or suffer
losses'[36]) and which takes as its ideal the consent of each to all (the model
being the *doing* of the market exchange rather than the *debating* of the
village meeting) ultimately arrives at the long-term perspective of quasi-
permanent rules of the game and multi-period precommitment of
citizens and their leaders that is captured by the notion of constitutionalism: 'In its most elemental meaning a constitution is a set of rules which
constrain the activities of persons and agents in the pursuits of their own
ends and objectives.'[37] Of citizens, since agreed guidelines laid down in
advance and properly enforced are the best bulwark against that
discretion which degenerates into disorder and leads to anarchy: 'To
expect the poker player with a pat hand to agree to a new deal is to place
entirely too much dependence on human ethics.'[38] Of leaders, since no
one with any personal experience of 'petty bureaucrats' and the 'power
of man over man'[39] will fail to recognise the potential resentments and
niggling nuisances that are eliminated where 'the range and scope for
collective political action are constrained or limited by constitutional
boundaries':[40] 'The enforcing agent is restricted by terms of the initial
agreement. Individuals hold rights or claims vis-à-vis the enforcing
agent as much as against other persons'.[41] Life is full of temptations, as
everyone who has ever deliberately refrained from keeping his alarm
clock within reach of his bed will be able to confirm. Constitutionalism
circumscribes the outlets for some at least of those temptations. In so
doing it reveals itself as incompatible with the eclectic, pragmatic
orientation which 'plays it by ear' and 'lives from day to day'; but not
incompatible *per se* with any particular party-political programme save
that of the anarchists or of the totalitarians. Nor need the constitution
be a written one. America has a written constitution while Britain does
not, and yet no one in Britain would deny that a Government was
behaving unconstitutionally which refused to call a general election at
least once every five years or to go to the nation after experiencing a vote
of no-confidence in the House of Commons. What matters, in short, is
not the specific form that the constitution takes so much as the fact that
individuals in society demonstrably opt for a binding and non-tem-
porary normative standard: 'By "constitutional" in all this discussion, I
mean only to refer to rules and institutions that continue in being from
period to period, independently of choices made within periods. I am not
concerned with semantics.'[42]

Seen from the perspective of economics, a constitution is by definition cost-effective precisely because stability of institutions obviates the need for decision-making costs to be incurred yet again. A society without a constitution is characterised by a frenzied and a permanent negotiating between coalitions which is, as may be illustrated by the case of public finance, all but financially ruinous for the nation: 'If individuals and groups, including politicians, came to consider seriously the possibility of manipulating basic fiscal institutions for the accomplishment of short-run purposes, bargaining elements will quickly swamp all efficiency considerations.'[43] A society with a constitution, on the other hand, is spared the need to waste resources in an in-period scramble for advantages that recommences the day after each new agreement is reached. It is also spared the unnecessary uncertainty of not having a clue as to the nature of future public policies that will impinge themselves on the business climate – a considerable benefit to a business man trying desperately to plan.

Seen from the perspective of politics, a constitution is a mode of limiting in advance the potentially self-perpetuating, self-enhancing powers of a Leviathan that is likely to get out of control. Likely to get out of control for a very simple reason: 'Individuals enjoy power. They relish opportunities to control the lives of others, and there are few exceptions to this generalization . . . The producer begins, all too naturally, to enjoy his role as chooser.'[44] Many ideas have been put forward over the years in an attempt to constrain the leadership – the separation of powers, the federal system, the superordination of Biblical and/or natural law to the man-made alternative. It is the conviction of the public choice constitutionalist that unanimity of consent is sufficient to legitimise the precise content of the clauses, but that the power of those anxious to wield power over others is best circumscribed by means of a multi-period set of ground-rules which they themselves are unable to alter to suit their own interests (ideological, pecuniary or whatever else these might be): 'It cannot be presumed that discretionary power possessed by agents under a particular institutional regime will be exercised in others' interests, unless there are constraints embedded in the institutional structure which ensure that effect.'[45] Power corrupts, power attracts the corrupt, and this the Italian thinkers who so much influenced Buchanan's intellectual system had correctly appreciated at a time when so many others took it for granted that politicians were naturally and exclusively public-spirited: 'The Italians had escaped the delusions of state omniscience and benevolence that had clouded the minds of England and German language social philosophers and scientists. The Italians had long since cut through the absurdities of Benthamite utilitarianism and Hegelian idealism.'[46] Buchanan shares their mistrust; and thence his insistence on the use of constitutional means to constrain the powers of those who would be powerful.

Seen, finally, from the perspective of moral philosophy, a constitution has overtones of equity and justice for the simple reason that it is binding upon an unknowable future and thus a means of compelling present-day decision-makers to decide what rules are 'fair' in advance of knowing their own future circumstances: 'The analogy with the choosing of rules for an ordinary game of poker is a close one. The individual will try to select rules that seem to be "fair". At this level of consideration, "fairness" and "efficiency" merge and come to mean the same thing.'[47] A self-interested rich man will be tempted to vote on the basis of perceived personal advantage if not placed behind a veil of uncertainty thick enough to hide from view the nature of his own personal cost/benefit position. The passage of time provides precisely such a veil: 'Reasoned, and reasonable, discussion should be possible on the most efficient structure of asset-transfer taxation that would come into effect in, say, a quarter or a half-century after decision. Individuals who participate in the discussion on this basis will be unable to identify their own positions so clearly'.[48] Thus do implementation lags, extended horizons and quasi-permanent standards come to focus self-interest on the general rather than the particular and thereby to generate consensual choices that would be unthinkable in the absence of unknowledge. To Buchanan as to Rawls, in other words, unknowledge is the parent of fairness; and that suggests that it is *moral* as well as rational to have a constitution.

Moral it may well be, but there is a problem nonetheless. On the one hand Buchanan is sympathetic to the idea of quasi-permanent, non-discretionary normative standards in areas of public life popularly regarded as of such great significance to life and property as to warrant the name of constitutional – inter-personal shifting of income and wealth being an obvious candidate:

> Fiscal institutions that will insure some net redistribution can be constitutionally selected, while at the same time effective constraints can be placed on the range of action taken operationally by dominant political coalitions. Day-by-day exploitation of the fiscal process to seek income and wealth must be abandoned in favor of quasi-permanent and built-in features of the structure which will implement transfers while at the same time restricting legislative authority.[49]

On the other hand, however, Buchanan is a strong advocate of revealed preference and citizen sovereignty, a social reductionist whose point of departure is the conception of democratic man as an active, creative, participative being: 'The individual, observed to make his own choices, is a better judge of his own better-offness than is any external observer of his behavior'.[50] Yet the Enlightenment vision of democratic man as an independent originator (neither the servant of God nor the slave of a tyrant) is in truth not easy to reconcile with the constitutionalist's perception of man as morally bound by a multi-period contract which was agreed in time past without the explicit consent of citizens present. To say that each citizen gives his implicit consent to an on-going and predetermined set of constitutional rules merely by virtue of the fact that he retains his membership in an established collectivity is not to say that each individual is happy with the legal burden bequeathed to him (along, one is tempted to say, with the burden of the national debt) by citizens past – only that he prefers the legal burden to the contracting-out alternatives represented by options such as suicide. Constitutional rules can, of course, be altered; but the very fact that to alter a constitutional rule by legitimate means requires, in Buchanan's intellectual system, as close an approximation to unanimity of consent as is possible does seem to build in a strong bias in favour of the *status quo*. That, indeed, is precisely the intended function of constitutional rules, and that which differentiates them most definitively from operational rules.

Even where constitutional rules are not altered, of course, there remains the possibility that they might be bent, twisted, manipulated or actually ignored by a cunning leadership determined to have its own way – a possibility which the libertarian Rothbard finds to be far more than merely a theoretical construct in the case of the United States experience: 'In a profound sense, the idea of binding down power with the chains of a written constitution has proved to be a noble experiment that failed. The idea of a strictly limited government has proved to be utopian'.[51] The First Amendment guarantees 'freedom of speech' (and yet cigarette advertising and pornography are restricted, seditious incitement to riot prohibited irrespective of whether or not the riot actually takes place, street-demonstrations outlawed on the dubious grounds that they might cause street congestion); the Thirteenth Amendment bans 'involuntary servitude' save for convicted criminals (and yet military-service and jury-duty have been made compulsory, a minimum school-leaving age instituted, the innocent detained in custody pending a trial at which they will be found not-guilty); and the conclusion which Rothbard draws is that, the leadership demonstrably being too cunning to allow itself to be entrapped by paper promises, 'some other, more radical means must be found to prevent the growth of the aggressive State'.[52] The means which he has in mind is the devolution of powers from governments to individuals and therewith the scrapping altogether of the coercive monopoly that gave birth to the constitutional idea: 'The libertarian alternative is to abstain from such a monopoly government to begin with.'[53] An alternative, needless to say, which Buchanan the libertarian would find by no means uncongenial, so strong is his personal attachment to 'the simple principle of laissez-faire', to 'the principle that results which emerge from the interactions of persons left alone may be, and often are, superior to those results that emerge from overt political interference'.[54] Whatever the position of Buchanan the optimistic libertarian, however, Buchanan the misanthropic Hobbesian will cry out to him not to forget that men are made of coarse clay, while Buchanan the cautious constitutionalist will insist that Ulysses' hands must be bound in advance lest he subsequently steer his ship on to the Sirens' rock. To all of which Rothbard will reply, simply, that Buchanan the libertarian ought to have had more confidence in his own instincts: the inescapable truth, Rothbard will say, is that it is in the nature of constitutional limits for them to be repeatedly breached, in the nature of governmental power for it to be fundamentally discretionary. Those who wish to see genuine consumer consultation, Rothbard will therefore recommend, would be better advised to devote their attentions to markets than to States.

Buchanan has a clear perception of the way in which subjects can come to feel alienated from politicians who exercise discretionary power without troubling to practice consumer consultation. It is in the circumstances surprising that he does not show a similar measure of understanding for the plight of citizens present, living as they do under the dominion of constitutional rules imposed on them by citizens past and strongly tempted to answer the cry from the veil of uncertainty that there ought to be no man a judge in his own cause with the countervailing cry that there ought to be no taxation without represent-ation. Yet it is just such taxation that the constitutional approach to economic policy decisions wishes to see levied – the precommitted ceiling on government expenditure (with its obvious implications for public finance) being one example, the precommitted rate of growth of the money supply (with its obvious implications for taxation by inflation) being a second. Faced with a choice between the tyranny of the past and the tyranny of the politicians, there is in the circumstances no particular reason to agree with Buchanan that the rational citizen should and will opt for the former solution. There is, indeed, good cause to suspect that citizens present whose attitudes and consensus have moved on significantly from those of citizens past will wish to retain flexibility in and control over economic policy decisions by rendering choices on such issues not quasi-permanent but rather expressly in-period.

To argue thus in favour of operational rules with respect to economic problems is not, of course, to deny the relevance of constitutional rules to other areas of social life: written or unwritten, few of us would feel entirely secure in a nation without enforceable multi-period guidelines in the field of human rights, while the very survival of the democratic system presupposes an institutionalisation of democratic practices and a tradition of rule-bound rulers. Revealed preferences of real individuals are unlikely, however, to provide much comfort to the constitutional political economist who wishes to consign a certain range of decisions on economic issues to the quasi-permanent category as well. Buchanan says little of the inter-party rivalries which compel vote-seeking politicians out of self-interest to respect the wishes of their constituents; nor of the role of the media in serving as a forum for discussion and documentation and as a watch-dog for the citizen-interest (not least for the sound commercial reason that abuses sell papers); nor of the self-regulation practised by responsible politicians who, morally committed to the democratic system, voluntarily reveal facts and seek out opinions. His writings focus not so much on the potential for good inherent in democratic institutions as on the dismal case of the worst-possible scenario – the case where moral men prove unable to bid successfully in the political auction for the monopoly franchise to rule, power-hungry self-seekers fight to win, and ultimately 'bad behavior drives out good'.[55] Real individuals, perhaps not quite so pessimistic about politics and politicians, will, arguably, perhaps not be quite so eager to precommit and preconstrain their elected leadership, beyond imposing requirements – multi-period or constitutional requirements – involving adequate disclosure of information and regular election of representatives. Were this to prove the case, then Buchanan's respect for persons and Buchanan's constitutional political economy would necessitate recommendations dramatic in their divergence.

That is why, returning to the perspective of economics, it would be unwise to assign too much significance to the least-cost argument that constitutional conservatism is good economics as well as good ethics because it economises on decision-making costs. It is true by definition that fewer decisions mean lower costs, but that statement is of broader applicability than to the multi-period constraint alone: the same criterion could be employed (although, speaking factually, it seldom is) to legitimise the social democratic ideal of the sensitive political leader with one finger in the wind, one ear to the ground, to whom fiduciary power may reasonably be delegated precisely because he is trusted independently to take initiatives with which unconsulted citizens will nonetheless reveal themselves *ex post* to be eminently satisfied. More important, perhaps, is the fact that decision-making costs are not the whole of the cost-function which Buchanan wishes to see minimised: to decision-making costs must be added external costs, and from external costs quasi-permanent rules can hardly be said to be exempt save in the first and original stage of constitution-making. At that moment in history the standard of full unanimity of consensus is applied. Thereafter it is not, and members of future generations belonging to the same society may come to experience felt externalities as a consequence of their being precommitted to an out-of-date way of life not of their own choosing. Those felt externalities are bound to be exacerbated when frustrated individuals, turning for advice to their elected representatives, learn that the politicians too are in the power of the past. The antidote to such felt externalities is freedom of choice. Freedom of choice for the individual. Freedom of choice for the society of which he is a part.

7 The Moral Dimension

It is tempting and easy to regard Buchanan as a moral nihilist who finds no place in his intellectual system for absolute moral values and absolute moral obligations, who has as little time for God as he does for philosopher-rulers, who assigns hardly any importance to evolution and none at all to natural rights. It is certainly the case that more than one commentator has complained that the model is ethically under-determined, focusing as it does on voluntary agreement and absence of coercion and little else. Norman Barry, for instance, who reflects that Buchanan's 'procedural liberalism' appears to him to be deficient in 'some background morality that would define and validate just procedures'[1] and who concludes that the approach is capable of generating outcomes which many observers would regard as absurd and unacceptable: it 'allows slavery to masquerade as freedom and theft to constitute a title of property'.[2] Or Scott Gordon, who expresses his concern that the centrality of revealed preference compels the system illegitimately to derive *ought-ness* from *is-ness* and who warns that contracting emanates purely from self-interest, rendering agreement *per se* 'without any input of moral consideration':[3] 'It seems to me that Buchanan is striving to commit what G.E. Moore called the "naturalistic fallacy": deriving moral principles without the aid of any moral premise . . . The attempt cannot succeed.'[4] Not, that is, unless one is prepared to accept the legitimacy even of slavery so long as it is voluntarily entered into, and this Gordon is not prepared to do:

> Long ago, Plato used the paradox of freedom (Cannot free men choose to be governed by a tyrant?) to attack the Athenian democracy; but liberty may suffer as much from its friends as its enemies when political philosophy is driven by 'inexorable logic'. Political space is curved, and political principles, when extended, turn round upon themselves. Even good principles must be tempered by moderation, lest one find oneself going round the circle and defending what one abhors.[5]

Neither Barry nor Gordon would appear keen to countenance the treatment of unfreedom as freedom simply on grounds of contract. Not so Robert Nozick, who asks the important question about the rational individual of 'whether a free system will allow him to sell himself into slavery' and then responds 'I believe that it would': 'Any individual may contract into any particular constraints over himself and so may use the voluntary framework to contract himself out of it.'[16] Nozick's reply is that of Buchanan as well. Buchanan points out that even at the stage of the initial contract concluded in the anarchic state of nature there is no reason to suppose that there obtains equality of strength as between the parties. He uses such an imbalance of powers to explain the possibility that the weaker might voluntarily opt for enslavement in preference to extinction – and that the stronger might rationally be prepared to offer them such an alternative: 'A contract of slavery would, as other contracts, define individual rights, and, to the extent that this assignment is mutually accepted, mutual gains may be secured from the consequent reduction in defense and predation effort.'[7] Both the weaker and the stronger reap perceived gains from trades of privileges; slavery is evidently regarded by all concerned as being more efficient than the relevant second choice; and considerations of Pareto optimality may therefore be said to support the in some ways surprising notion that a revealed preference may legitimately be recorded that leads to the suppression of revealed preference. Buchanan is, of course, speaking of micro-contracting. That a whole community might wish to sign a macro-contract with a Leviathan is not quite what he has in mind. Yet is is well-known that some dictators have enjoyed almost total unanimity of popular support (perhaps because they were believed to speak with the voice of the tribe, perhaps because under their firm guidance the trains ran on time); and it may also be the case that the high percentage of voters even in modern Western democracies who sit on their hands may indicate not the rational abstention of the individual all too conscious of his own insignificance so much as the deliberate decision of the dentist's patient to rank good government above representative government. Buchanan's own statistic that 45 per cent of the American electorate failed to register a preference in the 1972 Presidential election could thus be taken to mean, employing Buchanan's own logic, that those consumers not only knew best but also knew best that others knew best. There is no telling where such reasoning will lead.

It is tempting and easy, approached in this way, to regard Buchanan as a moral nihilist; and certainly Buchanan himself does little to dispel the impression that he presents not a single *ought-to-be* that cannot ultimately be factored down to *homo economicus* and contractual consent. He defends Order and Stability (the subject of the first section of the present chapter) not because these characteristics are ethically sound in their own right but because they form the substance of the moral package purchased by rational shoppers. He anticipates Maximin and Security (the subject of section 7.2) not because he is able to derive these standards from the holy writ of some nervous apocalyptic but because they are legitimated by the revealed preferences of real-world individuals who do not treat voluntary agreement lightly. He champions inter-temporal responsibility and truth-telling (the subject of section 7.3) not because pushpin is intrinsically better than poetry but because these guidelines are insisted upon by sensible citizens who demand to know what they are buying and how much it will cost. Buchanan on the moral dimension, it would appear, is like nothing so much as Henry Dubb in Petticoat Lane. Agreement is all.

Agreement is all; but it is still not possible to agree with Barry that Buchanan's democratic proceduralism is a boot-strap theory, a grin without a cat, a facade without a foundation, a self-validating system deficient in that background morality which alone can convert the random into the good. On the contrary, the background morality is very much there, and it is respect for persons – 'the basic Kantian notion', as we recorded in Chapter 6, 'that individual human beings are the ultimate ethical units'. It is this 'basic Kantian notion' and nothing else which confers legitimacy upon consent and constitutes the substance of the 'behavioral standards' and the 'ways of conduct' which Buchanan regards as the *sine qua non* for the harmonious functioning of a society of equals. It is that basic notion of people as ends, not means, which alone represents the meta-principle that renders good (and not merely random) the range of social *ought-to-be*s that we shall examine in this chapter. It is at that 'Archimedean point' and nowhere else that the real James Buchanan is to be encountered. His passionate plea for a remoralisation of social usages is nothing more nor less than a plea for the rest of the community to join him at that point; for only there and then, he would insist, do agreed-upon *ought-to-be*s acquire explicitly *moral* significance.

Buchanan's plea is a passionate one; and the reader who regards Buchanan as a strict legalist *pur sang* will in truth see only one side of a complex author whose political culture is actively populist (his grand-father, John P. Buchanan, was elected Governor of Tennessee in 1891 on the Farmers' Alliance ticket), whose formative years were spent in a rural community imbued with ethico-religious values (including those of his mother: her family had produced several Presbyterian preachers), and whose world-view was shaped at an impressionable stage by the mixture of markets and morals that so much characterises the work of Frank Knight ('*the* intellectual influence during my years at the

University of Chicago'⁸). The reader who focuses exclusively on the logician and the contractarian will in consequence of his intellectual myopia miss much of the passion of the prophet who, while stressing that his scientific investigations are studiously detached from his personal attitudes, would be the last to deny that it is ultimately his ethics which powers his economics and drives it along: 'We must all recognize, I think, that the ultimate purpose of positive analysis, conceptual or empirical, must be that of modifying the environment for choices, which must, in some basic sense, be normatively informed. The ultimate purpose is the "ought", no matter how purely we stick positively with the "is".'⁹ Behind the positive scientist, in other words, there quite clearly stands the moral crusader who, like Marshall, is exceptionally anxious to do good.

7.1   ORDER AND STABILITY

Buchanan is opposed to crime: 'The quality of life in major American cities since World War II has been affected much more by crime in the streets than by smog.'¹⁰ Buchanan in the circumstances would like to see at least as much attention devoted by his professional colleagues to the former category of environmental pollution as they currently devote to the latter. The methodology, however, must be different. In the latter case, the economist is quite correct, recognising as he should that extra cost and extra benefit are subjective perceptions resident nowhere save in individual actors' own minds, to set up a licence-to-pollute model such as would compel the tort-feasors to negotiate terms of compensation with holders of property-rights in claims to unspoilt facilities. In the former case, however, the situation is qualitatively different and the gains from trade approach is, quite simply, inappropriate. Not impossible to formulate – Becker's imaginative account of the way in which the potential criminal can set up in his own mind a hypothetical exchange-process as between probable loot and probable punishment clearly demonstrates the opposite. Rather, inappropriate – since the representative criminal is seldom a natural anarchist, but instead an anxious citizen sufficiently aware of his own vulnerability to rank the stability of the rules-governed order above the brutish beastliness of a society that has failed to make a social contract. The representative criminal is, in short, remarkably similar to the representative policeman in the sense that neither wants his money to be embezzled by an unscrupulous bank-manager, his new house to be fraudulently re-sold by a crooked conveyancer, the diamonds which he gives his wife to turn out to be glass. The representative criminal's lot is not a happy one where his life outside work is made a misery by scoundrels, and that is why that partial approach which focuses exclusively on his own cost-calculus when deciding whether or not to abstract the Koh-I-Noor is in truth so partial as to be misleading. A more general and therewith a less deceptive approach would range more widely than the act-calculus alone to embrace adherence to the legal order as a good thing in its own right: 'The law, as such, warrants moral support by citizens simply because it is the law.'[11] No hard-working criminal, after all, wishes to be mugged in the streets or find that some despicable wretch has indulged in an act of sequential alienation with respect to a much-loved Van Gogh; and thus it is that even the criminal has a vested interest in law and law-enforcement.

Ideally, of course, the criminal would prefer to be the only piggish violator in a pastry-shop community. What one can be, however, all cannot; and that is why the rational criminal should adhere to the implicit contract which is, admittedly, his second-best scenario. In so doing, he is gambling that his fellow-citizens will do the same – speculating, in effect, that they will pull their weight in the shared enterprise which is our society rather than seeking to ride free on the efforts of others. Such voluntary restraint clearly has overtones of individual interest, but it is to bed-rock interest in the sense of Hobbes rather than to immediate interest in the sense of Becker that Buchanan's appeal is in the last analysis directed. So too, Buchanan would add, was that of the great Scotsman who penned an account of the moral sentiments before he proceeded to an analysis of the wealth of nations. The Scotsman believed that moral capital and *homo economicus* were the twin sources of peaceful prosperity; and we today cannot do better than to keep in mind at all times 'Adam Smith's emphasis on the necessary mutuality of respect for law, without which markets cannot function. Such law-abiding behaviour cannot in itself be readily derived from a pure *homo economicus* model.'[12] Perhaps it cannot be; but then, if conduct not directly associated with a personal and direct *quid pro quo* is to be assigned so important a place in the system, Buchanan is himself being uncharacteristically piece-meal in stating that 'public choice . . . in summary terms is nothing more than the application and extension of economic tools to politics'.[13] Public choice would appear in practice to be significantly more than that where – as in the present instance – it both reverses the roles (since the appeal to the rational criminal is couched in the Hobbesian language of chaos versus State) and introduces a third element into the argument (in the form of socio-cultural background values such as condemn excessive self-seeking and antinomian attitudes). Multi-period cultural conventions might even usefully be regarded as having something of the legitimacy of multi-period (albeit unwritten) constitutional constraints about them – the logic behind Buchanan's assertion that American education is 'failing dismally' 'There is little or no transmission of the cultural-value heritage of the historically imagined American dream.'[14] Not so much the market orientation of the calculative hedonist – that aspect of the dream is catered for. Rather, the respect for law and sense of responsibility which typify the constitutional orientation – and without which maximisation without murder would vanish from the earth.

The criminal is stronger on the pragmatism of self than he is on the constitutionalism of community. So too is the student terrorist – at least to the extent that that student does not experience the psychic cost of a spoiled conscience when, having earlier internalised society's standards of right and wrong, he nonetheless turns to terror: 'He may have to overcome moral principle before embarking on action that involves destruction to property and harm to others. The existence of such moral principle seems more likely to be relevant in inhibiting behavior in Western than in Eastern cultures. This, in itself, may provide a partial explanation of the relative severity of student riots in Japan.' Buchanan's normal position has been one of hostility towards the 'constitutional illiteracy'[16] of the student activists, combined with the cultural conservative's resentment of any radical attempt to overthrow the traditional standards of decency imparted on behalf of the 'national moral community' by the 'elders' of an on-going tribe. The hostility towards constitution-breakers who impose upon their nation excrescences which the general public simply does not like to see ('burned-out buildings, broken windows, and widespread behavioral pollution',[17] for example) remains unremitting throughout the body of Buchanan's work – logically so, since he regards such confrontations and revolts as indicative not merely of an *ad hoc* abdication of authority on the part of spineless administrators who ought to be better role-models but indicative as well of a dangerous tendency which, left unchecked, could lead to the collapse of normative constraint itself: 'If attitudes in the society of the 1970's are such that they make individuals in positions of authority unwilling to punish defection, continued drift toward the chaos of anarchy must be predicted.'[18]

The resentment towards moral reformers who, opposed to conformity without consultation, question the precise content of the norms taught by the elders is, however, a different matter – and here Buchanan is prepared to be conciliatory: 'The students simply have different preference functions from those of their elders. They choose to live differently.'[19] Buchanan, hostile as he is to the idea of revolutionary disruption, is thus quite prepared to see change take place within the framework of proper procedures and rule-governed behaviour. The student's demand for consumer consultation is, after all, fully compatible with Buchanan's own views on the importance of revealed preference, constitutional reform and unanimity of consent. What Buchanan does say, however, is that the consumer cannot expect to be consulted where he is lacking in the appropriate claims and property-rights; and it is in this connection that Buchanan makes proposals not incompatible with privatisation, competition, flexible fees and flexible salary scales such as constitute in effect a far more radical breach with tradition than does the student activist's quaintly Establishment request that his elected representative be granted a seat on the board. The student activist wants consultation via the political route. Buchanan wants consultation on the apples-for-oranges model of gaining through trading. The extent to which activist and economist alike agree that consent is a good thing, other-directedness an evil to be eliminated, must not be neglected simply because the respective proposals for assessing and incorporating the views of discrete individuals of equal moral worth turn out in the event to be so divergent. Above all else, however, Buchanan is adamant that the ultimate decision for change must be taken by properly-authorised agents of the community – and not by means of bombs being planted in university offices. The criminal who has studied his Hobbes must recognise that there is no rational alternative to rules-governed procedures. The choice before the law-breaker who happens also to be a student is no different – which is the same as to say no choice at all.

Order and stability presuppose proper procedures. It is Buchanan's contention that the rule of rules is likely to be espoused by rational actors (whether criminals and students or accountants and lecturers) on grounds of self-interest alone even where there are no supplementary normative constraints that militate in the same direction. It would be surprising, however, if past generations had not proceeded by a similar chain of reasoning (reinforced in their time, one suspects, by non-rational conventions such as those of revealed religion, nowadays somewhat in decay); and this means that the self-interest of the present-day is positively magnified by the multi-period dimension of that which is 'ingrained in Western tradition'.[20] On-going traditions in this way reinforce the inter-temporal nature of social stability and that reminds the reader yet again of the strong overlay of cultural conservatism in Buchanan's libertarianism. Time once again, it would appear, here constitutes what Alfred Marshall described as 'the centre of the chief difficulty of almost every economic problem'.[21]

Time at the very least, it would appear, imposes upon Buchanan's political economy what some observers will find a contradictory orientation of the following nature. Buchanan, when speaking statically, tends to deny that the group or collectivity is an organic whole and to cleave instead towards 'the philosophy of individualism which presumes no social entity'.[22] Yet he also stresses that the representative individual, rather than myopically choosing statically, normally opts instead for a 'life style', a 'behavior pattern', a 'life plan', a 'sequence of actions' which he hopes will maximise his long-run utility in the light of the cumulative element which characterises human experience: 'Some futures must be deemed better than others, and choices in the present will tend to reflect these preferences . . . A person who has not trained for long-distance running cannot compete in the Boston marathon regardless of a strong desire to do so.'[23] The representative individual normally takes temporal inter-dependence into account – and so does Buchanan, when speaking dynamically and speaking of the social whole: *sui generis* or not *sui generis*, he seems to be saying, individuals come and go but the cultural macrocosm carries on recognisably regardless of the names of the individual players in the established game. The constitutional rules can be changed, but only by a large majority and subject to considerable costs being incurred: like it or not, 'we start from here'[24] and the onus is on the reformers to alter the decisions made by the past, *not* on the *status quo* to prove that it still commands unanimity of consent. Besides that, the teaching in the schools should in Buchanan's view favour rules-bound conduct, money-supply and balanced budget provisions should limit the discretionary power of politicians and bureaucrats, the locus of property-rights in public goods should be clarified and perhaps reformed – all of these ways in which the present imposes upon unborn generations a stock of moral capital which it might not unaided have come to demand. Just as people in England are normally precommitted to the mother tongue of English without full consultation, so individuals in the future would be likely increasingly to think stability and talk order, were the institutional reforms to be adopted to which Buchanan's constitutional political economy would seem to point. The present may thus be seen as training and educating the future, ensuring that the grandchildren speak a language reasonably consonant with that of their grandparents as represented by their parents. That language, in Buchanan's view, is the language of order and stability. It could just as easily be that of compassion and caring, in which case institutional reforms quite different from those of Buchanan are called for – a national health service (to ensure uniformity of experience regardless of race or class), or generous unemployment benefits (since many of those who lose their jobs do so as the price of economic progress upon which the rising living standards of their community inevitably depend), or blood donation from an early age (so as to train and educate the electorate in the profound satisfaction associated with what Richard Titmuss called the 'freedom of choice for the expression of altruism'[25]). Where a cultural conservative such as Titmuss says that it is compassion and caring that most need conserving and cultivating, a cultural conservative such as Buchanan identifies instead order and stability as the trunk of tradition, all else as the branches and the leaves. What divides the cultural conservatives is their disagreement as to the precise nature of that which is to be conserved and cultivated. What unites them is their conviction that institutional reform consolidates and enhances the normative standard. What makes Buchanan's position unusual is the presence of his libertarian individualism alongside his cultural conservatism: an advocate of revealed preference in the static case, of institutional predetermination in the dynamic, some observers will find a contradictory orientation in Buchanan's political economy insofar as it relates to the popular valuation of order and stability.

7.2 MAXIMIN AND SECURITY

Buchanan anticipates that rational citizens, sensible and self-aware as they are, will adopt the position that there *ought to be* order and stability. He also expects them to reveal the preferences of the risk-averter rather than those of the risk-lover, and for that reason to share his own conviction that there *ought to be* maximin and security.

Buchanan's views on maximin and security are firmly rooted in the venerable tradition of insurance and risk-avoidance that boasts the distinguished names of so many anxious thinkers, not least Edmund Burke (who wrote as Tawney records he was said to speak, 'with the expression of a man confronted by assassins'[26]) or, for that matter, the Founding Fathers of the American Constitution. The Founding Fathers built in checks and balances, separation of powers, a bicameral legislature, a bill of rights, a federal system and an electoral college, but amid that plethora of provisions and counter-provisions they did not include an upper limit on the centralised power of the modern State. There was, in their view, no need to do this: 'The writers of that document simply could not bring themselves to imagine governments with the authority and appetites that the modern Leviathan is observed to possess.'[27] This is not to say that *all* politicians are bloodthirsty scoundrels, *all* bureaucrats power-crazed psychopaths, and Buchanan is quick to pay tribute to the other-regarding orientation, the conscientiousness, the decency, the commitment to 'doing good' that is so often observed on the part of the leadership: 'Political decision makers, even if unconstrained directly by the citizenry, may be honorable men and women motivated by a genuine sense of public duty; kings may care about their subjects.'[28] No one is saying that good kings cannot exist, or even suggesting that the majority of elected and appointed officials are anything other than benevolent and responsible. When all is said and done, however, the contingencies against which people insure are normally the exceptional and the a-typical: 'We need not predict that each child will fall off the cliff to justify the installation of railings. Minimax is descriptive of deeply felt human precepts of rationality. We seek to ensure that the best remains a potentiality by guarding against the worst.'[29] As with the railings, so with the leadership: 'There is, in the evaluation of institutional alternatives, an intrinsic feature that imposes a sort of risk aversion on the evaluator . . . The harm inflicted on his fellows by a person who behaves "worse" than the average person in the community is greater than the benefits provided by another person who behaves "better" than the average person.'[30] It is in the circumstances entirely rational to err on the side of caution.

Consider the case of taxation, where precommitted ceilings should be imposed even where the extreme values in question are hardly the normal ones: 'The desire to limit government constitutionally, to define in advance the range and scope for the subsequent implementation of the taxing authority, arises only from a presumption-prediction that government may, *at least on some occasions*, act in ways that are not within the interests of taxpayers.'[31] Or the case of money-creation, where the State must maintain long-term confidence in paper if it is to continue to raise revenue via the issue of currency – but where even an 'occasional'[32] bad government can undo overnight the acceptability so carefully built up by a succession of good ones. The currency case reminds us that even responsible governments (which could well be the norm) need to be protected from the depredations of bad ones (which might be elected only infrequently) and returns us to the rationality of maximin which is at the centre of Buchanan's contractarian model: 'We use this model to generate predictions of a "worst-possible" sequence of outcomes, predictions that facilitate our analysis of ways and means of ensuring that such "worst-possible" results will not, in fact, be realized.'[33]

Maximin is the logic of the constitutional settlement which Buchanan wishes to impose on governments in order to limit in advance the external costs that might spill over on to the citizenry in consequence of the actions taken by politicians and bureaucrats. Normally in an economic model it is taken for granted that the interests of our trading-partners complement those of ourselves – that it is not from the benevolence of the brewer that the baker expects his beer but rather from the brewer's self-interested regard to his own bread – but, evidently, this rule sinks into abeyance when we come to apply economic analysis to the political market. There, presumably because the services are not well-defined in advance (Buchanan clearly rejects the equation of consumer sovereignty with 'overall satisfaction' and a popular perception of 'good performance') and because the self-seeking shopper apparently lacks adequate sanctions (Buchanan clearly rejects the idea that normal democratic processes such as regular elections provide these sanctions), the only option open to the anxious thinker is to institutionalise *ex ante facto* a set of restrictions on the discretionary powers of the leadership. Even 'social democrats' who are strong supporters of governmental pragmatism 'often at the same time strongly support constitutional guarantees of democratic decision-making procedures as such'.[34] To that extent they too are anxious thinkers – since they do not want to see a majority coalition once in power legally abolish all future elections, jail the members of the opposition, terminate the freedom of speech, muzzle the press: 'Almost all announced majoritarians will invoke *constitutional* protections and guarantees as the appropriate means of checking or limiting the unconstrained will of majority coalitions.'[35] Such 'social democrats', Buchanan would say, are entirely right to be anxious when they think of the multiple temptations to fallen man if clothed in power. They ought, he would add, to be more anxious still. Action can only be *ultra vires* if the *vires* are laid down in advance. Anxious 'social democrats' make a constructive contribution by specifying some of the *vires* that must be pre-limited. Anxious constitutional political economists make a more constructive contribution by providing a more extensive list.   '

The extensive list is rational, Buchanan argues, precisely because maximin is rational. Thus the harm done by the student revolutionary may be taken to exceed the benefits conferred by the student representative, the evils generated by the Supreme Court Justice who elects to play God to outweigh the good done by the law-abiding judge with a gentleman's attitude to that which is cricket. In the long-run, the simple truth being that 'malice is contagious',[36] there is a high likelihood that Gresham's Law will be operative in politics in such a way as to debase the quality of the product on offer: 'When many persons are involved in a social interaction, the narrow pursuit of self-interest by a subset will induce all persons to behave similarly, simply in order to protect themselves against members of the subset.'[37] Even before the moral average begins to fall, however, it is nonetheless rational to proceed with care and to assign disproportionate weighting to probable knavery as compared with probable saintliness of equivalent magnitude. It is rational in Buchanan's own choice-calculus, as is typified by the succinct statement that 'I am by nature a pessimist'.[38] It is rational in the choice-calculus of the community as a whole, the ordinary citizen being expected to experience so acute a case of anxiety as to tip the balance unambiguously in the direction of restricted political powers: given 'the elementary fact that more restrictive rules will not only help to prevent the occurrence of disaster but also preclude actions that may be intended to promote desirable outcomes',[39] nonetheless, in imagining alternative scenarios under different sets of rules, 'citizens will act as if they were risk-averse'.[40] It is thus to the revealed preferences of ordinary men and women as well as to his own that Buchanan makes appeal in building up his account of the relationship between rationality and risk.

Whether or not he has properly captured the essence of popular perceptions is, of course, a separate question, and one which can only properly be answered through in-depth psychological investigations relying extensively on the camera that photographs the contents of the mind. Until such a camera is invented, evidence will have to remain as inconclusive as the guesstimate, the hunch and the proxy; but the critic of Buchanan on maximin will nonetheless be able to make several comments. One is that all of economic action, being oriented by its very nature towards an unknown history-to-come, is fraught with risk – and yet entrepreneurial types do not for that reason rush to abandon entrepreneurial activity merely because the benefits come with costs attached. Another is that conservatism follows logically from the subjective aversion to the uncertain ('Hamlet said that it is better to bear those ills we have then to fly to others we know not of, but his statement applies also to benefits or pleasures'[41]) – and yet ordinary citizens frequently vote for major changes (as opposed to quasi-permanence of institutions) and, at least in the perspective of some theorists, normally spend on the basis of current income (as opposed to the long-term stability associated with life-cycle and permanent income hypotheses). Until the valuable camera mentioned above has been invented, the evidence on popular perceptions with respect to risk-taking and gambling, to risk-avoiding and insuring must remain problematic; but these observations do suggest that Buchanan may have exaggerated the extent to which maximin follows inevitably from the choice-calculus of the representative citizen. What does follow is a shrewd valuation of careful cautiousness (an asset without which few of us would manage to get safely across Oxford Road, let alone across Oxford Street). A shrewd valuation of careful cautiousness is, however, in and of itself hardly sufficient to produce the cry from the heart that is audible from one end of Buchanan's intellectual system to the other. To produce such a cry, passion as well as prudence is required, and most of all an anxiety threshold which many persons – perhaps because they have failed to grasp the truth about underlying social realities – will be inclined to regard as unacceptably low.

Nor will even all anxious persons necessarily adopt the uncontrolled and discretionary powers of politicians and bureaucrats as a central focus for their fears. Buchanan believes that rationally they will and makes the following statement on man behind the veil of uncertainty: 'For the rational individual, unable to predict his future position, the imposition of some additional and renewed restraints on the exercise of such legislative power may be desirable.'[42] Perhaps so; but it is salutary to remember that it was not fear of the protective State so much as fear of physical extinction *in the absence* of the protective State that induced the Hobbesian being of whom Buchanan has so much to say to hire a powerful Leviathan, and to do so without demanding that a single constitutional constraint be locked into a contract which as it stood placed no limits whatsoever on the liberty of the sovereign. Physical extinction is clearly a dreadful thing, the fear of physical extinction arguably a more dreadful one still; and the decision of anxious Adam to rank the protective State of authoritarianism above the anarchic state of nature is one which most readers of Hobbes would themselves probably have made. The employment of a protective State is not, however, by itself enough to drive the fear and the phenomenon of extinction from the world – extinction associated not with the *bellum* of anarchy nor with the *imperium* of Leviathan but with the inability to find employment or to pay for essential medical treatment. Anxious Adam made the aggression of his fellows the central focus for his fears and turned to the protective State for help. Anxious 'social democrats', out of work because there is none and in poor health because they have no money for fees, are known to argue by analogy when they take their fears to the productive State. Neither anxious Adam nor the anxious 'social democrats' would deny that considerable harm can be caused by the ambitious neurotic who, under stress, takes early retirement by pressing the button on the nuclear deterrent; or by the greedy hedonist who, unstoppable when in the shops, spends the taxpayers' money on clothes and jewels which the man in the street is unlikely ever to see. Both anxious Adam and the anxious 'social democrats' would accept that constraints and limits ought to exist such as would protect the employers from these and other abuses on the part of their staff. Simply, not all anxious persons will adopt, with Buchanan, the possibility of such tyranny as a central focus for their fears. Many anxious persons will regard the Buchanan problem, while a real one, as of secondary interest; and will argue that the problems which they themselves regard as most pressing are precisely those which cause them to look to the State for a solution.

Unemployment is a case in point. Buchanan, who was born in 1919, was a witness to the human tragedy of the Great Depression – and himself to some extent a victim of it: 'I was to be the lawyer-politician . . . Economic reality destroyed this dream; Vanderbilt moved beyond the possible as the Great Depression moved in. College was what I could afford, Middle Tennessee State Teachers' College in Murfreesboro, which allowed me to live at home and to earn enough for fees and books by milking dairy cows morning and night for four years.'[43] Others had experiences which were far more shattering; and discretionary macroeconomic stabilisation policies such as those which follow from Keyne's *General Theory* of 1936 undeniably possess great attraction in such circumstances.

Keynes himself, Buchanan believes, was in error in recommending that the requisite stimulus be fiscal in nature rather than monetary: deficit-finance via bond-issue means interest-bearing assets, and is thus obviously inferior on grounds of economic rationality to deficit-finance via money-creation (which, of course, involves no real resource cost save that actually incurred in the physical processes of minting and printing). Technique apart, however, Buchanan was prepared throughout much of his career to countenance quite a considerable measure of discretion with respect to the application of that stimulus. The following statement, dating from 1970, is indicative of his general position: 'If widespread unemployment of economic resources and much unutilized productive capacity exist (roughly the situation during the Great Depression in the United States), the government can and should adopt a fiscal policy which involves the financing of all or a portion of government expenditures through outright money-creation rather than taxation.'[44] In such a situation, after all, a currency-powered deficit is positively 'desirable'[45] precisely because it is nothing other than optimal in the sense of Pareto to call into productive employment the services of spare capacity that would otherwise have remained unemployed and wasted: 'Individuals owning the resources concerned are made better off, and no one in the economy is made worse off.'[46] No transfer of resources takes place from private to public sector where there is enough for both; there is no taxation through inflation in such a period because it is not price-levels but output and employment that respond to the rise in demand; and so great would seem to be the benefits from moderate and responsible pragmatism that it comes as somewhat of a surprise to find Buchanan, in the late 1970s and in the 1980s, increasingly adopting a position – with respect to the money supply rule, for instance, or the balanced budget amendment – that can only be described as that of the hard-line and inflexible legalist. Buchanan is fully aware that the replacement of the discretionary by the constitutional option might have its bad side as well as its good and that governance by the book 'might sometimes restrict well-intentioned and far-seeing politicians from securing macroeconomic stability . . . In one perspective on politics at least, any implied reduction in the governmental flexibility of response to unforeseen circumstances will embody potential costs that must be taken into account.'[47] Indeed they must; but the discretionary power to stabilise carries with it the potential to pollute, and the anxious thinker has a well-known propensity to rank the harm associated with the worst case above the gain associated with the best. The critic of maximin as applied to macroeconomic policy will reply that such a line of argumentation is tantamount to saying that the best way to prevent *some* shop-assistants from pilfering is to prevent *all* shop-assistants from entering the shop, tantamount to asserting that the best way to avoid disposing of the baby with the bathwater is to avoid bathing the baby at all. The critic of maximin might even accuse the anxious thinker of fiddling while Rome burns, of ranking his own fears with respect to discretionary demand-management above the no-less real fears of other members of the nation with respect to finding and retaining employment.

Buchanan, fortunately, has no need to answer these accusations. The reason is simple: just as he has become increasingly inflexible and legalistic in his approach to macroeconomic policy, so he has become increasingly sceptical about the capacity of the instruments actually to honour their promises. Considerations involving end states thus point in the same direction as considerations involving processes, the former morally subordinate to the latter but a source of reinforcement and support for the senior partner nonetheless. Theories of market failure and the corrective State were popular in the complacent 1950s when Buchanan was at the start of his academic career. Such theories were less widely accepted in the mistrustful 1970s, and not least because of the contribution of the public choice economists themselves in seeking to separate the concept of private sector inadequacy from the dentist model of State intervention: 'There is no necessary presumption that simply because markets are imperfect, political processes will work better. On the contrary, as public-choice theory reminds us, there are very good reasons for doubting the capacity of political processes to achieve Pareto optimality. The normatively relevant comparison is between two imperfect institutions.'[48] The fact that markets fail (to supply public goods, for example, or to combat generalised externalities, or to deal with powerful natural monopolies) does not mean that governments will not also fail, perhaps even more decisively. Macroeconomic policy provides one of the clearest instances of such failure, namely the Great Depression of the 1930s as interpreted in the following words by Milton Friedman: 'The Great Depression in the United States, far from being a sign of the inherent instability of the private enterprise system, is a testament to how much harm can be done by mistakes on the part of a few men when they wield vast power over the monetary system of a country.'[49] Buchanan, increasingly influenced by Friedman's monetarism, has become increasingly sceptical about the capacity of fine-tuning on the part of economic technocrats to produce targeted stability while avoiding unintended shocks. He has also become increasingly convinced that the supply-side solution to the problem of unemployment is the proper one; and that the road to recovery leads not through central banks and finance ministries but through free enterprise and competitive markets, spontaneous adjustment and flexible prices. Increasingly sceptical about the efficacy of discretion, increasingly convinced of the benefits of automaticity, Buchanan's position by the 1980s had in effect become this, that anxious persons who adopt unemployment as a central focus for their fears would be well-advised to seek the solution at the root of the problem, in the pricing system and not in the level of aggregate demand. The *bellum* of anarchy and the *imperium* of Leviathan constitute, at any rate, the central focus for Buchanan's fears – and unemployment does not.

Some anxious persons fear unemployment more than they fear either chaos or dominance. Other fear ill-health and loss of earning-power; and they too will be inclined to regard constitutionalism as of secondary interest in the light of the particular phenomena towards which their particular form of risk-averseness is principally directed. John Rawls, speaking of the veil of ignorance, derives a difference principle relating to ease of access to primary goods which is bound to provide considerable solace to the faint-hearted: 'We simply maximize the expectations of the least favored position subject to the required constraints.'[50] James Buchanan, speaking of the veil of uncertainty, removes that reassurance by indicating that he regards the difference principle as little more than a footnote to the procedural theory of justice as fairness: 'This distributional principle is only one from among a set of possible outcomes that might emerge from a genuine Rawlsian process of evaluation, any one of which would be equally deserving of the attribute of justice.'[15] Perhaps so; but only if the representative individual is taken to be risk-neutral. If, however, that individual is taken to be risk-averse (and that is a presupposition which Buchanan shares with Rawls), then maximin and the insurance principle come into play and strict logic suggests that human anxieties are indeed likely in and of themselves to encourage the levelling-up of the least-advantaged. A person dwelling in the veil of unknowledge, after all, both requires and develops the faculty of imagination. He learns to picture his own state of mind as it would probably be were the State without due process to confiscate his property; but also to conceive of the sensations he would probably experience were a car-accident suddenly and unexpectedly to deprive him of health and income. An enthusiastic supporter neither of Leviathan nor of calamity, he is likely, if active as well as fearful, to seek to protect himself against both contingencies.

Against *both* contingencies – and that is why, dwelling as he is in the veil of unknowledge, he will call not merely for elections at pre-specified intervals and a system of proper representation but also for generous unemployment-benefits, subsidised housing for the destitute, extensive assistance to one-parent families, and a variety of other measures to aid the Rawlsian less-advantaged. His motivation will be tinted with compassion (imagination being a great teacher of empathy and unknowledge a first-rate school) but its texture will be of the purest self-interest. No anxious person, if also rational, will prefer private-sector income-maintenance to State: cover up to a prearranged limit can easily be exhausted before the individual manages to escape from the state that caused the dependency, and private-sector income-maintenance is in any case notoriously difficult to arrange because of the spectre of moral hazard. Nor will a rational person, if also anxious, prefer commercial medicine to a National Health Service: few citizens can afford the premiums that would buy an open-ended entitlement, some will sympathise with their own position if rendered uninsurable by an incurable disease or incapable of insuring by a long spell of extreme penury, and many will also say that unequal power born of unequal knowledge leads to a conflict of interest on the part of the profit-maximising medical practitioner such as inevitably undermines patient confidence while raising the cost of care. A National Health Service assuages some at least of these anxieties. It does so by practising a system of pooling; and that, admittedly, means higher contributions for the good risks, lower for the bad, than would be expected *ceteris paribus* (*ceteris paribus*, since a full account would have to take into consideration additional variables such as central subsidisation of the system and economies of scale in the spreading of administrative overheads) by the individual's own personal actuary. Good risks would complain of discriminatory treatment, bad risks would dance in the street – except for one thing: today's good risk, looking at tomorrow, knows full well that permanent disability might in truth be as near as the nearest unhinged draper, dislodged girder or drunken driver. Life in the veil of unknowledge is significantly less restful than, let us say, life in the Vale of Evesham; and that is why even today's good risk might rationally demand the collectivist antidote to the great evil of anxiety. Certain it is that what might loosely be termed the 'fear motive' plays no small role in Kenneth Arrow's attempt to account for 'the general social consensus . . . that the *laissez faire* solution for medicine is intolerable':[52]

A good part of the preference for redistribution expressed in government taxation and expenditure policies and private charity can be reinterpreted as desire for insurance. It is noteworthy that virtually nowhere is there a system of subsidies that has as its aim simply an equalization of income. The subsidies or other governmental help go to those who are disadvantaged in life by events the incidence of which is popularly regarded as unpredictable: the blind, dependent children, the medically indigent. Thus, optimality, in a context which includes risk-bearing, includes much that appears to be motivated by distributional value judgements when looked at in a narrower context.[53]

That Buchanan's intellectual system can incorporate such a line of argumentation is not in question – particularly since Arrow himself pays tribute to the treatment of redistribution as 'income insurance'[54] that is to be found in *The Calculus of Consent*. What is to be questioned is the secondary status which Buchanan assigns, in his discussion of risk-aversion, to the fear of being rendered bedridden and impoverished relative to the fear of being made the obedient servant of non-accountable authority. Revealed preference, after all, is a hard task-master, and there is as little reason *a priori* to expect the members of the community to suffer from Buchanan-fear (i.e. a state of anxiety directed towards State direction) as there is to expect them to suffer from Tawney-fear (i.e. exceptional concern about health and money). Risk-averters suffering from Tawney-fear will look to the public sector for the cradle-to-grave security of the modern welfare state and will probably share Tawney's own view that the 'bloodthirsty Leviathan' can without insuperable difficulties be made into a 'serviceable drudge': 'We, in England, have repeatedly re-made the State, and are re-making it now, and shall re-make it again. Why, in heaven's name, should we be afraid of it?'[55] Risk-averters suffering from Buchanan-fear, convinced as they are that the road to the censor's office and the prison-camp is all too frequently paved with exemplary housing estates and first-rate dentists, will not be quite so sanguine. Milton Friedman is not quite so sanguine:

> The citizen of the United States who is compelled by law to devote something like 10 per cent of his income to the purchase of a particular kind of retirement contract, administered by the government, is being deprived of a corresponding part of his personal freedom . . . Underlying most arguments against the free market is a lack of belief in freedom itself.[56]

The real point is simply that different risk-averters will want to avert different risks; and that the revealed preferences of a democratic electorate could, conceptually speaking, be such as would impel anxious man to vote Socialist out of fear. The fear is not the Buchanan-fear of a monopoly of State power that crushes the spirit and even the life of the numerous perfect competitors who are the individual citizens. The fear is the Tawney-fear of the insufferable wretchedness that is the lot of the impoverished haemophiliac with dependent children and no job who has little to call his own besides a rat-infested slum dwelling. The actual distribution of fears in the community is, of course, an empirical matter to which the *a priori* has little to contribute. This much, however, can be said, that citizens who make ill-health and loss of earning-power the central focus for their fears are unlikely to read Buchanan on the *bellum* and the *imperium* with any real sense of immediacy or involvement. Fear is a dreadful thing, they will observe, and their own fears are elsewhere engaged. The subject of this section has been Maximin and Security. The argument has been that rational citizens might regard these as valued *ought-to-bes*. The criticism has been the risk-aversion in general, fear of the State in particular, are assigned disproportionate emphasis in Buchanan's intellectual system. The concluding topic is human nature.

Buchanan has no explicit theory of human nature – only a theory of revealed preference such as may be employed by the methodological individualist to infer the essence from the shadow. Buchanan has employed the apparatus and has had to report results fully consonant with his own personal pessimism and misanthropy: 'Each person seeks mastery over a world of slaves.'[57] Buchanan's starting-point, admittedly, was individualism. It was, however, not the hedonic individualism of the self-obsessed monad but rather the methodological individualism of the impartial spectator. The monad announces without hesitation that he is self-regarding and greedy. The spectator announces simply that his choice of apparatus precommits him to no conclusion in particular.

> This is not to suggest that each individual will be purely selfish in making his decision. An individual may or may not include certain social values in his own value scale which is relevant for his participating in collective decisions. For example, an individual may consider it beneficial to him individually to provide aid for the poor people of Tongatabu even though he realizes that this expenditure of public funds can in no way affect his own individual position in society.[58]

Such altruism is clearly not ruled out by assumption. Simply, Buchanan, having employed his chosen apparatus to illuminate the shadow that casts light on the essence, is forced to conclude that it is not as reliable and powerful a motivating factor as is purposive self-interest: 'Altruism, like good manners, can be appreciated but not "presumed upon".'[59] All in all, conflict and bellicosity are all that can be predicted in an uncertain world; and the fact that the obsessive drive to win and dominate might recur even amidst the superabundance of the society that knows no scarcity ('Social strife might arise in paradise'[60]) suggests that the nature of the failing is psycho-biological rather than economico-social in origin.

Whatever its origin, it is the empirically-ascertained existence of that failing that turns the true Hobbesian to the protective State: 'To the individualist, utopia is anarchist, but as a realist he recognizes the necessity of an enforcing agency, a collectivity, a state.'[61] Not only to the protective State, moreover, but to the precommitted State, for the truth is that individuals 'whose passions include the desire to wield power over others'[62] are almost by definition likely to exercise their dominance in ways uncongenial to their subjects and victims: '"Ordered anarchy" remains the objective, but "ordered" by whom? Neither the state nor the savage is noble, and this reality must be squarely faced.'[63] It is not squarely faced by those most extreme of economic contractarians who argue that the cement of society is not the exercise of power but the complementarity of interest: 'The libertarian anarchists who dream of markets without states are romantic fools, who have read neither Hobbes nor history.'[64] Buchanan has read both and both have led him to the conclusion that the state of nature resembles less the Garden of Eden than it does the state of Texas. Buchanan has read both but he has read both selectively; and more extreme libertarians will certainly wish to point out that his exceptional risk-averseness would seem to have caused him to dwell disproportionately on instances of predation and aggression relative to evidence of charitable gifts, blood donation and the organic solidarity of the butcher, the brewer and the baker. Such selectivity is to some extent to be expected, it being a characteristic feature of the maximin perspective to weight the harm done above the equivalent good. Yet the unintended outcome is inevitably to convey an impression of human nature that is deceptively one-sided. One-sided, and sociologically impoverished as well, to the extent that no attempt is made to classify observations according to time and place; or systematically to explain variations with reference to key causal variables such as philosophical ideals, social pressures, and economic institutions. Should human nature be consistently egocentric, then, clearly, there is no alternative but to sway with the blow and live with the stigma of the ineluctable failing. Should human nature be genuinely malleable, however, then the possibility opens up of reforming persons by means of reforming the influences that shape the persons. Should human nature be susceptible of significant improvement, needless to say, then the position of the anxious thinker is itself significantly improved. He will, one feels certain, continue to share with other rational risk-averters the conviction that there *ought to be* maximin and security – but he will also, presumably with some pleasure, come to see that the probability of his being confronted by assassins is greatly reduced.

7.3   TIME AND TRUTH

Public choice emerged from public finance – the 'parent discipline',[65] historically speaking, for political economists concerned with the relationship between governments and individuals. It is in the circumstances no surprise to find that so much of what Buchanan says about inter-temporal responsibility and truth-telling is said in connection with the contract made in a modern democracy between the State and the citizens. The question of the national debt in particular is assigned by Buchanan a central position at the very crossroads of social experience – at the very spot, in fact, where ethics and economics happen to meet. Obsessive and even excessive though his concern with budgets and deficits may well be, one thing is certain: seldom if ever has so aridly technical a topic been invested with so much moral fervour. The reader is forewarned that he or she is about to enter the territory of 'myopic hedonism' and 'thrift as a moral virtue',[66] of 'public profligacy' and 'fiscal prudence'.[67] Young ladies and persons of a nervous disposition are advised that Buchanan on the rise of the national debt is likely to prove at least as distressing as Mill on the fall of the rupee – more so, in fact, since the story of public spending without public earning is also the story of how, thanks to the 'Keynesian apologetics', Victorian moral precepts and 'traditional ethical considerations'[68] have been swept aside by an insidious and short-sighted philosophy of 'enjoy, enjoy' that is bound ultimately to leave the nation the poorer. Moral rules, after all, 'like more formal legal rules, are public capital, and they may carry positive weights in a properly constructed national balance sheet'.[69] No one but a prodigal or a spendthrift wishes to see the running-down of any part of his national capital; and that is why Buchanan is clearly so confident that his jeremiads with respect to public-sector borrowing requirements will not fail ultimately to persuade.

Buchanan's discussion of the national debt at the crossroads of ethics and economics draws attention in particular to the importance and value of two ethical imperatives. It is with these two sets of *ought-to-bes* that we shall be concerned in the two parts of this section.

(a)   Inter-temporal responsibility

Democracy means consultation and consent such that 'the social or collective choice finally made reflects widespread participation by individuals and ultimate consensus'.[70] Debt-finance is therefore fundamentally non-democratic: 'Public debt is necessarily a tax on future income',[71] some of that future income belongs to future generations who never shared in the 'degree of reasonable acquiescence'[72] which gave birth to the burden, and such inter-temporal taxation without representation must inevitably merit the same moral condemnation as would the Hobson's choice offered by the highwayman between your money and your life. Of course there is, for fallen man, aware that his personal time horizon is short and seeing no reason to act as if his life were eternal, a strong temptation to binge today and to leave the bill for posterity: no one would nowadays assert that family relations were 'so close that fathers considered their sons as parts of themselves for estate planning purposes',[73] and that honest decency which a father is unprepared to show towards his own sons he is even less likely to show towards the unborn offspring of unknown others. Of course there is, for vote-seeking politicians, aware that their constituents smile on public spending but resent the taxes that might pay for it, an equivalent temptation to bash the future in order to benefit the present – and to legitimise their moral decadence with reference to the macroeconomic prescriptions of the Keynesian economics: 'The Keynesian arguments were effective in providing politicians with excuses for acting out their natural proclivities to spend without taxing, as they responded to constituency pressures. These proclivities had previously been held in check, both for politicians and for constituency groups, by moral constraints.'[74] The effect of the Keynesian economics was thus to turn both the fathers and the politicians loose, and to cause them to yield to temptations which any responsible citizen in the good old days of the *self*-policing Victorian moral code would have striven hard to resist. Thence the case for the legally-enforceable balanced budget rule that compels each year's collective expenditure to be financed out of each year's national income – and not out of national borrowing such as precommits cohorts to come to carry a burden of service and amortisation that they never offered to shoulder.

It is the absence of consultation and consent that renders debt-finance fundamentally at odds with democratic values. At odds as well, therefore, with the normal public choice mode of making significant statements about desiredness on the basis of individuals' revealed preferences. No group setting can, obviously, produce results that as sensitively reflect actors' perceptions as does the two-person, apples-for-oranges swap; and to that extent the pooled observations of public sector economics are by their very nature a second-best index of utility. That they are *some* index of thoughts and feelings is not, however, in dispute: in the static case, after all, democracy dictates some consultation and some consent. Not so in the dynamic case, and that is why the choices made by the concrete present on behalf of the nebulous future cannot be taken as serious indicators of *what* future citizens will actually want and of *how strongly* they will experience those desires: 'The subjective evaluation which compares the individualized benefits with the real costs in the tax-expenditure decision is missing.'[75] Even if the unconsulted future is in fact offered percentagewise more or less the public package it desires (half defence, half education, let us say), still the quantitative dimension is lacking in that the future citizen is never given the opportunity to say precisely how much extra payment would just equal, in his own mind, the extra worth to him of the expenditure being undertaken: 'There is little reason or use in attempting to measure in some objective manner the benefits from the public project. The subjective evaluation made by individuals in their roles as choosers provides a much superior guide to the "correctness" of the social decision.'[76] Superior, inferior or indifferent, the point is that such a guide is simply not to be had; for the truth is that there exists no known technique for obtaining from future generations their considered opinion on the sacrifice of relevant alternatives.

Future generations have no opportunity *ex ante* to reveal their preferences, but it would be a misleading exaggeration to say that they are never tolerably satisfied *ex post* with the nature of the product that is provided. Suppose, for example, that 'the public funds are used to ward off disaster, that is, to finance a war': 'The taxpayer will find his net worth increased on balance in spite of the necessity to service the debt.'[77] The 'will' reflects the confidence of an author who is thinking of the psychic income accruing to the campaign against the *Volksfeind* and not of the Dien Bien Phu of My Lai, but the meaning is clear enough, that the citizen who is coerced to forego present enjoyment in order to pay interest on bonds issued to finance a past World War may well find the national survival thereby made possible a bargain at the price. The services of wartime defence evidently yield long-term benefits; and where the future unambiguously derives rewards, it has long been a tenet even of fiscal conservatism that the future should make some contribution to the costs. Buchanan himself has been known to adopt this position with respect to long-lived capital assets such as roads, dams, parks and schools: 'It should perhaps . . . be noted that the ethical principle against the issue of debt which embodies some transfer of net fiscal liability to future generations of taxpayers does not fully apply when debt is limited to financing genuinely long-term projects. In this case, future genera-tions enjoy the benefits as well as inherit the liability.'[78] Buchanan makes clear that it would not, in his view, be morally acceptable to transfer real burdens to the future where the spending in question is consumption and current: 'For those public expenditures or outlays that are expected to yield up all or a major portion of public service benefits in a reasonably short period of time, taxation should be employed.'[79] Where public investment is involved such as 'yields benefits over a whole series of time periods',[80] however, there Buchanan has in some of his writings taken a positive stance on proposals to relate the life of the debt to the life of the asset. He has even gone so far as to support such proposals with the argument that debt-finance is a valuable hedge against under-investment on the part of a rational and a selfish present generation: 'Private people discount future taxes and future benefits too heavily in the making of social or collective decisions.'[81] Just as the future is not keen to pay for the present, so the present has an understandable reluctance to finance facilities which will only be accessible to the future. All of which gives the impression of a man of not inconsiderable moderation. A man who accepts that an unconsulted future can nonetheless be tolerably satisfied with the dishes cooked up for it by an imaginative present. A man who writes in places as if in support of the double budget – one for current expenditure, one for capital – that had been advocated by Keynes in *The Means to Prosperity*[82] and subsequently made by Abba Lerner an integral part of the theory of functional finance.[83] A man whose natural conservatism could even be cited in support of an evolutionary perspective such as would cause the believer in *natura non facit saltum* to expect that our children will want roads for their cars and schools for their children, very much as our parents did – an argument which suggests that guessed-at preference might in an on-going society prove a close substitute for revealed, and that the debt we pass on finds its moral counterpart in the debt we inherit. A man, in short, of not inconsiderable moderation.

Potential moderation rather than actual moderation, however; for it is, at the end of the day, maximin and not eclecticism that enjoys the last word when Buchanan, having explored a world of possibilities, ultimately opts for the constitutional expedient of the balanced budget amendment. One reason for this rejection of discretion and authorities in favour of predictability and rules is the purely technical one that macroeconomic stability is better promoted by clearly-defined institutional parameters ('rules which are constructed once and for all, and which are, in a real sense, relatively absolute absolutes'[84]) than it is by *ad hoc* tinkering and *ad hominem* bungling: 'Collective decisions must be made in terms of organizational rules or constraints that are expected to prevail over a sequence of results. Non-optimality in a single case does not imply potential consensus on a change in the organizational rules.'[85] The reference to 'consensus' moves the argument on to a not-unexpected next step, that ordinary citizens normally reveal a strong preference for a stable environment: all change, they will say, is *per se* suboptimal since it erodes what little foreknowledge we have and makes the task of adaptation to need that much more difficult. Whether or not ordinary citizens would continue unanimously to reject discretion if the authorities were widely believed to be as knowledgeable and skilled as the Harley Street surgeon Buchanan does not say. In view of his own lack of confidence in the omniscience and beneficence of the policy-makers, he evidently sees no need to explain how rational citizens would react if the techniques were in fact capable of producing the desired result. If rational citizens wished to opt against automaticity, however, then his methodological individualism would commit him to taking a good photograph of their revealed preferences, while his democratic contractarianism would compel him to urge an interventionist State to act on the principle that the consumer knows best. It is that same individualism, that some contractarianism, needless to say, which provides the last but also the strongest of the reasons which might be adduced to explain Buchanan's commitment to the annual balancing of public expenditure and taxation: the future have not given their consent (which renders any lien on their incomes morally unacceptable) and they are all too often starved so that the present might be stuffed (an intergenerational transfer of resources away from the unconsulted such as is indicative of a deplorable deficiency in the *mens democratica*). One is tempted to say that few investments would ever be made, either in the public or the private sector, if the future had in each case to be consulted and to give its consent. Buchanan, here as usual, however, is one jump ahead of the critic: nowadays, he insists, only a relatively small share of governmental outlays' can be seen as embodying a capital component – so small, in fact, that 'the analytical treatment of all public outlays as current public consumption does not seem far off the mark, and surely not far enough off to yield wildly misleading conclusions'.[86] It is a clear case of inter-temporal irresponsibility, Buchanan concludes, where the future is asked to make sacrifices in order to pay for the 'TV dinners purchased by food stamps'. Debt means shifting of burdens. Shifting of burdens is morally wrong.

There is a second moral absolute in Buchanan's discussion of the national debt at the crossroads of ethics and economics. Before we can turn to it, however, there is a final observation that must be made about the shifting of burdens. It has been made by a number of economists, including Ricardo,[87] Pigou[88] and Barro.[89] It is, in effect, that burdens are not shifted at all. Should there be no problem of postponement, of course, should there be no inter-temporal transfer, then it becomes quite possible to enjoy the benefits of a substantial national debt without simultaneously committing an act of gross irresponsibility.

The Ricardo-Pigou-Barro position (also that of Wicksell on the debt, incidentally) is that it is the present, not the future, that bears the burden: it is the present, after all, that has to give up an equivalent amount of private consumption or private capital formation when bonds are purchased and resources thereby transferred to the State. Future generations of taxpayers do, admittedly, have to pay interest on the debt; but then, future generations of bondholders are only too happy to receive those transfers – leaving the (internally-held) stock of wealth in net totally unaffected on a generation-for-generation basis. Various arguments against deficit-finance can no doubt be accommodated within the broad church of this perspective (the upward impetus to interest-rates, for example, or the disincentive effect on work and investment of higher taxes to service greater borrowing). Inter-temporal irresponsibility is not, however, among their number.

Buchanan's position and perspective are different, and most of all because of a significant difference in methodology. Buchanan does not deny that the physical flows of resources are for all intents and purposes those which objectivist economists such as Ricardo, Pigou and Barro assert them to be. What Buchanan does add, however, is that data on physical flows is of very limited relevance where it is with constructs such as 'burden' and 'sacrifice' that the economist is concerned – subjective perceptions, in other words, and thus not to be confused with the number, weight and measure of the accountancy calculus. The simple fact is that 'the mere shifting of resources from private to public employment does not carry with it any implication of sacrifice or payment',[90] and that for any meaningful statement about utility and disutility to be made some insight must first be won concerning the precise perceptions of the individual actors themselves. The precise perceptions are, of course, non-observable. Revealed preference in voluntary exchanges is, however, a reasonable proxy – and a reasonable demonstration that no sacrifice at all but rather a psychic gain is made when a consumer rationally and willingly decides to spend his money on debt: 'If an individual freely chooses to purchase a government bond, he is, presumably, moving to a preferred position on his utility surface by so doing. He has improved, not worsened, his lot by the transaction.'[91] He was, one must assume, reasonably aware of the delights (ranging from Skilauf in the Tyrol to Sachertorte in the Hofburg) that constituted the opportunity cost of his purchase. That he opted nonetheless not for the guided tour of Mozart's birthplace or the posed photograph on Freud's couch but for the acquisition of a piece of paper promising principal with interest in future time must therefore be taken as a reasonable indication that he ranked what he bought over that which he rejected. One man spends his money on a book by Carl Menger, another buys an empty box – and a third, also involved in maximising satisfaction given scarce resources, lends to the government. Objectively speaking, resources, quite obviously, were thereby transferred to the State, just as resources which might have been utilised to purchase a life-size model of the hunting-lodge at Mayerling were undeniably transferred to Johannes Jodelmeister by a consumer who wished to purchase yodelling-lessons. Subjectively, however, it makes no sense to speak of 'burden' or 'sacrifice' when the individual would feel *less* happy if denied the opportunity to acquire the debt than he would if offered the chance to lend. The expenditure financed by the debt might also please the present-day lender (icing on the cake, as it were) – as, indeed, it might the future taxpayer (*ex post* but still possible, as has been recorded). Pleased or not, and even if the TV dinners have long since been gobbled up and the new missile system written off as an expensive failure, the future taxpayer is still under obligation to accept a lower net income in order that funds might be transferred to the bondholder. Unless the future taxpayer happens to share the revealed preferences of the past decision-makers who selected the project, the inference is inescapably that the burden of sacrifice is borne not by the cohorts who create the debt but by their successors, who have to service and repay it. The burden is shifted, such shifting is immoral; and thus does the association of inter-temporal responsibility with the balanced budget follow logically, given Buchanan's methodological subjectivism. Ricardo, Pigou and Barro do not share that methodological subjectivism and cannot therefore share the diagnosis of shifting which results from it. Whether or not they would share the moral outrage if they were in a position to share the analytical apparatus is an entirely separate question. Perhaps they would not; for the fact is that not every economist shares Buchanan's desire to become involved in *ought-to-bes*. Nor, incidentally, his indignation when decision-makers are seen to behave in a manner which is taken to be irresponsible.

(b) Truth-telling

Inter-temporal responsibility is the first of the two moral absolutes that emerge from Buchanan's discussion of the national debt at the crossroads of ethics and economics. Truth-telling is the second. The villain of the piece is real-world man when put in a position of power: 'Elected and appointed politicians and bureaucrats are not different from other men. They are motivated at least in part by their own interest, not by some higher version of the "social good".'[92] Politicians court popularity and votes, bureaucrats want extra benefits and expanded bureaus, and no one in either Westminster or Whitehall would wish to deny the possibility that the leadership might feel tempted to treat the citizenry more like an opponent in a game of poker than as a valued ally in a common struggle. Allies put their cards on the table and tell one another the truth. Opponents, on the other hand, go in for bluffs and secrets, stratagems and tricks. Whatever happens in the world of poker, Buchanan argues, such conduct is totally inappropriate in the world of democratic politics – where, when all is said and done, the leadership is not the master but the servant of the citizenry, and morally bound by the spirit of the contract to table the truth.

The whole truth, moreover; and this in the field of fiscal affairs, as it happens, is a clause that is not always honoured. It is certainly not honoured when a rational leadership, aware that expenditures win votes while taxes elect oppositions, opts to finance current benefits without incurring current costs by means of a deliberate budgetary deficit. The citizen is made in this way the victim of fiscal illusion (since he thinks public spending costs less than it does) and of fiscal error (since he orders more of public spending than he would do if told the real price). A citizen who is suffering from fiscal illusion and fiscal error can hardly be said to be in a position rationally to participate in the utility-maximising process of fiscal exchange: he cannot compare the extra benefits from spending with the extra costs from taxing (as he would be able to do were the budget to be a balanced one) and he lacks the information he requires to make an intelligent decision. He could, of course, make a Downs-type private investment in overcoming ignorance (say, by buying a scholarly tract on public finance and learning how a State can live beyond its means); but no amount of information-gathering can make an uncertain future fully knowable (as where a leadership as yet unborn hasn't itself a clue as to the probable size of deficits to come, let alone whether these deficits will be financed mainly by new bonds or mainly by new money).

He could, alternatively, rely on politicians voluntarily to disclose how much of present-day spending is being financed by means of burdens left for the future to settle: assuming that the citizen has a genuine sense of inter-temporal responsibility (that, in other words, he for some reason hesitates to confiscate the property of future cohorts of his fellow nationals despite the fact that he knows little more about them than he does about 'the poor people of Tongatabu' as they live and work today), assuming further that the leadership has a non-rational commitment to duty such as is not always found in, let us say, the second-hand car market (that, in other words, politicians eschew considerations of electoral expediency and say precisely what percentage of today's TV dinners consumed by Scotsmen in kilts will be paid for by the grandchildren of Welshmen currently playing hide-and-seek in primary schools), this is undeniably the option with the greatest appeal to the sincere and committed moralist. To the moralist, perhaps, but not to ancient Adam, who, pointing out that the voluntary method presupposes a healthy supply of enthusiastic volunteers, will say that his belief in maximin combined with his pessimistic view of human nature have led him to the conclusion that the *best* and the *best-possible* modes of promoting truth-telling with particular reference to the national debt are, sadly, two quite different things – and that the best-possible option is, here once again, that which is associated with 'membership in a collectivity that is constitutionally empowered to make decisions under predetermined rules'.[93] The best-possible option is, in short, the multi-period law which *compels* political decision-takers to tell the truth precisely because that option then blocks off access to each and every alternative avenue: a balanced budget is a budget that is (and that is seen to be) balanced, and that fact even the most unbalanced of politicians has no choice but to take to heart save in the truly exceptional case where his accountancy is as fantastic as his righteousness. Ancient Adam will no doubt look back with some nostalgia on those summery days before the Fall when men (and, indeed, women) told the truth because of a voice within that imposed the necessary discipline on action without. That voice within was for all intents and purposes a constitutional settlement – all personal morality is for all intents and purposes a constitutional settlement. Where, however, that voice within shows itself incapable of maintaining the necessary standards, then some functional equivalent must be found. The legally-enforceable balanced budget is such a functional equivalent: where taxation and spending are bound together by hoops of iron, the room for obfuscation of the actual fiscal burden is thereby reduced.

Reduced, but not eliminated; for the unbalanced budget is, clearly, only one instance of fiscal immorality, only one illustration of the manner in which an unconstrained leadership can seek to turn fiscal illusion and fiscal error to its own selected advantage. Thus a sensitive politician, even one who has not personally studied the nervous Machiavellians such as the wise Puviani, is quite capable of devising a way fiscally to exploit the psychological uplift of a happy event (say, by charging for a marriage licence); or of sowing terror in order to harvest tax (say, by warning the haves that society will break down in the absence of greater public expenditure favouring the have-nots); or of marrying the displacement effect of wartime emergency with the ratchet effect of inertial conservatism in order to breed a permanent increase in State spending and control (say, by slipping in a welfare state in a period of disarmament as an alternative to a return to the *status quo ante*). Nor will a sensitive politician fail to reflect that the 'tax consciousness' of the individual taxpayer can be significantly reduced where the tax is levied 'painlessly'. Thus, since 'individuals are likely to be less informed about the costs that indirect taxes impose on them than they are about the costs of direct taxes'.[94] the lesson for the political imperialist wanting to better the share of the State is clear – avoid *ex post* reclamation of income once in the pocket, flirt with income tax deducted at source, opt first and foremost for tax carefully concealed in the sale-price of the goods: 'Individuals are not conscious of the real costs which the payment of the tax imposes on them.'[95] Individuals can be confused further still through the deliberate fragmentation of the tax-load (a person likely to be shocked by the magnitude of a single levy might hardly be conscious of many small ones), combined, perhaps, with an imaginative variety of different rates (a person capable of remembering a single rate of 10 per cent is unlikely to have at his fingertips the 59 per cent on a packet of cigarettes, the 8 per cent on a pound of sugar, the 12.75 per cent on a rail ticket from Leeds to Bradford which he must know if appropriate comparisons of the tax-wedge are to be made). Individuals, in short, would be well advised, in Buchanan's view, to fear manipulated intelligence and false perceptions such as it is in the interest of the leadership to foster: there is something singularly immoral, he reasons, in asking people to pay more for public services than they would rationally choose to do if presented with a carefully itemised bill. It is the study of the leadership to obscure the opportunity-cost of State spending, to dull the tax-awareness of the sensible citizen – and thence to produce a higher share of government involvement in the economy than would have resulted had the true cost not been papered over with illusion and error by an elite bent on dominance. It is the study of the constitutional political economist to ensure that the revealed preferences of the men and women in the street are given the attention they deserve – and this points to a prearranged figure for public spending. The figure can be changed in the same way as any other part of the constitutional *status quo* can be changed (and subject, it must be added, to the surmounting of the not inconsiderable difficulties which always attend upon the application of the unanimity rule). The crucial point is that such change involves a deliberate and conscious popular choice. It is not change without consultation. It is change which institutionalises transparency of burdens and puts public officials in a position where they have no option but to tell the truth.

As with the balanced budget norm and the public expenditure ceiling, so with the money supply rule. Currency (unlike bonds) bears no rate of interest, inflation is a tax on money-holders of which they are normally oblivious, rising prices mean falling real burden of debt service; and there is, all in all, a genuine incentive to irresponsible leaders to finance projects by means of paper. As long as the resultant inflation is unanticipated, they will reason, as long as their employers, the citizens, continue to suffer from money illusion, the fact is that 'the tax is concealed. Individuals are subjected to a burden of tax without knowing it . . . This method of taxation seems contrary to the whole ethos of democratic society.'[96] Indeed it is; for no hidden sacrifice can ever be compatible with the concepts of disclosure and consultation which characterise that ethos. This coerced transfer is, of course, a current burden, and for that reason arguably less attractive to the present generation than is the shiftable sacrifice of the national debt. Even so, however, ancient Adam when elected to Parliament will seek to shift the blame even if not the burden; and will seek to persuade the electorate that it is not the government at all but rather, say, the unions that are inequitably gnawing away at the community's real balances. One would have thought that a democratic electorate upon whose revealed preferences Buchanan's entire intellectual system is founded would not have been as easily conned by the half-truths of political persuaders as is the Galbraithian consumer by the calculated mendacity of Madison Avenue; but an informational deficiency, here as elsewhere in connection with illusion and error, does seem to be among the social forces which open wide the water-gates to the flood-tide of vested interest. Existing checks on abuse of position Buchanan brushes aside. He is perhaps wrong to do so. Excessive inflation, once anticipated, causes citizens to run down stocks of interest-free debt while demanding indexation of bonds. Both fixed and floating exchange rates come under pressure due to the balance of payments problems that result. A government wishing to be re-elected in the future dare not over-use the trick of unanticipated inflation lest this be exploited by opposition and media alike to deplete its reputational capital. All of these checks are indicative of a constitutional settlement, loosely defined; for all of them are, undeniably, multi-period constraints on the financing of projects by means of printing paper. To that extent every responsible democrat is also a constitutional political economist. Whether the *further* constraint of a money-supply rule is needed is more controversial. The technical difficulties involved in relating money to prices are well-known even to the school-certificate candidate, and embrace problems such as velocity, interest-sensitivity, asset-substitutability and definition of terms. More significant, however, is the possibility that a money-supply rule is all but unnecessary in a well-functioning democracy precisely because alternative checks fulfilling an equivalent function are already in operation. One is tempted to say that a money-supply rule might be more appropriate for countries with a low level of economics literacy, weak opposition parties and a media-famine than it is in, let us say, modern Britain or the United States. Ancient Adam would, however, reply that politics is politics and discretion is always and everywhere a dangerous phenomenon.

Inflation reduces the real value of interest payable and is to that extent a mode of partial default on debt. Agreement being the very essence of *ought-ness*, even partial default on a contract once concluded is unambiguously unjust and immoral. Total default is that much more unethical, and in this form of truth-telling as in others, the leadership should set a good example of 'moral worthiness' by means of adherence to commitments (however ill-advised they may with hindsight appear) into which the State has entered: 'Unless there is a general set of attitudes that embodies respect for past legal commitments, the very existence of an ongoing legal-political order is called into question. If each new legislature should simply repudiate the enactments of its predecessor, political chaos would quickly replace political stability and continuity.'[97] There would clearly not be much of economic life (nor, for some at least, much of any life at all) were anarchy to replace order; and the ever-present spectre of a potential return to the state of nature is in itself a good enough reason for the State not to establish an all-too-risky precedent by means of reneging on a claim. A good enough reason, certainly, but not the only one – since agreed-upon conduct has moral value in its own right: 'It seems clear that there is moral value, over and beyond economically measurable worth of socio-legal stability, in membership in a polity where promise-keeping extends to the government as well as to citizens in their personal capacities.'[98] A voluntary undertaking to repay borrowed money is a serious business. Provided that agreement was uncoerced and the contract fully legitimate, the right to employ the lender's funds carries with it a duty to return the funds in due course. States as well as individuals are morally bound to honour their agreements and to do their duty. Morally *and legally* bound, moreover, since, in the case of default as in the three previous cases we have examined (those of the budgetary balance, the public expenditure ceiling and the money supply rule), the present is able, within the framework of the democratic order, to precommit the future. All that is required for this to be possible is for citizens to be empowered to take legal action against a defaulting State in the same way as they would sue and pursue any other borrower who sought to breach his contract. All that is required, in other words, is for an independent judiciary to be established with full powers to hear cases against a State which demonstrates behaviour-patterns that more closely resemble those of the criminal or the student revolutionary than they do those of the broker whose word is his bond.

The multi-period expedient of the constitutional solution is one which has a great appeal to the anxious moralist whose views on order and stability, risk-avoidance and insurance, inter-temporal responsibility and truth-telling have formed the substance of this chapter. So great an appeal, indeed, that the reader rises from the table with the strange feeling that he has been served up only half the dishes which the anxious moralist clearly meant for him to taste. The sensation is simply explained. Buchanan the political economist makes proposal after proposal for precommitting politicians and preconstraining bureaucrats, for protecting the community from depredation and dominance on the part of servants who seek to act as masters. Buchanan the economic sociologist has, however, somewhat less to say about the manner in which the criminal or the student revolutionary might come to build up the stock of moral values that so clearly precommits the actions of the broker whose word is his bond, that so frequently deters from 'fiscal fraud' the author of an income-tax form whose truthfulness is the basis for his burden. Self-reporting presupposes such truthfulness: 'The effective administration of the tax depends upon a rather high degree of taxpayer morality. It works well only if the number of persons who seek deliberately to disobey the law remains relatively small.'[99] Functional equivalents for such truthfulness can unquestionably be found, just as heightened coercion of the individual and increased spending on the police are the functional equivalents for self-enforcement and self-regulation. Buchanan's point is that such functional equivalents are poor substitutes indeed for the real thing:

> Individuals must abide by behavioral standards which dictate adherence to law, respect for property and personal rights, fulfillment of contractual agreements, standards which may not, in specific instances, be consistent with objectively measurable economic self-interest. Absent such standards as these, markets will fail even when there are no imperfections of the sort that have attracted the attention of the welfare theorists.[100]

Markets will fail – strong words indeed; and that is why the reader rises from the banquet of Buchanan's intellectual system with the strange feeling that he has been served up only half the dishes. The constitutional precommitment of politicians and bureaucrats, he will reflect, however necessary in itself to prevent government failure, is but a part of the whole. Additional precommitment is evidently needed, he will reason, if ethical failure is not to create a normative vacuum so extreme that the participants in market capitalism will beg for the return of Leviathan. That precommitment must take the form of a 'common set of moral precepts' (precepts that 'include respect for individual rights, once these are defined in law and/or customary standards of behavior'[101]), of a consensual adoption of ethical guidelines, of a 'general acceptance of a minimal set of moral standards': 'Well-defined laws of property and freedom of market exchange minimize the necessary scope and extension of such standards, but they by no means eliminate them.'[102] The analysis of that precommitment is the study of the economic sociologist. It is a study to which Buchanan turns far less frequently than one would expect from a cultural conservative convinced that social values are primary inputs in a nation's production function – and fearful lest social change bring with it an erosion of moral capital such as to call into question the very survival of the market exchange system.

Encroaching *anomie* in the work of Buchanan being in some sense the functional equivalent of the revolutionary proletariat in the work of Marx, it is surprising that he does not have more to say about the origin and nature of multi-period normative standards. Be that as it may, Buchanan has the temperament of the Old Testament prophet, and his various writings reveal a deep-seated concern with social values which is none the less real for clearly interesting him less than do the machinations of the mighty. At times he is apocalyptic about the imminence of moral collapse, as in the following, dating from 1977: 'The basic structure of property rights is now threatened more seriously than at any period in the two-century history of the United States.'[103] At other times he is more confident about the resiliency of stable institutions, as in the following, only four years its junior: 'Perhaps the excesses of the 1960s were aberrations from the more orderly development of a social order embodying affluence, justice, and freedom. Perhaps. But hoping will not make things so.'[104] At no time, however, does he play down the importance of social values – nor, indeed, make any effort to conceal his own anxiety when he looks into the future. In the 1930s, Buchanan says, 'rare indeed were those who felt themselves morally capable of choosing individually determined norms for obedience'.[105] What was then rare, he believes, is now commonplace; and the half-century which separates Murfreesboro from Fairfax has, in his view, borne witness to increasing demands on the part of sovereign consumers for the same freedom of choice in the market for morals as they are used to enjoying in the market for tomatoes. Those increasing demands, he is convinced, are the cultural counterpart of the very similar demands increasingly made in the same period by politicians and bureaucrats for more extensive discretionary powers. Such demands are to be regretted, their further increase to be feared; for it is the conviction of the constitutionalist that precommitment and preconstraint in the markets for ethical standards and political services are, far from being incompatible with the *regime* of revealed preference in the market for tomatoes, positively the precondition for its healthy functioning. How best to halt the advance of the antinomian culture then becomes a question of paramount importance. It is a question which can only be answered by a constitution-maker who is prepared to devote to ethics the same detailed attention that Buchanan devotes to politics. Buchanan does not himself say precisely how best to bring about the necessary remoralisation of social usages. What he does indicate are some at least of the causes of the moral decay which he believes was the experience of the United States in the half-century from Roosevelt to Reagan.

Thus there has been a diminution in the importance of the family as an agent of socialisation: 'The family's role in transmitting moral values, including a sense of respect and honor for the institution itself, has been undermined by the shift from the extended unit to the nuclear cell.'[106] There has been a shift of population from the morally-supportive village community to the rootless anonymity of the modern town: 'Can urbanized man be expected to live by the moral precepts ideally characteristic of the sturdy yeoman farmer?'[107] There has been, parallel-ing the improvement in transportation which is the complement to the premium on mobility, an improvement in mass communications which has had an unexpected outcome: television exposure of political wrong-doing (ranging from the Stalinist purges to the Watergate break-in) may act as a deterrent to future abuse, but such publicity also undermines confidence in legal processes and loyalty to the leadership. Family, community, mobility, publicity – in all four instances the direction of economic and technological change has been such as apparently to weaken the institutional supports which once had 'tended to establish and to maintain order and stability in society'.[108] The revealed preferen-ces of sovereign consumers suggest that that economic and technological change was in itself probably worthwhile – that it was in itself probably indicative of progress and not of retrogression. Yet the fact remains, in Buchanan's view, that that change has brought with it 'disintegrating institutions', and therewith the 'predictable effects of such disintegration on individual adherence to traditional moral norms'.[109] Traditional moral norms in the absence of which, Buchanan insists, *markets will fail.* Economic and technological advance to that extent may be said to carry the seeds of a contradiction capable of converting progress into something ugly and malign.

It is not economic and technological advance, however, to which Buchanan assigns the lion's share of the blame for moral decay. Never a strong evolutionist, always disposed to place mind over matter in the explanation of events and to stress the frequency with which ideas provide the key that unlocks the cage of circumstance, it is principally to institutions that trade in concepts that Buchanan turns when he seeks to explain the erosion in his nation's stock of moral capital which he believes to have taken place.

Consider the church. With his own personal attachment to the work-ethic, to deferred gratification, to radical individualism, one would have expected Buchanan to see in religion in general, Calvinist Protestantism in particular, a powerful ally on the ideational and ideological front. Significantly, it is from none other than Benjamin Franklin – constitu-tion-maker and advocate of free enterprise – that Max Weber chooses to quote when he seeks to show that the essential elements of the spirit of capitalism are identical with 'the content of the Puritan worldly asceticism'.[110] Buchanan himself, however, is unprepared to put much faith in an institution which no longer enjoys the power to influence which it once had – and which is all too often prone to encourage not law-abiding conduct so much as anarchy and outrage: 'If anything, the modern church has become itself subversive of existing and traditional moral standards, changing its color from an institution of order to one promotive of disorder and instability.'[111] Nor is the school much better: 'Within the context of strong and stable institutions of family, church, and state, the school can appropriately combine a rational transmission of moral values with a critical and searching reexamination of these values. As the offsets are weakened, however, and as the internal mix within the school changes toward criticism and away from transmitting value, this institution becomes one of disorder and instability in modern society.'[112] The position of the university has already been noted, where the old-style emphasis on critical intelligence, freedom of speech, open competition of ideas has come to be challenged by the intolerance of student activists in an institutional setting where it is the denial of individual choice, the lack of product differentiation, the neglect of technical innovation, the absence of consumer consultation that must bear the bulk of the responsibility for the unhealthy attitudes that frustration has engendered: 'The liberal academician refuses to face the apparent fact that he and his own kind have been instrumental in undermining constitutional order and attitude in the society at large. The student sees through the sham; he properly understands that if modern liberal attitudes toward sociopolitical processes are turned inward to the university setting, the existing structure of the university must be dramatically reformed.'[113]

Then there is the over-expansion of the productive State, which infringes rights without due process, imposes decisions without democratic involvement, inspires in the citizen feelings of resentment and alienation, and ultimately leads to still further other-directedness on the part of the leadership – since in such circumstances it is only to be expected that 'the protective state must ride herd on the possible excesses of the productive state'.[114] And there is accelerated inflation, diminished frugality and an over-arching atmosphere of lawlessness brought about not so much by bad men as by bad rules such as are common given the dangerous combination of Keynesian economic theories and democratic political structures: 'Our specific hypothesis is that the Keynesian theory of economic policy produces inherent biases when applied within the institutions of political democracy. To the extent that this hypothesis is accepted, the search for improvement must be centred on modification in the institutional structure.'[115] The church, the school, the university, the productive State, the Keynesian macroeconomic mind-set – all have contributed significantly to the erosion in the stock of moral capital which Buchanan believes to have occurred in his country and in his lifetime. The inference is then that encroaching *anomie* might significantly be stemmed were order and stability to come to be ranked above Christian charity, maximin and security above joyful spontaneity, inter-temperal responsibility and truth-telling above pragmatic response and paternalistic manipulation. Ranked, needless to say, not simply by the odd moral philosopher in his book-lined study but rather by the general social consensus which alone, in Buchanan's perspective, has the power to legitimate a stock of binding social *ought-to-be*s in a world characterised by Kantian respect for persons.

Should that social consensus perversely support the churches, the students and the Keynesians, Buchanan's position would, of course, be a difficult one indeed. On the one hand he would remain committed to specific normative standards such as he would regard as the functional *sine qua non* for peaceful coexistence within the framework of an ongoing community. On the other hand he would have to admit that sovereign citizens have a presumptive right to their own revealed preferences and that a nation which knowingly wishes to return to the state of nature cannot reasonably be arrested in its chosen course by the extraneous authority of One Who Knows Best. On the one hand Buchanan would remain deeply concerned about the erosion of traditional standards, the primacy of the hedonistic self, the triumph of the permissive orientation such as Daniel Bell deems an essential characteristic of the journey into advanced technocratic capitalism:

What has been happening in Western society for the past hundred years, I believe, is a widening disjunction between the social structure (the economy, technology, and occupational system) and the culture (the symbolic expression of meanings), each of which is ruled by a different axial principle. The social structure is rooted in functional rationality and efficiency, the culture in the antinomian justification of the enhancement of the self . . . The result has been a disjunction within the social structure itself. In the organization of production and work, the system demands provident behavior, industriousness and self-control, dedication to a career and success. In the realm of consumption, it fosters the attitude of *carpe diem*, prodigality and display, and the compulsive search for play.[116]

On the other hand Buchanan would have to say that even feckless gamblers and Bohemian types who flaunt their disrespect for routines have nonetheless an absolute property in their individual preferences; and that if the members of the community genuinely display no disposition to agree, then the classical liberal's respect for persons leaves him with no choice but to rank individual autonomy above orderly process.

Buchanan no doubt hopes that individual autonomy will favour agreement on the moral values that are the *sine qua non* for the society founded on agreements. Choice, however, is queer. Buchanan is too sceptical about evolutionary theory to produce a more reassuring schema than that of Bell. He is fully aware that his own proposals for moderate social engineering (the extension of Mill's best-judge principle to the free choice of university education being only one illustration of the reformer-missionary at work) will appeal most of all to precisely those compactual collectivities least in need of moderate social engineering. He cannot be unaware that vested interests, nepotism, deceit, the disproportionate influence of a powerful multinational over a corrupt elite, militaristic bullying and institutionalised privilege-selling are likely to render the adoption of a constitutional solution based upon the moral values of the democratic contractarian all but impossible in some societies without the antecedent cataclysm of the violent revolution or the invasion from abroad such as have little attraction for the consensual gradualist. He must see that agreement to agree might presuppose a *specific* agreement constraining private power alongside the protection of the citizen from 'the *politically* orchestrated tyranny of others' that is the central obsession of this quintessentially anxious thinker who describes as 'perceptive' the view that 'we are motivated primarily by fears rather than by aspirations':[112] minimum wages, maximum hours, statutory guarantees to unions and the right to strike, maternity and re-training leave, the defence of the environment via zoning and anti-pollution schemes, the introduction of a negative income tax to widen access to contractual agreements made via market exchanges, all of this might be demanded by an electorate committed not simply to agreement *per se* but to agreement to a *specific* agreement. Choice, in short, is queer; and Buchanan never entirely convinces the reader that the functional need will in the event produce the particular agreement that, in his view, alone legitimates the requisite values. That he hopes it will do so is not, however, in question.

It must therefore be concluded that Buchanan can hardly be called the optimistic observer of the social scene that he would be if genuinely able to derive *ought-ness* from *is-ness* in the manner imputed to him by Barry and Gordon. Like any committed moralist, he would naturally be pleased if the functional *ought-to-be* were indeed to coincide with the consensual *is*; while like any democratic thinker who eulogises the reasoned response, he would no doubt be prepared to predict that the requisite coincidence would indeed come about in a society peopled exclusively by the rational and the sensible. All of which is well and good – but we start from *here*.

8 Economics and Beyond

James Buchanan, reflecting on the substance of his own self-image as it was when in 1986 he was awarded the Nobel Prize in Economics, was capable of making a declaration which in other circumstances could all too easily have caused him to be ostracised as an eccentric and ridiculed as a crank:

> I am not, and have never been, an 'economist' in any narrowly-defined meaning. My interest in understanding how the economic interaction process works has always been instrumental to the more inclusive purpose of understanding how we can learn to live one with another without engaging in Hobbesian war and without subjecting ourselves to the dictates of the state. The 'wealth of nations', as such, has never commanded my attention save as a valued by-product of an effectively free society.[1]

An academic economist who thus defines his field of inquiry to be more nearly consensual order and conflict resolution than allocative efficiency and general equilibrium is bound to be somewhat of an outsider, and Buchanan has no doubts as to the overall attitude of the uni-disciplinary Establishment to the work of the multi-disciplinary iconoclast: 'I would not presume to think that my own views on methodology would convince more than a minority of my professional collegues.'[2] This lack of enthusiasm on the part of his professional colleagues would be, one fears, as nothing compared with the downright hostility of student activists, Keynesian interventionists, itinerant pragmatists, officials with discretionary powers – and those spokesmen for the poor and the unemployed who take the absence from Buchanan's work of concrete recommendations intended specifically and significantly to assist the disadvantaged as proof positive that the multi-disciplinary iconoclast in effect prefers contract to compassion and the *haves* (with the effective demand to trade, market and exchange) to the *have-nots* (whose only capital is their crying need and their unsatisfied wants). It cannot, however, be said that the scholarly achievements and missionary zeal of other influential academic scribblers – of Marx and Keynes, of Tawney and Galbraith – met initially with unqualified approbation and widespread acceptance. Buchanan's prolific output, relentless logic and obvious commitment undeniably made his, in the three decades from the mid-1950s to the mid-1980s, less and less of an out-of-tune voice in the wilderness, whatever the professional and popular opposition that his ideas have evoked; and that success in itself is a tribute to the fascination which his intellectual system has held for students of the social condition, whatever may be their academic training or ideological persuasion.

It is with the position of economic science within the whole of that intellectual system that we shall be concerned in this, the concluding chapter of this book. Our observations will be grouped into three sections. The first section, headed Subjectivism, will examine the linkages between catallactics and revealed preferences in a world where each actor is alone competent to assess his opportunities and evaluate his choices: 'Utility is a subjective phenomenon, and it is not something that can be externally or objectively measured.'[3] The second section, headed The Mixed Economy, will look at the relationship between private and public in the light of Buchanan's own personal predilection for 'advance towards the libertarian ideal of a minimal protective state in which the massive government economy of our present is dramatically reduced in size, scope and power, and in which the generative forces of the market are allowed much more room to play, thereby ensuring both increased productive performance and economic growth'.[4] The third section, headed Politics, Economics and Political Economy, will consider Buchanan's important contribution to the 'exciting and new field of theoretical inquiry . . . emerging on the borderline between two disciplines'[5] and taking as its goal the removal of those intellectual blinkers that have long obscured the two-way relationship between markets and States: 'We reject this set of blindfolds. We step back one stage, and we try to observe the political along with the economic process. We look at the *political economy*.'[6] Our conclusion will be that Buchanan has dared to think big at a time when it was standard professional practice to look through microscopes; and that this loftiness of aspiration is in itself no small contribution in an era increasingly threatened by technocracy without vision and specialisation without purpose.

8.1 SUBJECTIVISM

Economics is about many things, but most of all it is about the making of choices in situations where means are perceived to be inadequate relative to ends: 'Choice implies that alternatives are mutually conflicting, otherwise, all would be chosen, which is equivalent to saying that none would be chosen.'[7] Central to the economist's concerns is therefore the notion of opportunity cost, of options foregone, of next-bests sacrificed. Scarcity of resources sees to that: 'Cost is the obstacle or barrier to choice, that which must be got over before choice is made. Cost is the underside of the coin, so to speak, cost is the displaced alternative, the rejected opportunity. Cost is that which the decision-maker sacrifices or gives up when he selects one alternative rather than another.'[8] No one, be he prince, pauper or cost-accountant, is able to consume his cake and save it for his tea. The benefit of *having* carries with it the cost of *not-eating*. The benefit of *eating* carries with it the cost of *not-having*. All cost, in short, is opportunity cost.

All cost, therefore, is quintessentially subjective; for the trade-off between A and B is not in truth a trade-off between A and B at all. Rather, it is a trade-off between the amount of satisfaction that the decision-maker expects to derive from A, as compared with the quantity of enjoyment which he anticipates that B will afford him. Such a psychic calculus is by its very nature an intensely personal one in a way that a calculus involving a physical magnitude (one piece of cake) or a monetary measurement (£10 000) is not – the requisite information residing, after all, nowhere else than in the mind of a discrete and unique individual: 'In a theory of choice, cost represents the anticipated utility loss upon sacrifice of a rejected alternative. Because utility functions are necessarily personal, cost is tied directly to the chooser and cannot exist independently of him . . . Cost cannot be measured by someone other than the decision-maker because there is no way that subjective experience can be directly observed.'[9] Only the decision-maker can estimate his own pleasures or evaluate his own trade-offs or say which alternatives he regards as relevant for himself; and that is why the economist who wishes meaningfully to identify the *what* and to quantify the *how much*, unable as he is to look directly into the minds of the choosers, has no alternative but to fall back upon the proxy values thrown up at the moment of exchange. His approach, in other words, is that of revealed preference within the context of catallactics: 'The opportunity costs that are relevant for individual choice are necessarily subjective, and these costs cannot be measured independently of choice itself.'[10] Only by observing actual choices being made, in other words, does the economist learn something of the true nature of values quintessentially subjective.

The economist must, however, be quick on his feet; for the sad fact is that values observed all too quickly freeze into values historic, the record of past choices and not an indicator of current decisions. Genuine costs, by definition, are date-stamped once-for-alls that 'exist in the mind of the individual choice-maker only at the moment of decision'.[11] Genuine costs, by definition, are *ex ante* values, forward-looking and future-oriented constructs, not the *ex post* retrospectives of the cost-accountant who has eaten his cake and found it mouldy. Sympathising as one must with his regret and his disappointment, the economist has no choice but to inform the accountant that sunk costs and by-gones are no longer of any interest to the student of choosing behaviour: 'Only at the moment or instance of choice is cost able to modify behavior', the economist will say, and that means that values with genuine behavioural content simply 'cannot be measured after the fact'.[12] Since all of human life involves the making of choices at the margin in conditions of considerable uncertainty concerning future time, quite a number of people are likely to change their minds after they have incurred a cost. Those persons can expect little interest from the economist in the burden they have borne: 'Since choice has been made,' he will insist, 'this cost is irrelevant excepting insofar as the experience may modify anticipations about choice alternatives in the future.'[13] Thus it is that the economist, situating revealed preference within the context of catallactics as the subjectivist will, must be quick on his feet: 'Cost can never be realized because of the fact of choice itself: that which is given up cannot be enjoyed.'[14] Valuations are always correct at the planning stage of the individual actor: 'Cost consists therefore in his own evaluation of the enjoyment or utility that he anticipates having to forgo as a result of choice itself.'[15] Valuations never have economic significance once the moment of choice is in the past. With respect to valuation as with respect to justice, it would appear, attention remains properly focused on process and not on outcome.

Process which is, moreover, on-going and continuous – not the once-for-all gravitating to the inertial position of equilibrium so much beloved of first-years who worship at the Marshallian cross but rather the perpetual searching and imagining, becoming and trading, that characterises the economics of uncertainty and time of the genuine Austrians such as Menger, or the celebrated subjectivists of the LSE such as Hayek, Robbins and Coase in the 1930s, Thirlby in the 1940s and 1950s, Wiseman in the 1950s, or the still-less-orthodox theorists of alertness and vision such as Kirzner and Shackle. Hayek had supervised Shackle's Ph.D thesis (on Keynes) at the LSE in the 1930s and throughout his life Shackle remained, in Geoff Harcourt's words, 'an ardent admirer and friend'.[16] Many readers familiar with the ideas of both Shackle and the LSE agnostics will, one suspects, wish to take issue with Buchanan's observation that 'Shackle does not, to my knowledge, make the obvious linkage between his provocative and important work on decision, uncertainty, and time and the work on opportunity cost carried forward by his LSE counterparts',[17] but Buchanan ultimately does concede, speaking of Shackle, that 'his whole approach to decision is fully consistent with that developed by the London theorists.'[18] That approach had been foreshadowed in the 1920s by the seminal papers (and by the influential *Risk, Uncertainty and Profit* of 1921) of Buchanan's great mentor, Frank Knight, on uncertainty, history-to-come and the probability calculus. Of those contributions Buchanan has written as follows: 'The fact remains . . . that there exist certain uninsurable uncertainties in the institutional environment of modern business operation . . . To this extent, therefore, genuine Knightian uncertainty must exist in a world where decisions must be made and where decisions must be erroneous. As Knight quite explicitly stated . . . where there is no genuine uncertainty, there are no decisions.'[19] An approach bound to appeal to the celebrated subjectivists of the LSE – as, according to Buchanan, indeed it did: 'His influence was notable at the London School of Economics, where, largely at the urging of Lionel Robbins, Knight's work become a necessary part of reading for an economics degree.'[20]

Buchanan, directly influenced by Frank Knight and personally much in sympathy with the perspective that sees microeconomics not so much as comparative statics as dynamics without end, is himself very much in the sceptical tradition which eulogises searching while tending to treat finding as somewhat of a fortuitous accident. One implication of this methodological orientation is that, even making the standard assumption of rationality, it is inappropriate to expect realised experience to be an objective measurement of subjective anticipation: *ex post* consequences can only be a proxy for *ex ante* sensations in (general) equilibrium states and these the process perspective tends to discount as uncommon and a-typical in a changing environment. A second implication is that, quantification of variables only being appropriate when those variables are significantly more concrete than is the entrepreneurial fantasy in a world of fog that is the stuff of economics, there is not much need for 'the conceptualization of economics as a branch of applied mathematics'[21] which the constrained maximisation orientation breeds and forms: acceptable perhaps as part of a theoretical exercise in the efficient allocation of a fixed endowment, the simple computational approach which treats optimality in economics as a sub-topic in 'the mathematics of applied maximization' is misleading and unhealthy where it diverts the attention of the investigator from the far more fruitful 'analysis of exchange processes'.[22] Economics being first and foremost about human actions and interactions while seeking to effect market exchanges, the fact is that neither empirical evidence nor 'the excess baggage of modern mathematics'[23] can possibly be as helpful to the scholar as would be a sound appreciation of the gains from trade ('the basic wisdom that Adam Smith discovered')[24] combined with the sensitive exercise of the faculty of imagination ('as G.L.S. Shackle should have taught us all'[25]): 'The problems in economics are not amenable to scientific solutions, and progress is not to be expected by pushing back the frontiers of science.'[26]

Only a minority of present-day economists would, of course, be fully in sympathy with this proposition or genuinely prepared to join Buchanan in ranking catallactics and imagination, Smith and Shackle, above induction and deduction, fact-hoarding and symbol-flaunting. The result is more or less what one would expect, that 'exciting young minds' tend to look elsewhere and economics departments tend to 'attract and turn out dullards': 'Instead of evidence of progress . . . I see a continuing erosion of the intellectual (and social) capital that was accumulated by "political economy" in its finest hours. I look at young colleagues trained to master regression routines who are totally uninterested in, and incompetent to examine, elementary economic propositions.'[27] These 'young colleagues' are unlikely to find much in Buchanan's work that engages their interests; while Buchanan, for his own part, feels so alienated from the over-confidence with which the 'dullards' cling to their maximisation paradigm that he has gone so far as to threaten an essay entitled 'Why I am Not an Economist'. That title would be a sad reflection on the state of economic science, for the truth is that Buchanan *is* an economist (albeit an unorthodox economist) – and an economist with a deep-seated moral conviction 'that the perspectives of an economist are valuable in the discussion of basic issues of social philosophy'.[28] Individualism is one – as witness 'the more or less natural proclivity of economists to look at individual behavior, at individual choice'.[29] Purposive rationality is a second – as where, *ceteris paribus*, 'to say that an individual behaves *economically* we really mean that, when confronted with a relevant choice, he chooses "more" over "less" '.[30] *Homo economicus* is a third – the assumption, in other words, 'that men behave in behalf of narrowly defined and objectively measurable self-interest'.[31] Market between anarchy and Leviathan most of all – since, however valuable, 'the principle of order that economics teaches is in no way "natural" to the human mind which, in innocence, is biased towards simple collectivism': 'As a discipline or area of inquiry, economics has social value in offering an understanding of the principle of order emergent from decentralized processes, of spontaneous coordination.'[32] The Scotsman had said as much when, reflecting that 'nobody ever saw a dog make a fair and deliberate exchange of one bone for another with another dog', he then recorded that the butcher, the brewer and the baker were very definitely animals of a different breed when it came to proposing bargains and contracts grounded in an appeal to self-love and personal advantage: 'Give me that which I want, and you shall have this which you want, is the meaning of every such offer; and it is in this manner that we obtain from one another the far greater part of those good offices which we stand in need of.'[33] Thus does the science of catallactics acquire the morally beneficent character of symbiotics, where 'symbiotics is defined as the study of the association between dissimilar organisms' and 'the connotation of the term is that the association is mutually beneficial to all parties.'[34] Trade and exchange mean complementarity of interests (an alternative to conflict between individuals) and a heightened level of perceived satisfaction (since without this anticipation of something better no one but a dullard would seek to make a swap in the first place). Trade and exchange evidently possess philosophically-desirable properties in their own right; and nowhere more so than when they are interpreted by means of a subjectivist methodology which makes much of perceptions and processes while playing down the value to the useful economist of constructs such as equilibrium conditions and end states. Buchanan sees himself as a modern missionary anxious to do good. He is also a puritan and an ascetic who has little time for toys.

8.2 THE MIXED ECONOMY

Buchanan is a proceduralist and a democrat, adamant that his principal contribution is to the theory of just and orderly processes, insistent that his insights and schemata are value-neutral with respect to the choice between alternative economic and social systems: 'I do not offer a description of the "good society", even on my own terms.'[35] A proceduralist and a democrat though he undeniably is, Buchanan is, however, very much the moralist and the prophet as well – a man who, even before he reached the University of Chicago in 1945, had thought long and hard about public and private and formulated a personal ideology which even then was unfriendly to other-directedness: 'When I reached the University of Chicago, I was what I now best describe as a libertarian socialist. I had always been anti-state, anti-government, anti-establishment. But this included the establishment that controlled the United States economy. I had grown up on a reading diet from my grandfather's attic piled high with the radical pamphlets of the 1890s. The robber barons were very real to me.'[36] Even before he reached the University of Chicago, it would appear, Buchanan's own personal perception of the 'good society' was that of the advocate of autonomy and initiative who was groping towards the institutionalisation of a decentralised decision-making mechanism such as he rapidly identified in market capitalism. The robber barons quickly disappeared, however, and with their disappearance any need to build in constitutional safeguards against the sustained abuse of concentrated power on the part of giant corporations and counterpart associations. Textbook models of perfect competition have much to answer for.

Buchanan makes no secret of his 'strong advocacy of the market organization of the economy'[37] or of the 'return to the stance of the classical political economists'[38] which he would himself very much like to see. The wisdom of Mandeville (that private vices can be public virtues, that beneficent mutuality can be an unintended outcome) has, he believes, gone into eclipse – and masterless men have, to their discredit, filled the vacuum by opting for a master: 'The faith in politics exhibited by twentieth-century man, at least until the 1960s, stems ultimately from his loss of faith in God, accompanied by an ignorance about the effective working of organizational alternatives.'[39] Ignorance about alternatives can never be a good thing for a shopper in the marketplace for institutions who genuinely wishes to reveal preferences that are other than random; and in that sense it is clear that Buchanan's writings, together with those of other committed advocates of market capitalism, cannot but have a didactic function. A didactic function of a constructive nature in stressing that, owing to uncertainty and change, there is a need to keep one's options open not so much for the instrumental benefit of maximisation as because, quite simply, one hasn't a clue: 'Man wants liberty to become the man he wants to become. He does so because he does not know what man he will want to become in time.'[40] A didactic function of a negative nature in pointing out the perceived unpopularity of the interventionist State and contrasting it with that more moderate polity that leaves its citizens room to breathe: 'Politics that is confined to a few and well-defined tasks cannot be seriously predatory.'[41] Thus Buchanan states that the government should police conflicts, enforce laws, provide certain essential goods and services; but that, 'beyond these limits, the "good society" of the constitutionalist embodies the Jeffersonian ideal of "least government"'.[42] Buchanan should perhaps have made clear that by *the* constitutionalist he means no more than *a* constitutionalist; and that his own personal perception of the 'good society' should not be confused with the broader methodological orientation which his rigorous proceduralism represents. That point having been clarified, however, there is no question that Buchanan's own sympathies are definitely engaged; that the founder of the Thomas Jefferson Center cleaves to the 'civic religion' of the Enlightenment thinkers that, so sceptical about the State, focused particular attention 'on the *rules that constrain governments* rather than on innovations that justify ever expanding political intrusions into the lives of citizens';[43] and that at least one strict constitutionalist happens also to be a staunch libertarian. In the on-going debate about public versus private, in other words, it would appear that Buchanan has a personal bias for private.

It is inviting to regard that personal bias as no more nor less than a personal credo – an intelligent man's statement of what he as an individual feels to be right and proper, but not in any sense the inevitable outcome of a commitment to the constitutionalist paradigm. Buchanan himself would no doubt wish to present his world-view in this way, maintaining as he consistently does that propositions concerning good procedures are entirely separable from images of good societies. Just as Adam Smith's personal preference for books over belt-buckles had little to do with his general advocacy of the market mechanism, Buchanan would no doubt suggest, so his own personal preference for private over public is not to be confused with his support for order and process. The distinction between mechanism and end state is entirely clear and is in effect encapsulated in Nozick's procedural framework for utopia, 'namely, one which leaves liberty for experimentation of varied sorts'[44] without rigidly specifying in advance the precise pattern that that process will produce. The relevance of the distinction in the specific case of the political economy of James Buchanan is, however, somewhat more problematic. The difficulty arises because of the very nature of the paradigm itself. The two dimensions which cause the difficulty are the primacy of revealed preference and the urgency of political precommitment. Given such strands in his argument, the unsympathetic commentator will observe, what Buchanan is really saying is that the consumer can select a car of any colour he likes so long as it is blue.

Consider first revealed preference. As a subjectivist Buchanan is of the opinion that all cost is perceived alternative and that no one but the discrete individual concerned can be in any position to quantify utility or measure sacrifice. As an economist Buchanan takes the view that the psychological information, the experiential data, which is the *sine qua non* for welfare-orientated decision-making, can only be collected by means of observing real world choices actually being made. Life would no doubt be very much simpler if *ex ante* valuations possessed an objective identity independent of the acting subject's unique gut reactions; or if some remarkable machine were to be invented that permitted policy-makers directly to make inter-personal comparisons of the contents of men's minds; or if unexpected access to God's filing cabinet were to produce unimpeachable statistics leading to the estimation of a social welfare function without the need for the sceptic's time-consuming detour through each and every exchange made by each and every actor. Of course life would be very much simpler if these enviable conditions were to obtain (just as it would be infinitely healthier if all contagious diseases were to vanish overnight). We start from here, however, and not from there, and thus it is, in Buchanan's perspective, that private negotiation is always the more sensitive indicator, State-imposed taxes, guidelines and bounties always the blunter instrument: 'In the classic example, how much would the housewife whose laundry is fouled give to have the smoke removed from the air? Until and unless she is actually confronted with this choice, any estimate must remain almost wholly arbitrary.'[45] No housewife seeking compensation for an extern-ality would, if also rational, show any real enthusiasm for an almost random number; and that is why she is likely to rank the spontaneous and voluntary contract indicative of revealed preference above the edict of the *one* that is imposed, without any allowance being made for human diversity, across the board upon the *many*. As with the housewife, so with the nation; since the logic of political unknowledge is that the citizen, if also rational, will probably wish to maximise the scope for individual search and conscious choice, agreed-upon side payments and mutually-satisfactory bribes, self-interested reciprocity and personally perceived betterment, the exchange of rights and the gains from trade. The citizen will probably wish, in other words, to maximise the scope for the market and significantly to reduce the role played by the State.

Consider now political precommitment. Buchanan conceives of the democratic process as a political market and of his own public choice approach as 'a straightforward extension of the exchange nexus.'[46] That being the case, one would expect him to have what might be called a proceduralist's confidence in the viability of the public sector. Of course the leadership cannot conceivably know the precise rankings and utility-fields of each and every actor – and for that reason there is bound by definition to be an inefficient and unsatisfying dimension to any *fiat* system: 'What does the economist mean by an "optimum allocation of resources"? He really means that allocation which is produced by the uninhibited interplay of private individual choices and nothing more.'[47] Yet it is and must be the study of that leadership to keep the efficiency and the satisfaction slippages to the bare minimum, to act in all cases *as if* in possession of proper information on revealed preferences. The incentive is the vote motive and the desire, in a competitive political market, so greatly to please sovereign citizens as to continue to enjoy the privilege of power. It is easy enough for the academic observer to set up a two-pole model in which the alternative to divine omniscience is presented as radical ignorance. No political entrepreneur, if also rational, could, however, afford himself the luxury of employing so tidy an either/or construction or of conflating for convenience the problem of imperfect knowledge (the central difficulty in any instance of human action) with that of no knowledge at all (as where a greengrocer, mistaking his market, offers nails when his customers demand pears): to do this would be to conceal the very nature of the political profit which he anticipates will be the reward to his investment of alertness and sensitivity. The market for political services being, in the public choice perspective, very much like the standard economic market, one would have expected Buchanan to adopt the eclectic position of the political entrepreneur rather than the dogmatic stance of the academic observer – and to have shown a proceduralist's confidence in the one market as in the other. It is a matter of record that such an expectation would have been ill-founded. Buchanan proposes no quasi-permanent multi-period checks on potential abuses in the private sector. He does propose a considerable measure of constitutional precommitment in the public sector. He would not, if also rational, propose the unanimity rule, the money supply target, the balanced budget, the expenditure ceiling if he were not deeply concerned about the power of politicians, bureaucrats and special interest groups significantly to pervert the public purpose, significantly to palm off upon the citizens policies which are vote-winners only so long as the master is oblivious to the chicanery of the servant.

And there is more. Buchanan records with regret the fact that an irresponsible leadership employs inflation as a mode of invisible taxation levied without democratic consultation – and proposes that such reprehensible conduct, such betrayal of trust, be blocked off by a multi-period law such as would prohibit this form of vote-buying through creeping default. Buchanan notes with sorrow the propensity of today's decision-makers cynically and immorally to make tomorrow's taxpayers bear the cost of public goods that future generations will themselves never see – and recommends that the hands of those who go in for deliberate manipulation of 'fiscal perceptions'[48] Ulysses-like be tied in advance lest they cede to the temptations proffered by fiscal illusion. Yet Buchanan must know that a cunning entrepreneur, frustrated in one area, will then simply turn to another; that unanticipated inflation and the shifting of burdens are only the tip of a fearsome iceberg; and that political marketeers, callously prepared as Buchanan asserts they are *de facto* to defraud widows and orphans, will simply think up new tricks the moment that existing avenues are closed to them. Buchanan the constitutional political economist explicitly advances proposals of a legalistic nature aimed at reducing the opportunities for predatory behaviour. Buchanan the libertarian implicitly indicates that there is a viable alternative solution to the problem of the non-beneficent leadership in the form of greater dependence on market, reduced reliance on State. The sheer pessimism about politics which led Buchanan to formulate the former approach would seem to impel him automatically to rank the latter very highly indeed – as he himself in some places seems openly to declare: 'Public choice, along with complementary empirical observation, has defused enthusiasm for collectivist solutions to social problems. In this negative sense, public choice has exerted, and continues to exert, major ideological impact.'[49] On balance, however, it is Buchanan's consistent practice to adopt a cautious and guarded posture – as where, comparing the market failure concept of welfare economics with the government failure construct of his own school, he comes down unambiguously on the side of ambiguity: 'I am *not* saying that public choice implies government failure *relative* to market alternatives. I am saying that *relative* to the images of government prevalent in the 1940s, public choice has embodied a theory of government failure.'[50] To which the unsympathetic commentator will reply that Buchanan the libertarian obviously has a healthy respect for market processes; that Buchanan the constitutional political economist would never have formulated so complex a theory of political precommitment if he had had any real faith in the public sector; and that what Buchanan is really saying is that the consumer can select a car of any colour he likes so long as it is blue.

The unsympathetic commentator will say that the very structure of the political economy of James Buchanan is such as to promote a bias within the mixed economy away from public and in favour of private. The more sympathetic observer will take the concerned social philosopher at his word when he says that his proper focus is on procedures, not end states, on good rules, not desirable outcomes. The position of a libertarian who is also a proceduralist is difficult to interpret at the best of times. Nor can it be said that Buchanan goes out of his way to assist the reader, sympathetic or not, to grasp the precise manner in which the pieces of the puzzle in fact fit together to constitute a coherent and a consistent whole: hidden assumptions may determine the cut of the cloth in the case of Marshall, but to Buchanan they influence the choice of the fabric and the shape of the tailor's eyebrows as well. Ambiguities abound, but the sympathetic observer will wish nonetheless to maintain that Buchanan's proceduralism is intellectually separable from Buchanan's libertarianism – and that a bias away from private and in favour of public can actually be derived from a system of which the point of departure is radical individualism.

The key is consent; for one of the eventualities which the tolerant theorist of freedom of choice must take on board is that the revealed preferences of real world individuals will not only converge but will converge on the need for the interventionist State. Thus it happens that Buchanan, who must therefore be counted such a tolerant theorist, insists on defining a public good not in terms of its objective characteristics but, employing socio-political rather than economic terminology, as '*any* good or service that the group or the community of individuals decides, for any reason, to provide through *collective* organization'.[51] Free State education falls into the category in both Britain and the United States. Consensus varies as between the two democracies, however, with respect to the provision of free State health care: 'Great Britain has chosen to define medical care as a quasi-collective service to the fullest extent; the United States has chosen to leave this service to the market economy, although the quasi-collective nature has been acknowledged by the provision of care to those financially unable to purchase services in the market.'[52] Consensus may vary but the principle does not, that 'the citizens of a governmental unit, acting collectively through the legislative process'[53] should be given or not given that which most of them most want to be given or not given. The graduated income tax, for example, in a country where 'income redistribution, at least in some indirect sense, is treated as a public "good"':[54] 'This tax . . . can be made as progressive in rate as social attitudes permit.'[55] Alternatively, the direct prohibition by law of a commodity such as a narcotic drug to which the 'overwhelming consensus' is unquestionably hostile: 'Laws such as these will normally be used only when the predominant majority of the citizens consider the consumption of the item in question undesirable.'[56] That some hypothetical student of society might prefer health care to be rationed by markets, income tax to be proportional and self-immolation via substance-abuse to be legal is not of any great relevance to the choices that must be made: that student is no more than one among equals, good procedures are essential if political decisions are sensitively to reflect popular attitudes – and the key to the door of decision simply cannot be other than consent.

The key being consent, there is much to be said for considered reform in processes, for careful improvements in rules, for 'institutional change', in short, such as would 'allow the operation of politics to mirror more accurately that set of results that are preferred by those who participate'.[57] Such change is Pareto-efficient (in the sense that all parties benefit, not merely some). Applied to the mixed economy, three structural alterations suggest themselves. All three would move the society closer still to the regime of unanimity of agreement which remains the ideal and the benchmark; and not one is in itself unfavourable to the public sector as compared with the private. The unsympathetic commentator who sees Buchanan first and foremost as a libertarian and only then as a proceduralist is unlikely in the circumstances to find much support for his contention in the three proposals which follow.

The *first* proposal involves geographical decentralisation of political authorty: 'Clearly, for many of the more specific public functions, decisions can be more rationally made at the local government level than at any higher level in the political hierarchy.'[58] For there to be a meaningful devolution of the decision-making powers, it must be stressed, there must also be an appropriate devolution of responsibility for finance and provision. In some cases (national defence is the obvious example) such subdivision of responsibility is simply not feasible and there remains in consequence no serious alternative to Big Government. In other cases, however, finance and provision on an area-by-area basis is a genuine option – the local police services, say, or the collection of refuse – and one which ought, moreover, to be examined carefully by every committed democrat who believes that the supply of public functions ought to respond as sensitively to individuals' preferences as does the supply of private goods. It is, indeed, the model of the consumer buying a radio as applied to the community buying a park that ought, theoretically speaking, to determine the actual size of the relevant deciding, financing and providing unit: 'Each collective good or service is "collective" to only a limited group. The extent of the group determines the "economic" size of the governmental unit which should perform the function.'[59] Different governmental units for each and every public function (reflecting the fact that each and every public function has its own unique externalities and set of spillovers) represent an ideal situation. The costs of administration will probably dictate a far more limited number of areas – the nation, the state or province or county, the local community certainly, perhaps also the agglomeration (a consideration which will not have failed to capture the attention of the student of municipal transport in the suburbs of London, Paris or New York). The number of areas will be limited by the economist's constraint of affordability, but the inference is clearly that the selection of the area-by-area option will have more than a marginal impact in terms of the decentralisation of political authority. Smaller units mean lower decision-making costs. A more diversified product means greater freedom of choice. Migration from one region to another puts pressure on unresponsive leaders and thereby helps to check abuse of power. Most of all, the decentralisation of authority maximises *ceteris paribus* the opportunity for each social actor to reveal his preferences and to make his voice heard. Red or blue, at least his views will be on record and his consent more likely to count when it comes to actually plotting the course of the mixed economy than if his were no more than a tiny face in an overwhelming crowd.

The *second* proposal involves the matching of a particular tax to a particular benefit: 'Effectively designed earmarking may limit the extent to which government, any government, can exploit the taxpaying public; government may be given a positive incentive to provide the goods and services that taxpayers want.'[60] Public spending at the present time is a bundle. So is public revenue. Buchanan recommends that the black box be opened, the bundles broken up, and specific costs paired with specific benefits in order that the individual citizen may see quite clearly in what way he is spending his money. In the private sector it is standard practice for the rational shopper, proceeding item by item, to seek to proportion marginal burden to marginal satisfaction – consciously to decide, in other words, to sacrifice one more penny to buy one more apple. Buchanan's proposal is that the standard practice of the private market be made, via earmarking, standard practice for the public sector as well. Wily politicians will gnash their teeth at the loss of obfuscatory and discretionary powers with respect to the budgetary mix while entrenched bureaucrats (already upset, no doubt, by proposals for devolution that challenge top-heavy structures) are bound to be concerned lest greater transparency prove a threat to existing privileges. Buchanan's reply to all of this would be in effect that it is undemocratic and patronising to conceal from the purchaser the true cost of any good or service in which he has expressed an interest; or to marry an unpopular service to a popular one in such a way as to force a would-be host to invite both the friend and the spouse lest he otherwise be deprived of the friend. Buchanan would say that what the community should do is to opt wherever economically feasible (wherever administrative costs do not, that is, dwarf anticipated benefits) for *à la carte* in place of *carte blanche*, for a system under which a vote for better fire-protection or a new opera house is directly matched with a specific levy intended to finance the project agreed upon and no other. Earmarking involves higher decision-making costs than does the general fund system (the obvious reason being the fact that there are more decisions to be made) but it also brings with it the not inconsiderable benefit of improved revelation of preferences. Unpopular projects will lose their funding (or at least the bulk of it: passionate minorities will retain access to the more restricted but non-zero – and non-earmarked – general budget with respect to which legislative logrolling will continue to apply), but this in itself need not mean an overall cut in public spending. On the contrary, it might mean an overall rise, as where improved citizen consultation breeds reduced taxpayer alienation and increased public willingness to support public projects. Whether the outcome is an overall cut or an overall rise, however, the purpose behind the proposal is clear: earmarking increases the ability of individuals to say for themselves what they see as better and what they see as worse. The purpose behind the proposal, in short, is no more nor less than an improvement in procedures that brings the democracy that much closer to Wicksellian optimality.

The *third* proposal involves the financing of collectively-provided services not out of tax revenues at all but rather via direct charges payable exclusively by users. Under the access-without-price system, the individual tends quite rationally to 'demand more services privately than he will supply publicly' – 'the kernel of the internal conflict in the National Health Service'.[61] 'In their *private or individual choice* behaviour as potential users or demanders of health-medical services, individuals are inconsistent with their *public or collective choice* behaviour as voter-taxpayers who make decisions on supplying these same services.'[62] The inconsistency lies not in the individuals' preference but rather in an institutional setting which causes consumers to ignore the opportunity cost of resources which are made available to them free on demand. The solution lies in a reform of that institutional setting such as would integrate the services in question into the standard decision-making framework which currently applies in the case of normal consumables like apples and pears, beef and beer. User-charges would reduce non-urgent consumption by giving the individual an incentive to restrain himself from luxuries which become that much less attractive at a positive price. User-charges would permit the making of direct comparisons between alternative utilities and promote in that way a more efficient allocation of national endowments. User-charges would in themselves be equitable precisely because, as the name suggests, it is the beneficiary who pays the fee: ethically speaking, there is 'little basis for supporting the subsidization of the users of the mails by the general federal taxpayer',[63] and the same might reasonably be said with respect to the metering of domestic water supplies, the rationing by tolls of access to congested highways, bridges and tunnels, the pricing of places in universities and colleges – and, of course, the National Health Service. User-charges, finally would serve as a measure of desiredness and an indicator of revealed preference: uneconomic due to administrative costs in some cases, unfeasible due to indivisibility of benefits in others, it is arguably because of the valuable information they contribute to the process of consumer-consultation that user-charges most of all recommend themselves to the student of democratic procedure and should therefore be employed as extensively as possible. Charges in the public sector are intentionally similar to prices in the private. Their imposition (or non-imposition) is of little further relevance, however, to the broader question of whether a sensible society ought to promote a bias within its mixed economy away from public and in favour of private: public sector or private sector, Buchanan would say, it is right and proper that the gatekeeper to the postal services should be the sticking of the stamp.

Buchanan is a proceduralist in the Wicksellian mould. He is also an advocate of individual autonomy in the tradition of classical liberalism. As a proceduralist he makes proposals for a more sensitive taking of the national pulse – geographic decentralisation of political authority, the matching of a particular tax to a particular benefit, the imposition of user-charges on the consumers of collectively-provided services. As a libertarian he makes clear his own personal preference for private over public but manages to situate within his schema no concrete recommendation more anti-Statist than the moderate suggestion that arbitrary action by the government should be suppressed where it is incompatible with voluntary contractual arrangements: 'For example, minimum-wage legislation and most restrictions on entry into professions, occupations, types of investment, or geographical locations could be rejected, as could all discrimination on racial, ethnic, and religious grounds.'[64] Bad laws should be repealed, individuals' preferences maximally revealed, self-seeking leadership maximally pre-constrained;

but with respect to the precise mix of the mixed economy the methodology of constitutional political economy provides, in the last analysis, no usable blueprint whatsoever.

The silence is not *obiter dictum*. On the contrary, it is an essential part of the story; for it is the avowed intention of the committed proceduralist not to impose his own preferred structures and outcomes on others but rather to suggest good processes by means of which the community as a whole can articulate a social consensus and formulate a social compromise. The precise content of the rules and the rights that are thrown up by good processes is a matter of complete indifference: 'The conceptual agreement may range from an assignment that involves relatively little "law" in the formalized sense to an assignment that rigidly constrains individual behavior over many dimensions of adjustment.'[65] What is of over-arching concern to the committed proceduralist is, after all, not content but consent:

> Mutual agreement, backed up if necessary by effective enforcement, is a necessary condition for social interchange. But this agreement may embody any one of an almost infinite variety of actual distributions and/or imputations of rights among persons, constrained by any one of an equally large number of possible sets of rules for personal behavior. Neither the specific distribution of rights among separate persons, nor the general characteristic of the rights structure itself is relevant directly to the issue of mutual agreement, certainly in definition and enforcement. Physical facilities may be variously partitioned among individuals as units of 'private property'. Or, alternatively, such facilities may be organised under rules that dictate common usage by large groups of persons, including the whole membership of the community. If the limits to individual behavior are well defined, voluntary social interaction can proceed in an orderly fashion under any structure.[66]

A spirited defence of tolerance, open-endedness and non-specificity on the part of Buchanan the proceduralist which is likely, as it happens, to cause a certain amount of anxiety with respect to precise social arrangements on the part of Buchanan the libertarian. What would happen, the latter Buchanan will ask the former, if his fellow-citizens consciously selected a money supply rule that, while scrupulously non-discretionary, was also astoundingly inflationary? Or if they deliberately decided, putting equity above efficiency because of sympathy with the deprived, to opt for a constitutional ceiling on public expenditure higher than any budget any responsible social democrat has ever proposed? Or if they, duty-bound patriots imbued with national pride, voted overwhelmingly for military conscription in preference to the priced alternative, despite the voluntarist's warning that a 'hidden tax . . . imposed quite arbitrarily on a small set of persons'[67] hardly appears to him to be a fair one? Buchanan the proceduralist will not be able to reassure Buchanan the libertarian as to the precise mix of the mixed economy that will be ground out by means of good processes – and will plump instead for a joke: 'I lack the enthusiasm for science fiction that seems to be required to qualify as a futurist.'[68] Buchanan the libertarian, convinced as he is that the unemployed are not about to give up their TV dinners nor those protected by minimum wage laws renounce their privileges that 'a good part of the observed unemployment among teenagers'[69] be reduced through more flexible contracting, will not be amused by the proceduralist's levity – and will opt in its place for a note of realism such as he would greatly prefer not to have to sound: 'As social scientists, our predictions must, it seems to me, remain pessimistic . . . We are whistling in the wind if we anticipate breakdown and reversal.'[70] The most that can be said is that perhaps the stress of Buchanan the proceduralist on revealed preference and political precommitment will make some contribution to the institutional shift away from State and in favour of market which Buchanan the libertarian would so much like to see come about. Perhaps it will.

8.3 POLITICS, ECONOMICS AND POLITICAL ECONOMY

Political scientists have traditionally studied State power. Economists have traditionally studied voluntary exchanges. There has been little love lost between the dismal practitioners of the disparate disciplines, largely because there was little love to begin with. Good fences make for good neighbourliness. A wide no-man's-land makes for no neighbourliness at all. Unsightly and neglected, it has the advantage of keeping in separate pens savage animals prone to meet trespass with terror. It has the disadvantage of preventing cross-breeding and cross-fertilisation such as might lead to the birth of something genuinely new. It has the further disadvantage of representing in itself unexplored territory possessing inestimable potential. The political economy of James Buchanan is situated in that no-man's-land. Intentionally so, for it is there and nowhere else that some of the most interesting and important issues of public policy are in effect to be encountered: 'The student of economics can examine the working of a market system within a specified set of constraints; the student of politics can examine the organization and the processes through which social decisions are made. But the two must join in studying the effects of political or collective decisions on the economy.'[71] The alternative to the adoption of so inter-disciplinary a research programme is for all intents and purposes to fail to understand the origin and impact of those decisions; and that, Buchanan feels, no responsible social scientist can afford to do.

Here at least Buchanan sees some grounds for optimism. The independence of pure economics from its neighbouring disciplines is already becoming less (despite the obvious spread of specialisation and professionalisation *within* the discipline); and one reason for that reorientation of emphasis is almost certainly the example provided by the 'cross-disciplinary field'[72] of public choice itself. The political scientist as well as the economist is increasingly attracted by the new field. So is the game theoretician, the organisational psychologist, the small group sociologist, the anthropologist interested in cooperative structures – with all of whom, in the 'interdisciplinary communication network' that is emerging, the socially-responsible economist finds it easier to interact effectively than he does with some of the scholars in his own professional category such as the 'growth-model macroeconomist, with whom he scarcely finds any common ground. This specialized interdependence, if it is, in fact, general over several emerging specializations, can be expected to result, ultimately, in some movements toward professional institutionalization.'[73] Like the apocryphal blind men who strove collectively to build up a composite picture of an elephant from the knowledge of each of one separate part, these specialists are now increasingly striving to come together to share information gathered from a variety of different perspectives. The end result, Buchanan is convinced, will be the breaking down of the traditional disciplinary borderlines and the development of revolutionary new paradigms.

With much of this a heterodox and evolutionary economist such as Galbraith would have a considerable amount of sympathy; for he, like Buchanan, feels that the contribution of the economist would be more relevant if it paid more attention to institutions and more useful if it sought more intensively to incorporate the variable of power.[74] Galbraith, however, would as a social democrat want to model his political economy on the conscious direction of politics; and would point with approbation to Tawney's declaration of 1949 that

the increase in the freedom of ordinary men and women during the last two generations has taken place, not in spite of the action of

Governments, but because of it. It has been due to the fact that, once political democracy had found its feet popularly elected chambers began, under the pressure of their electors, to prescribe minimum standards of life and work, to extend public services, to pool surplus wealth and employ it for the common good . . . The mother of liberty has, in fact, been law.[75]

Buchanan's conceptualisation of political economy is therefore rather a different one, taking as it does as its point of departure not the political commitment to design but rather 'the work that has been done by economists of extending the simple principles of their discipline to political decision-making, to the making of decisions in a nonmarket context'.[76] The social democratic approach is first to enumerate the objective functions of the beneficent State and then to express the belief that wise voters may be relied upon to hound from office all but good men. Buchanan's political economy of methodological individualism, on the other hand, reflects the professional orientation of a trained economist who sees about him exchange wherever he looks: 'Governmental decisions are no more exogenous than are those made in the private economy. Collective decisions arise out of the behavior of individuals responding to alternatives placed before them. Any approach to a complete or satisfactory treatment of the public economy must examine as a central feature the way in which collective decisions are made.'[77] And that, needless to say, is not by State *qua* State but by persons *qua* persons: 'The state has no ends other than those of its individual members and is not a separate decision-making unit. State decisions are, in the final analysis, the collective decisions of individuals.'[78] Such methodological individualism does not, as we have seen, rule out the possibility that individuals will demand welfareism of the type advocated by Galbraith and Tawney. A procedure and not an end state, what it does is to suggest that any approach to collective decision-making which does not rely heavily on the concept of self-interested individuals rationally involved in voluntary exchanges is bound to yield a misleading picture of external reality.

In that sense the revolutionary new paradigm in terms of which Buchanan wishes to model the interdisciplinary synthesis of political economy is not new at all, but rather as old as the first dyad to have mouthed the words subsequently recorded by the celebrated Scotsman as 'Give me that which I want and you shall have this which you want.'[79] Smith was referring to an obviously economic market inhabited by self-avowed tradesmen such as the butcher, the brewer and the baker.

Buchanan proposes no more than that the voter, the politican and the bureaucrat be regarded in the same way, as self-oriented buyers and sellers with a healthy interest in the *quid pro quo*. Some observers will complain that to treat government as exchange is to treat a dog as a cat; and will warn against the 'attempt on the part of economics to take over all the other social sciences' which Kenneth Boulding has castigated as no less than 'economics imperialism'.[80] Others, more convinced, perhaps, of the centrality and universality of the 'disposition to truck, barter, and exchange',[81] will say that the adoption of a unitary approach to human striving at least makes possible a unitary theory of human action; and that that theory has aesthetic as well as descriptive merit precisely because it stimulates and encourages the weaving of a seamless web. Buchanan's intellectual system is such a seamless web. The pattern which affords the continuity is the principle of exchange.

The interpretation of the political process as a political *market* is the essential characteristic of Buchanan's political economy; and it has thus become his study to apply the basic economic constructs of higgling and bargaining to the political theory of democratic decision-making. Private exchange being based upon cost of search, cost of negotiation, calculative rationality, expected utility, anticipated complementarity of interest, ultimately upon unanimity of consent, it is only to be expected that a public choice approach following in its foot-steps will incorporate constructs such as minimisation of cost (decision-making plus external), conflict-resolution by means of contracted agreement (the case of vote-trading, vote-selling, package deals, compensation, compromise), freedom of choice, the self-interest axiom, the best-judge principle, the notion of revealed preference. Neither private exchange nor public choice, Buchanan stresses, is capable *ex ante* of specifying the goal or end towards which action (individual or collective) ought to be directed – a point about process which the materialistic maximiser would be well advised to take to heart: 'There is no need to assign net wealth or net income a dominating motivational influence on behavior in order to produce a fully operational economic theory of choice behavior, in market or political interaction.'[82] Both private exchange and public choice do, however, predict the generation of philosophically-acceptable albeit unintended outcomes through invisible hand mechanisms only on the assumption of purposive human action: *homo economicus* need not be fully informed but he is presumed nonetheless not to act at random. Given rational striving, in both the economic and the political market, theory suggests that trading partners will gravitate to the contract curve (the Pareto-optimal locus along which, the slack having been taken in, Jack's gain can only be Jill's loss) and will then, while there, proceed to make compromises with one another as to where, between maximum and minimum acceptable values, each will finally put down his equilibrium and cease his bargaining. They will strike compromises and not one another – and will in that way demonstrate the extent to which political action is on all fours with economic because of the ubiquity of reciprocity and the mutual gains from trade.

A lesson, needless to say, which all economists with any sense of social responsibility should now make it their business to learn: 'Economists should cease proffering policy advice as if they were employed by a benevolent despot, and they should look to the structure within which political decisions are made.'[83] Economists should, of course, show exemplary scientific detachment when ferreting out the facts; and they should take particular care to extend that neutrality of orientation to other people's *ought-to-be*s irrespective of whether those values happen to coincide with their own. That having been said, however, economists should never forget either the direct relevance of political economy to 'practical questions of public policy'[84] or the missionary role that must be played by politically-informed economists in helping their society to better its stock of procedures. *Must be played* (since it is exclusively 'in the context of voluntary exchange' that there is a 'precise correspondence'[85] between the twin norms of equity and efficiency) and *will be played* – since, and despite the undeniable presence of the 'highly intelligent technicians', the 'dullards' and the 'ideological eunuchs', the happy truth is that 'economics, as a discipline, will probably continue to attract precisely those scholars who desire to assist in policy formation and to do so professionally. The social role of the economist remains that of securing more intelligent legislation.'[86] The political economy of James Buchanan is an object lesson in the manner in which a socially-committed economist anxious to do good might wish to exercise that role. It is a role which Buchanan has made his own with a crusader's zeal that even non-contractarians and non-constitutionalists such as political pragmatists, Keynesian economists and student activists cannot choose but respect. The political economy of James Buchanan is the political economy of democratic responsiveness, social purposiveness, and ethical constraint. Whether or not one entirely accepts the methodological individualism, the *homo economicus*, the politics-as-exchange and the other specific details of the rigorous intellectual system which this most cautious and careful of social philosophers seeks to advance, it cannot be denied that the work of this controversial and ambitious thinker has conferred upon his discipline a *raison d'être* that converts the dismal science of scarce resources into the moral science of negotiated consent.

And yet some economists, oblivious to social role and devoid of crusader's zeal, continue to indulge in 'piddling trivialities'[87] – and thereby to 'opt out of their essential moral responsibility'[88]. They should, Buchanan is adamant, be studying and teaching the way in which exchange processes reconcile conflicts and render goals mutually compatible; and they should also be playing an active part in contemporary debates on rules, roles and institutions. Instead they are 'shifting attention to trivialities'.[89] They are abandoning their proper post, and that is not without danger for the rest of us: 'To the extent that they do so, their functional roles can only be filled by the charlatans and the fools, whose presence about us requires no demonstration.'[90] A statement with which no one who is not himself either a charlatan or a fool would wish to disagree.

Notes and References

A complete bibliography of the publications of J.M. Buchanan will be found in the *Southern Economic Journal*, vol. 54, 1987, pp. 1–18.

1 INTRODUCTION

1. J.M. Buchanan, *Liberty, Market and State (LMS)* (Brighton: Wheatsheaf, 1986), pp. 14–15.
2. *LMS*, p. 15.
3. *LMS*, p. 75.
4. *LMS*, p. 20.
5. *LMS*, p. 15.
6. J.M. Buchanan, *The Limits of Liberty (LL)* (Chicago: University of Chicago Press, 1975), pp. 91, 92.
7. *LL*, p. 170. That this is a highly controversial interpretation of Smith's position is not relevant for our present purposes.
8. *LL*, p. 170.
9. *LMS*, p. 10.
10. *LMS*, p. 5.
11. T. Hobbes, *Leviathan* (1651) (Oxford: Basil Blackwell, 1957), p. 82.
12. *LMS*, p. 267.
13. See R. Nozick, *Anarchy, State, and Utopia* (New York: Basic Books, 1974), p. ix for a concise explanation of the term.
14. M. Friedman, *Capitalism and Freedom* (Chicago: University of Chicago Press, 1962), p. 34.
15. *LL*, p. 7.
16. *LL*, p. 166.
17. *LMS*, p. 67.
18. *LL*, p. 178.
19. *LMS*, p. 23.
20. *LL*, p. 38.
21. K. Wicksell, 'A New Principle of Just Taxation', selection from *Finanztheoretische Untersuchungen* (1896) transl. by J.M. Buchanan, in R.A. Musgrave and A.T. Peacock (eds) *Classics in the Theory of Public Finance* (London and New York: Macmillan, 1958), pp. 89–90.
22. *ibid.*, p. 97.
23. *ibid.*, p. 118.
24. *ibid.*, p. 90.
25. *ibid.*, p. 79.
26. See in particular, in this connection, J.M. Buchanan and Marilyn Flowers, 'An Analytical Setting for a Taxpayers' Revolution', *Western Economic Journal*, vol. 7, 1969.
27. J.M. Buchanan, *Fiscal Theory and Political Economy (FTPE)* (Chapel Hill: University of North Carolina Press, 1960), p. 65.

28. Buchanan *and* his colleagues, since the fact is that Buchanan has published jointly with some of the most able socio-political economists of his time (Gordon Tullock, Geoffrey Brennan and Richard Wagner, to name but three) to such an extent that it has been suggested that the whole public choice school, and not Buchanan alone, should have been awarded the Nobel Prize. The view taken in this book (which is explicitly about James Buchanan) is that, whether the authorship is sole or joint, Buchanan's work may be taken as indicative of Buchanan's thought.

2. THE CONSTITUTION

1. See, for example, L. von Mises, *Human Action*, 3rd ed. (Chicago: Contemporary Books, 1966), esp. ch. 14.
2. *LMS*, p. 20.
3. *LL*, p. *x*.

2.1 The Individual

4. *LMS*, p. 51.
5. H.G. Brennan and J.M. Buchanan, *The Reason of Rules (RR)* (Cambridge: Cambridge University Press, 1985), p. 21.
6. *LMS*, p. 249.
7. *LMS*, p. 51.
8. J.M. Buchanan and G. Tullock, *The Calculus of Consent (CC)* (Ann Arbor: University of Michigan Press, 1962), p. 315.
9. *RR*, p. 50.
10. See A. Downs, *An Economic Theory of Democracy* (New York: Harper & Row, 1957). To judge by the number of references to Downs in his published work, however, Buchanan would not appear to have been much influenced by this important contribution.
11. *LL*, p. 34.
12. *LL*, p. 92.
13. *LL*, p. 23. Which is not to deny that 'those goods that are not superabundant' (*LL*, p. 28) *can* be a cause of conflict.
14. *LL*, p. 92.

2.2 The Agreement

15. *CC*, p. 81.
16. *RR*, p. *ix*.
17. *LMS*, p. 255.
18. *LL*, p. *ix*.
19. *LL*, pp. 93, 94.
20. *LMS*, p. 47.
21. *RR*, p. 7.
22. *RR*, p. 3.
23. *LL*, p. 20.
24. *LL*, p. 5.
25. *LL*, p. 94.

26. *LL*, p. 25.
27. *CC*, pp. 250–1.
28. *CC*, p.. 254.
29. *CC*, p. 79.
30. *CC*, p. 78.
31. *CC*, p. 78.
32. *CC*, p. 78.
33. *CC*, p. 96.
34. *CC*, pp. 79–80.
35. *CC*, p. 251.
36. *CC*, p. 191.

2.3 The Notion of Justice

37. *LMS*, p. 126.
38. *RR*, p. 98.
39. *RR*, p. 97.
40. *RR*, p. 100.
41. *LL*, p. 87.
42. *RR*, p. 98.
43. *LMS*, p. 258.
44. *RR*, p. 45.
45. *RR*, p. 99.
46. *RR*, p. 18.
47. *RR*, p. 102.
48. *LL*, p. 11.
49. *LL*, p. 25.
50. *LL*, p. 50.
51. *CC*, p. 253.
52. *RR*, pp. 104–5.
53. *RR*, pp. 101–2.
54. G.S. Becker, 'Crime and Punishment: An Economic Approach', *Journal of Political Economy*, vol. 80, 1968, p. 195.
55. *ibid.*, p. 176.
56. *RR*, p. 101.
57. J. Rawls, *A Theory of Justice* (1971) (Oxford: Clarendon Press, 1972), p. 31. Even before the appearance of his celebrated book, it should be noted, Rawls had made influential contributions to the contractarian theory of justice. See, for example, his 'Justice as Fairness', *Philosophical Review*, vol. 57, 1958, for an early and important statement of his position. Rawls does not appear to be mentioned in *The Calculus of Consent*, however, despite the fact that that book was first published in 1962. *The Calculus of Consent* has no index.
58. *ibid.*, p. 21.
59. *ibid.*, pp. 139–40.
60. *ibid.*, p. 302.
61. *ibid.*, p. 154.
62. *ibid.*, pp. 542–3.
63. *ibid.*, p. 261.
64. *ibid.*, p. 137.

65. *ibid.*, p. 543.
66. *ibid.*, p. 542.
67. *ibid.*, p. 158.
68. *ibid.*, p. 542.
69. *ibid.*, p. 86.
70. *ibid.*, p. 136. Emphasis added.
71. *ibid.*, p. 258.
72. *ibid.*, p. 16.
73. *ibid.*, p. 62.
74. *ibid.*
75. *ibid.*, p. 302.
76. *ibid.*, p. 527.
77. *ibid.*, p. 522.
78. *ibid.*, p. 114.
79. *ibid.*, p. 488.
80. J.M. Winter and D.M. Joslin (eds) *R.H. Tawney's Commonplace Book* (Cambridge: Cambridge University Press, 1972), pp. 53–4.
81. R.M. Titmuss, *The Gift Relationship* (Harmondsworth: Penguin, 1973), p. 274.
82. *ibid.*, p. 273.
83. R.M. Hare, 'Rawls' Theory of Justice', in N. Daniels (ed.) *Reading Rawls* (Oxford: Basil Blackwell, 1975), p. 84.
84. Rawls, *Theory of Justice*, p. 154.
85. *ibid.*, p. 155.
86. *ibid.*, pp. 152–3.
87. *ibid.*, p. 168.
88. *ibid.*, p. 172.
89. See on this *ibid.*, pp. 62–3.
90. *ibid.*, p. 157.
91. *ibid.*, p. 137.
92. *CC*, p. 14.
93. J.M. Buchanan, *Freedom in Constitutional Contract* (*FCC*) (College Station and London: Texas A & M Press, 1977), p. 210.
94. J.M. Buchanan, *The Public Finances: An Introductory Textbook* (PF), 3rd ed. (Homewood Illinois: Richard D. Irwin, 1970), p. 140. See also *PF*, pp. 84, 125, 141, 279, and *FCC*, pp. 187, 189.
95. Nozick, *Anarchy, State, and Utopia*, pp. 153, 156–7, 159.
96. *LL*, p. 167.
97. *RR*, p. 15.

3 OPERATIONAL RULES

1. *CC*, p. 284.
2. *LMS*, p. 239.

3.1 The Decision-Making Rule

3. *CC*, p. 251.
4. *CC*, p. *vii*.
5. *CC*, p. 69.

6. *CC*, p. 65–6.
7. *CC*, p. 292.
8. *CC*, p. 70.
9. *CC*, p. 81.
10. *CC*, p. 81.
11. *CC*, p. 80.
12. *CC*, p. 112.
13. *CC*, p. 112.
14. *CC*, p. 113.
15. *CC*, p. 115.
16. *CC*, p. 115.
17. *CC*, p. 116.
18. *LL*, p. 118.

3.2 Pareto Optimality

19. *LMS*, p. 87.
20. *RR*, p. 68. Passages such as this demonstrate the strong similarities between Buchanan's thinking and that of Shackle. See in particular G.L.S. Shackle, *Epistemics and Economics* (Cambridge: Cambridge University Press, 1972). University Press, 1972).
21. *LMS*, 102.
22. *RR*, p. 136.
23. *LMS*, pp. 180, 179.
24. *RR*, p. 138.
25. *RR*, p. 29.
26. *RR*, p. 139.
27. *CC*, p. 95.
28. *CC*, p. 92.
29. *CC*, p. 14.
30. *CC*, p. 94.
31. *CC*, p. 5.
32. Letter to W. Samuels dated August 8, 1973. In J.M. Buchanan and W.J. Samuels, 'On Some Fundamental Issues in Political Economy', *Journal of Economic Issues*, vol. 9, 1975, p. 27.
33. Letters to W. Samuels dated 18 May 1972, 27 March 1973 and August 8, 1973. In Buchanan and Samuels, 'Fundamental Issues', pp. 19, 25, 27.
34. *LL*, p. 85.
35. *LL*, p. 149.
36. *LL*, p. 160.
37. Letter to W. Samuels dated 18 May 1972. In Buchanan and Samuels, 'Fundamental Issues', p. 19.
38. Letter to W. Samuels dated 16 November 1973. In Buchanan and Samuels, 'Fundamental Issues', p. 33.

3.3 The Microeconomics of Consent

39. See on this *LL*, p. 178, which should be read in conjunction with the relevant sections in *The Calculus of Consent*.
40. Nozick, *Anarchy, State, and Utopia*, p. 41.
41. *ibid.*

42. *CC*, p. 91.
43. *LL*, p. 4.
44. *CC*, p. 190.
45. *CC*, p. 125.
46. *CC*, p. 133.
47. *CC*, p. 135.

4 INSTITUTIONAL FAILURE

1. J.M. Buchanan and N.E. Devletoglou, *Academia in Anarchy* (*AA*) (New York: Basic Books, 1970), p. 122.
2. *AA*, pp. *xi*, 4, 5, 64.
3. *AA*, p. 97.
4. *AA*, p. 104.
5. *AA*, p. 4.
6. *FCC*, p. 112.
7. *LL*, p. 162.
8. J.M. Buchanan, 'Why Does Government Grow?', in T.E. Borcherding (ed) *Budgets and Bureaucrats: The Sources of Government Growth* (Durham: Duke University Press, 1977), p. 3.
9. *LL*, p. 161.
10. *LMS*, p. 116.
11. *LL*, p. 14.

4.1 The Over-Extended State

12. *AA*, p. 103.
13. *LMS*, p. 116.
14. *LMS*, p. 116.
15. *LMS*, p. 108.
16. *LMS*, p. 117.
17. *LL*, p. 157.
18. 'Why Does Government Grow?', p. 13.
19. 'Why Does Government Grow?', p. 11.
20. *FCC*, p. 122.
21. *FCC*, p. 252.
22. *LL*, p. 157.
23. *LL*, p. 158.
24. *LL*, p. 163.
25. *LL*, p. 173.
26. *LL*, p. 172.
27. *LL*, p. 169.
28. *LL*, p. 164.
29. *LL*, p. 160.
30. *LL*, p. 161.
31. *LL*, p. 160.
32. *LL*, p. 91.
33. *LL*, p. 91.
34. 'Why Does Government Grow?', p. 6.

35. 'Why Does Government Grow?', p. 10.
36. 'Why Does Government Grow?', p. 6.
37. *LL*, p. 169.

4.2 Decision-Making Rules

38. *CC*, p. 96.
39. *CC*, p. 74.
40. *CC*, p. 82.
41. *CC*, p. 73.
42. *CC*, p. 74.
43. *CC*, p. 82.
44. *CC*, p. 194.
45. *CC*, p. 164.
46. *CC*, p. 74.
47. *CC*, p. 109.
48. *LL*, p. 104.
49. *FCC*, p. 273.

4.3 Keynesian Economics

50. J.M. Buchanan and R.E. Wagner, *Democracy in Deficit (DD)* (New York: Academic Press, 1977), p. 65.
51. H.G. Brennan and J.M. Buchanan, *The Power to Tax (PT)* (Cambridge: Cambridge University Press, 1980), p. 203.
52. *DD*, p. 7.
53. *DD*, p. 96.
54. *DD*, p. 4.
55. *DD*, p. 56.
56. *DD*, p. 140.
57. *DD*, p. 140.
58. *LMS*, p. 189.
59. *LMS*, p. 192.
60. *DD*, pp. *ix–x*.
61. *DD*, p. 101.
62. *DD*, p. 67.
63. *DD*, p. 143.
64. *DD*, p. 129.
65. *LMS*, p. 206.
66. *LMS*, p. 207.
67. *DD*, p. 65.
68. *DD*, p. 182.
69. *DD*, p. 88.
70. *DD*, p. 165.
71. *DD*, p. 167.
72. *DD*, p. 167.
73. See M. Friedman, 'The Role of Monetary Policy', *American Economic Review*, vol. 58, 1968, and 'Inflation and Unemployment', *Journal of Political Economy*', vol. 85, 1977, for Friedman's own development of the arguments. Friedman has become increasingly influenced over the years by

the work of public choice thinkers such as Buchanan: see, for example, his acknowledgement in *Free to Choose* (Harmondsworth: Penguin, 1980), p. 10. As this section indicates, Buchanan returns the compliment. Buchanan is, however, more friendly than is Friedman to some commodity base money or a Fisher index rule as (non-discretionary) alternatives to the (non-discretionary) money growth rule.

74. *DD*, p. 171.
75. *DD*, p. 154.
76. *DD*, p. 171. This passage was written in the mid-1970s and may well refer to the rumours of a military coup which circulated briefly in Britain at that time. It was not intended to refer to the Government and personality of Mrs Thatcher. Even so, the arguments concerning anarchy, leadership and monetarism which Buchanan advanced at that time are clearly not without relevance for the Conservative administration which assumed power in 1979.
77. *DD*, p. 171.
78. *DD*, p. 171.
79. *DD*, p. 64.
80. *DD*, p. 184.

5 A CHARTER FOR DEMOCRATS

1. *LL*, p. 167.
2. *RR*, p. 149n.
3. *LL*, p. 194n. The precise reference is to F.A. von Hayek, *Law, Legislation and Liberty* (London and Henley: Routledge & Kegan Paul, 1979), vol. I, esp. pp. 153–76.

5.1 Constitutional Reform

4. Letter to W. Samuels dated August 8, 1973. In Buchanan and Samuels, 'Fundamental Issues', p. 28.
5. *LL*, p. 96.
6. *LL*, p. 108.
7. *CC*, pp. 260–1.
8. *RR*, p. 145.
9. *PT*, p. 25.
10. *RR*, p. 146. This is a rather controversial statement in view of the obvious gains that a sensitive political entrepreneur would stand to make in such circumstances. It does offer considerable hope for constitutional reform, however, *even when* the normal sources of leadership demonstrably fail to show the requisite imagination and drive.
11. *RR*, p. 147.
12. *LMS*, p. 56.
13. *RR*, p. 139.
14. *RR*, p. 106.
15. *FCC*, p. 252.
16. *FCC*, p. 278.
17. *FCC*, p. 274.

18. *PT*, p. 7.
19. *DD*, p. 175.
20. *DD*, p. 176.
21. *CC*, p. 14. *As if*, of course, since Buchanan does say that most states emerged by conquest of the weak by the strong. Still, the key point is that 'existing rules can be changed contractually even if they did not so emerge' (*RR*, p. 22).
22. *CC*, p. 77.
23. *CC*, p. 77.
24. *CC*, p. 15.
25. See, for instance, *PT*, p. 202.
26. J.M. Buchanan, J. Burton and R.E. Wagner, *The Consequences of Mr. Keynes* (London: Institute of Economic Affairs, 1978), p. 83.
27. *CC*, p. 73.
28. *FCC*, p. 274.
29. *CC*, p. 291.
30. *CC*, p. 115.
31. *FCC*, p. 295.
32. *PT*, p. 204.

5.2 The Role of the State

33. A. Smith, *The Wealth of Nations* (1776), ed. E. Cannan (London: Methuen, 1961), vol. II, p. 209.
34. *ibid.*, p. 208.
35. *ibid.*, p. 209.
36. *FCC*, p.116.
37. *FCC*, p. 117.
38. *FCC*, p. 117.
39. *FCC*, p. 288.
40. *LMS*, p. 117.
41. *LMS*, p. 117.
42. *LL*, p. 177.
43. *AA*, p. 27.
44. To whom, incidentally, *Academia in Anarchy* is dedicated.
45. *AA*, p. 142.
46. *AA*, p. 83.
47. Smith, *Wealth of Nations*, vol. II, p. 158.
48. *AA*, p. 28.
49. *AA*, p. 105.
50. *AA*, p. 43.
51. *FCC*, p. 248.
52. *AA*, p. 170.
53. *CC*, pp. 82–3.
54. *CC*, p. 203.
55. *CC*, p. 204.
56. *LMS*, p. 104.
57. *LL*, p. 72.
58. *LL*, p. 100.

5.3   Macroeconomic Policy

59. *PT*, p. 192.
60. *FCC*, p. 269.
61. *PT*, p. 108.
62. *PT*, p. 38.
63. *PT*, p. 25.
64. *FCC*, p. 296.
65. *PT*, p. 24.
66. *LL*, p. 155.
67. *LL*, p. 178.
68. *LMS*, p. 185.
69. *LMS*, p. 184.
70. *LMS*, p. 193.
71. *LMS*, p. 217.
72. *LMS*, p. 194.
73. *LMS*, p. 194.
74. *DD*, p. 176.
75. *DD*, p. 139.
76. *PT*, p. 123. Brennan and Buchanan present the problem as a *de facto* Prisoner's Dilemma: the State, they say, knows that excessive inflation causes households to run down cash balances (and therefore limits the issue of fiat money), while the private sector believes the government will not maximally inflate (as otherwise it would refuse to hold non-indexed claims such as make up the money-supply). The State thus watches the citizens (to ensure that they continue to hold money) while the citizens watch the State (to ensure that it is not excessively issuing new money); and this process of watching and ensuring would seem to place a ceiling, as if guided by an invisible hand, on the extent to which public finance can proceed through the printing-press. Always assuming, of course, that households correctly perceive the link between money and prices. If, however, they do, then expectations become rational expectations, and unanticipated inflation – which figures prominently in Buchanan's monetarism, as it does in that of Friedman – becomes exceptionally difficult to explain.
77. *DD*, p. 117. Even pre-announced cash limits or money-supply targets count as political interference where they emanate from the Treasury.
78. *RR*, p. 150.
79. *DD*, pp. 4, 5.
80. *DD*, p. 182. The amendment in question is not just a constitutional rule but a *specific* constitutional rule. It thus goes beyond procedure to include end state or outcome as well – something that is, of course, not in keeping with Buchanan's normal approach. Strictly speaking, one *democratically*-established rule is as good as another in the perspective of constitutional political economy, provided that it is properly pre-announced and enforced.
81. H.G. Brennan and J.M. Buchanan, *Monopoly in Money and Inflation* (London: Institute of Economic Affairs, 1981), p. 40.
82. *Monopoly in Money and Inflation*, p. 65.
83. *PT*, p. 126.
84. *PT*, p. 127.

85. *DD*, p. 60.
86. *PT*, p. 129.
87. *DD*, p. 170.
88. R.M. Titmuss, *Commitment to Welfare* (London: Allen & Unwin, 1968), p. 157. Aware that a shift into a balanced budget regime from a deficit regime will cause dislocation, Buchanan does, however, implicitly answer objections such as that made in the text by recommending gradual and not sudden change.

6 THE DEMOCRATIC STATE

1. J.M. Buchanan, 'Better than Plowing', *Banca Nazionale Del Lavoro Quarterly Review*, 159 (1986), p. 374.
2. 'Better than Plowing', p. 371.
3. J.M. Buchanan, *The Inconsistencies of the National Health Service* (London: Institute of Economic Affairs, 1965), p. 15.
4. *Inconsistencies*, p. 15.
5. *Inconsistencies*, p. 16.
6. *PF*, p. 30. Emphasis added. The diagnosis is made looking backwards from 1970 over two decades of experiences and attitudes. It is not intended to be read as an account of attitudes in all periods of economic experience – not least because no one can foresee future perceptions.

6.1 Individualism

7. *LL*, p. 167.
8. *LL*, p. 164.
9. *LMS*, p. 248.
10. *FTPE*, p. 4.
11. A proposition which recurs throughout the whole of Buchanan's work, and nowhere more clearly than in his approach to the national debt. See, for example, J.M. Buchanan, *Public Principles of Public Debt (PPPD)* (Homewood, Ill.: Richard D. Irwin, 1958).
12. J.M. Buchanan and G. Tullock, 'An American Perspective: From 'Markets Work' to 'Public Choice', in A. Seldon (ed.) *The Emerging Consensus . . .?* (London: Institute of Economic Affairs, 1981), p. 88.
13. 'Better than Plowing', p. 366.
14. J.M. Buchanan, *What Should Economists Do? (WSED)* (Indianapolis: Liberty Press, 1979), p. 141.
15. *FCC*, p. 299.
16. *WSED*, p. 152. Emphasis added.
17. *FCC*, p. 259.
18. *FCC*, p. 244.
19. *FCC*, p. 113.

6.2 Unanimity

20. 'Better than Plowing', p. 363.
21. 'Better than Plowing', p. 363.
22. J.M. Buchanan, *The Demand and Supply of Public Goods* (*DSPG*) (Chicago: Rand McNally, 1968), p. 155. Buchanan clearly sees it as a significant part of his own contribution to have drawn attention to this relationship and also to the political-choice dimension in Wicksellian economics. This latter aspect of Wicksell's work Buchanan regards as having been particularly neglected before he brought it into prominence. As he explains (*DSPG*, p. 156): 'Wicksell and Pareto were roughly contemporaries and worked independently one from the other. Pareto's genius in developing the welfare criteria has been properly recognized. Wicksell's genius in relating political rules to orthodox efficiency notions in economics has not yet received its due.'
23. J.M. Buchanan, *Public Finance in Democratic Process* (*PFDP*) (Chapel Hill: University of North Carolina Press, 1967), p. 285.
24. *FCC*, p. 102.
25. 'Better than Plowing', p. 362.
26. *PFDP*, p. 253.
27. *LMS*, p. 191.
28. *LMS*, p. 103.
29. See R. Coase, 'The Problem of Social Cost', *Journal of Law and Economics*, vol. 3, 1960, esp. pp. 2, 4.
30. *LMS*, pp. 102–3.
31. *DSPG*, p. 96.
32. *CC*, p. 209.
33. *PF*, p. 68.
34. *LL*, p. 162–3.
35. *WSED*, p. 150.

6.3 Constitutionalism

36. 'Better than Plowing', p. 366.
37. *FCC*, p. 292.
38. *PFDP*, p. 300.
39. *AA*, p. 36.
40. *LMS*, p. 248.
41. *LL*, p. 83.
42. *DSPG*, p. 160.
43. *PFDP*, p. 300.
44. *AA*, p. 36.
45. *RR*, p. 65.
46. 'Better than Plowing', p. 365.
47. *PFDP*, p. 293.
48. *PFDP*, p. 299.
49. *FCC*, pp. 250–1.
50. *WSED*, p. 152.
51. M. Rothbard, *For a New Liberty* (New York: Libertarian Review Foundation, 1985), p. 67.

52. *ibid.*
53. *ibid.*
54. *LL*, p. 91.
55. *RR*, p. 60.

7.1 THE MORAL DIMENSION

1. N.P. Barry, 'Unanimity, Agreement, and Liberalism: A Critique of James Buchanan's Social Philosophy', *Political Theory*, vol. 12, 1984, p. 586.
2. *ibid.*, p. 595.
3. Scott Gordon, 'The new Contractarians', *Journal of Political Economy*, vol. 8, 1976, p. 584.
4. *ibid.*, p. 583.
5. *ibid.*, p. 585.
6. Nozick, *Anarchy, State, and Utopia*, p. 331. Such servitude must, of course, be non-hereditary.
7. *LL*, p. 60. To complete the trio, the position of Rawls seems to be that (a) 'It is always those with the lesser liberty who must be compensated' and that (b) 'slavery and serfdom . . . are tolerable only when they relieve even worse injustices' (*A Theory of Justice*, p. 248). Whether this evaluation of loss of liberty legitimises the contractual alienation of liberty is not made clear.
8. 'Better than Plowing', p. 363.
9. *WSED*, p. 176.

7.1 Order and Stability

10. *FCC*, p. 208.
11. J.M. Buchanan, 'The Ethics of Debt Default', in J.M. Buchanan, C.K. Rowley and R.D. Tollison (eds) *Deficits* (Oxford: Basil Blackwell, 1986), p. 365.
12. *LMS*, p. 238.
13. *LMS*, p. 13.
14. *WSED*, p. 106.
15. *AA*, p. 123.
16. *RR*, p. *ix*.
17. *WSED*, p. 268.
18. *FCC*, p. 210.
19. *WSED*, pp. 249–50.
20. *AA*, p. 122.
21. A Marshall, *Principles of Economics*, 8th ed. (London: Macmillan, 1949), p. *vii*.
22. See *FTPE*, pp. 117–18.
23. *RR*, pp. 69, 70, 71.
24. *LL*, p. 78.
25. Titmuss, *The Gift Relationship*, p. 253.

7.2 Maximin and Security

26. R.H. Tawney, *The Attack* (London: George Allen & Unwin, 1953), p. 93.
27. *PT*, pp. 25–6.
28. *PT*, p. 148.
29. *PT*, p. 207.
30. *RR*, p. 55.
31. *PT*, p. 194. Emphasis added.
32. *PT*, p. 125.
33. *PT*, p. 188.
34. *LMS*, p. 257.
35. *LMS*, p. 60.
36. *RR*, p. 61.
37. *RR*, p. 60.
38. *WSED*, pp. 269–70.
39. *RR*, p. 54.
40. *RR*, p. 55.
41. *PFDP*, p. 71.
42. *CC*, p. 82.
43. 'Better than Plowing', p. 360.
44. *PF*, p. 292.
45. *PFDP*, p. 269.
46. *PPPD*, p. 125.
47. *RR*. p. 54.
48. *RR*, p. 116.
49. Friedman, *Capitalism and Freedom*, p. 50.
50. Rawls, *A Theory of Justice*, p. 80.
51. *FCC*, p. 123.
52. K.J. Arrow, 'The Welfare Economics of Medical Care' (1963), in M.H. Cooper and A.J. Culyer (eds) *Health Economics* (Harmondsworth: Penguin, 1973), p. 41.
53. *ibid.*, p. 20.
54. *CC*, pp. 193.
55. R.H. Tawney, *The Radical Tradition* (Harmondsworth: Penguin, 1966), p. 172.
56. Friedman, *Capitalism and Freedom*, pp. 8, 15.
57. *LL*, p. 92.
58. *PPPD*, p. 155n.
59. *RR*, p. 63.
60. *LL*, p. 23.
61. *LL*, p. 12.
62. *RR*, p. 64.
63. *LL*, p. x.
64. *WSED*, p. 282.

7.3 Time and Truth

65. *WSED*, p. 183.
66. J.M. Buchanan, C.K. Rowley and R.D. Tollison, 'Government by Red Ink', in *Deficits*, p. 6.

67. J.M. Buchanan, 'Budgetary Bias in Post-Keynesian Politics: The Erosion and Potential Replacement of Fiscal Norms', in *Deficits*, p. 180.
68. *PFDP*, p. 103.
69. 'Budgetary Bias in Post-Keynesian Politics', p. 184.
70. *PPPD*, p. 155.
71. H.G. Brennan and J.M. Buchanan, 'The Logic of the Ricardian Equivalence Theorem', in *Deficits*, p. 83.
72. *PPPD*, p. 155.
73. *PPPD*, p. 161.
74. 'Budgetary Bias in Post-Keynesian Politics', p. 183.
75. *PPPD*, p. 167.
76. *PPPD*, p. 155.
77. *PPPD*, p. 58.
78. *PFDP*, p. 265.
79. *PF*, p. 311.
80. *PFDP*, p. 264.
81. *PPPD*, p. 160.
82. See J.M. Keynes, *The Means to Prosperity* (1933), in *The Collected Writings of John Maynard Keynes* (London: Macmillan, 1972), vol. IX.
83. See, for example, Abba P. Lerner, 'Functional Finance and the Federal Debt', *Social Research*, vol. 10, 1943.
84. *PPPD*, p. 195.
85. *FCC*, p. 233.
86. *LMS*, p. 201.
87. See D. Ricardo, *The Principles of Political Economy and Taxation* (1821), in P. Sraffa and M. Dobb (eds), *The Works and Correspondence of David Ricardo* (Cambridge: Cambridge University Press, 1951), vol. I, esp. pp. 244–9.
88. See A.C. Pigou, *A Study in Public Finance* (London: Macmillan, 1928), esp. pp. 231–249.
89. See R.J. Barro, 'Are Government Bonds Net Wealth?', *Journal of Political Economy*, vol. 82, 1974. See also J.M. Buchanan, 'Barro on the Ricardian Equivalence Theorem', *Journal of Political Economy*, vol. 84, 1976, which is followed by a rely from Barro.
90. *PPPD*, p. 34.
91. *PPPD*, pp. 34–5.
92. *WSED*, p. 211.
93. *LL*, p. 73.
94. *PFDP*, p. 186.
95. *PF*, p. 385.
96. *PF*, p. 296.
97. 'The Ethics of Debt Default', p. 365.
98. 'The Ethics of Debt Default', p. 365
99. *PF*, p. 237.
100. *WSED*, pp. 210–11.
101. *WSED*, p. 212.
102. *WSED*, p. 211.
103. *FCC*, p. 93.
104. *WSED*, p. 217.

105. *WSED*, p. 215.
106. *WSED*, p. 214.
107. *WSED*, p. 214.
108. *WSED*, p. 215.
109. *WSED*, p. 215.
110. M. Weber, *The Protestant Ethic and the Spirit of Capitalism* (1904–5), transl. by T. Parsons (Lond: Allen & Unwin, 1930), p. 180.
111. *WSED*, p. 214.
112. *WSED*, p. 215.
113. *FCC*, p. 111.
114. *LL*, p. 105.
115. *DD*, p. x.
116. D. Bell, *The Coming of Post-Industrial Society* (Harmondsworth: Penguin, 1976), pp. 477–8.
117. Letter from J.M. Buchanan to the author dated 13 June 1988. Emphasis added.

8   ECONOMICS AND BEYOND

1. 'Better than Plowing', p. 373.
2. *FCC*, p. 241.
3. J.M. Buchanan, *Cost and Choice* (*CAC*) (Chicago: Markham Publishing, 1969), p. 9.
4. J.M. Buchanan, 'Our Times: Past, Present and Future', in M.J. Anderson (ed.) *The Unfinished Agenda* (London: Institute of Economic Affairs, 1986), p. 34.
5. *WSED*, p. 158.
6. *DD*, p. ix.

8.1   Subjectivism

7. *FTPE*, p. 96.
8. J.M. Buchanan, 'Introduction: L.S.E. cost theory in retrospect', in J.M. Buchanan and G.F. Thirlby (eds) *L.S.E. Essays on Cost* (New York and London: New York University Press, 1981), p. 14.
9. *CAC*, p. 43.
10. *PFDP*, p. 60.
11. *PFDP*, p. 60.
12. *CAC*, p. vii.
13. *CAC*, p. 43.
14. *CAC*, p. 43.
15. 'L.S.E. cost theory in retrospect', p. 14.
16. G. Harcourt, 'Notes on an economic querist: G.L.S. Shackle', *Journal of Post Keynesian Economics*, vol. 4, 1981, p. 140.
17. *CAC*, p. 36.
18. 'L.S.E. cost theory in retrospect', p. 12n.
19. J.M. Buchanan, 'Knight, Frank H.' in D.L. Sills (ed.) *International Encyclopedia of the Social Sciences* (Glencoe, Ill.: The Macmillan Company & The Free Press, 1968), p. 425.

20. 'Knight, Frank H.', p. 425.
21. *WSED*, p. 202.
22. 'L.S.E. cost theory in retrospect', p. 3.
23. *WSED*, p. 282.
24. *WSED*, p. 282.
25. *WSED*, p. 281.
26. *WSED*, p. 280.
27. *WSED*, p. 279.
28. *FCC*, p. *ix*.
29. *WSED*, p. 155.
30. *PFDP*, p. 170.
31. *WSED*, p. 206.
32. *WSED*, p. 282.
33. Smith, *Wealth of Nations*, vol. I, pp. 17, 18.
34. *WSED*, p. 27.

8.2 The Mixed Economy

35. *LL*, p. 167.
36. 'Better than Plowing', p. 362.
37. *LMS*, p. 3.
38. *LMS*, p. 10.
39. *LL*, p. 170.
40. *WSED*, p. 112. Emphasis deleted.
41. *LMS*, p. 90.
42. *FCC*, p. 116. In a letter to the author dated 13 June 1988, Buchanan has re-stated this point as follows: 'For me, government has always been something to be protected from rather than to be the provider of assistance to. Perhaps this attribute is located in my *southernness*.'
43. *RR*, p. 150.
44. Nozick, *Anarchy, State, and Utopia*, p. 329.
45. *CAC*, p. 72.
46. *LMS*, p. 270.
47. *PFDP*, p. 290.
48. *DD*, p. 142.
49. *WSED*, p. 271.
50. *WSED*, p. 271.
51. *PFDP*, p. 11.
52. *PF*, p. 355.
53. *PF*, p. 364.
54. *PF*, p. 84.
55. *PF*, p. 434.
56. *PF*, p. 364.
57. J.M. Buchanan, 'The Constitution of Economic Policy', *American Economic Review*, vol. 77, 1987, p. 247.
58. *PF*, p. 413.
59. *PF*, p. 419.
60. *PT*, p. 152.
61. *Inconsistencies*, p. 12.
62. *Inconsistencies*, p. 4.

63. *PF*, p. 196.
64. *FCC*, p. 17.
65. *LL*, p. 34.
66. *LL*, p. 21.
67. *PF*, p. 176.
68. 'Our Times: Past, Present, and Future', p. 31.
69. *WSED*, p. 176.
70. 'Our Times: Past, Present, and Future', pp. 34, 36.

8.3 Politics, Economics and Political Economy

71. *PF*, p. *ix*.
72. *WSED*, p. 138.
73. *WSED*, p. 139.
74. See J.K. Galbraith, 'Power and the Useful Economist', *American Economic Review*, vol. 63, 1973.
75. Tawney, *The Radical Tradition*, p. 169.
76. *WSED*, pp. 138–9.
77. *FTPE*, p. 3.
78. *FTPE*, p. 12.
79. Smith, *Wealth of Nations*, vol. I, p. 18.
80. K.E. Boulding, 'Economics as a Moral Science', *American Economic Review*, vol. 59, 1969, p. 8.
81. Smith, *Wealth of Nations*, vol. I, p. 20.
82. 'The Constitution of Economic Policy', p. 245.
83. 'The Constitution of Economic Policy', p. 243.
84. *PPPD*, p. *v*.
85. 'The Constitution of Economic Policy', p. 247.
86. *FTPE*, p. 105.
87. *WSED*, p. 216.
88. *WSED*, p. 208.
89. *WSED*, p. 208.
90. *WSED*, pp. 208–9.

Index